PSYCHOLOGY

and the question of

AGENCY

SUNY SERIES,

ALTERNATIVES IN PSYCHOLOGY

MICHAEL A. WALLACH,

EDITOR

PSYCHOLOGY

and the question of

AGENCY

JACK MARTIN, JEFF SUGARMAN, JANICE THOMPSON

STATE UNIVERSITY OF NEW YORK PRESS

Published by
STATE UNIVERSITY OF NEW YORK PRESS,
ALBANY

For information, address
State University of New York Press
90 State Street, Suite 700, Albany, NY 12207

Production, Laurie Searl
Marketing, Fran Keneston

Library of Congress Cataloging-in-Publication Data

Martin, Jack, 1950–
    Psychology and the question of agency / Jack Martin, Jeff Sugarman, and Janice
    Thompson.
        p. cm. — (SUNY series, alternatives in psychology)
    Includes bibliographical references and index.
    ISBN 0-7914-5725-7 (alk. paper) — ISBN 0-7914-5726-5 (pbk. : alk. paper)
        1. Autonomy (Psychology) I. Sugarman, Jeff, 1955– II. Thompson, Janice, 1964– III.
Title. IV. Series.

BF575.A88 M37 2003
155.2—dc21   2002075854

10 9 8 7 6 5 4 3 2 1

CONTENTS

PREFACE

Most contemporary persons believe in both science and their own ability to direct their lives, a joint commitment reflected and encouraged by disciplinary and professional psychology. Nonetheless, it is by no means clear that such a commitment can be coherently maintained. While the determinism of science might fit well with the inevitability of death and taxes, it seems decidedly at odds with much of our everyday experience of ourselves as agents capable of choice and action that make a difference in our lives. On the other hand, a certain amount of order and predictability in our physical and social world seem necessary if we are to exercise any control over our circumstances. After all, chaos hardly seems conducive to self-determination.

In this volume, we argue for a kind of agency that is both determined and determining and strongly recommend that both disciplinary and professional psychology embrace such a conception as central to their inquiries and practices. In fact, we go so far as to suggest that it is precisely because mainstream psychology has not developed an adequate conceptualization and theory of human agency that it has fallen prey to an overly reductionistic scientism that has failed to draw necessary distinctions between natural and human phenomena. More particularly, most scientific and professional psychology has failed to provide an adequate account of self-determination as emergent from, yet irreducible to, its sociocultural constituents and physical–biological requirements. We maintain that such an account is exactly what is required for a coherent conception of human agents as both determined and determining, in a manner that fits both our everyday experience of ourselves and acceptably rigorous forms of psychological inquiry and practice. The purpose of our book is to argue for and theoretically elaborate this position.

Readers familiar with the philosophical canon will realize that the conceptualization of agency with which we will be concerned is a form of compatibilism. However, it is a kind of compatibilism that goes beyond voluntarism alone to allow for a modest kind of origination. In other words, our agency is not restricted to the kind of thing that the Stoic philosopher

Epictetus (ca. C.E. 50–130) apparently had in mind when he proffered his famous advice: "Do not seek to have events happen as you want them to, but instead want them to happen as they do happen" (Epictetus, 1983, p. 13). Our kind of agency is not restricted to such attitudinal accomplishment alone. Instead, we believe that the inevitable uniqueness of any individual life within its sociocultural, developmental context, together with emergent capabilities such as imaginative projection, critical self-reflection, oppositional thinking, and dialogical engagement, enable an agency, which while certainly not radically free, is nevertheless capable of generating possibilities for action that might deviate somewhat from possibilities already experienced.

Of course, how well we succeed in our attempts to argue for and theorize a situated, emergent, and deliberative agency ultimately is up to readers to determine. We are pleased to have the opportunity of placing our ideas in front of such a readership and want to express our gratitude to Jane Bunker, Michael Wallach, James Peltz, Laurie Searl and others at State University of New York Press for including our work in their "Alternatives in Psychology" series. We also want to acknowledge the assistance of Chris Holoboff in helping to prepare our manuscript. Thanks also to our friends and colleagues in the Division of Theoretical and Philosophical Psychology (of the American Psychological Association) for many informative conversations and for their general support of us and our work. Finally, we thank Robin Barrow, our good friend and Faculty Dean at Simon Fraser University for always encouraging us to put "ideas ahead of committees," an all-too-rare bias in today's university administrator.

Some of the ideas set forth in chapters 3, 4, and 5 of this book have been developed previously, although much less formally and fully, by Jack Martin and Jeff Sugarman in articles in the *Journal of Theoretical and Philosophical Psychology* (1999), the *American Psychologist* (2000), *Theory and Psychology* (2001), and the *Journal for the Theory of Social Behavior* (2001), and in a chapter in the volume *Between Chance and Choice*, edited by Harald Atmanspacher and Robert Bishop (Imprints Academic, 2002). We thank Imprints Academic, and the publishers of the journals in which these articles have appeared (Sage, the American Psychological Association, Basil Blackwell) for permission to use some of those ideas here.

Chapter One

Psychology and the Question of Agency

PROBABLY NO CONCEPT is as central to psychology and its aspirations, yet as poorly articulated within psychology, as that of *human agency*. Broadly speaking, agency is the freedom of individual human beings to make choices and to act on these choices in ways that make a difference in their lives. Exactly what is implied by such a freedom has been the subject of heated debate since at least the time of the Stoic sage Chrysippus (ca. 280–206 B.C.E.). Nonetheless, the assumption of some such freedom to choose and act as we will clearly undergirds much of our everyday activity. If we cannot be said to play an active role in the initiation of our actions, it is difficult to understand how we might be said to deserve the fruits of our achievements, to have moral responsibility for our conduct, or to be suitably in receipt of the admiration, gratitude, indignation, or resentment of others. Moreover, without some conception of agency it is difficult to conceive of ourselves as autonomously creative, as active contributors to our own lives and destinies, and as capable of giving and receiving meaningful friendship and love. In short, to dignify our very sense of ourselves as fully human seems to require the idea that we can initiate actions in relation to our hopes for our lives within the context of an open (not predetermined) future.

To date, disciplinary psychology has failed to achieve a coherent conception of agency. This failure is attributable, in large part, to disciplinary psychology's seemingly untenable joint commitment to fashioning a highly deterministic, reductive science in the manner of some branches and approaches to physical science, while simultaneously appearing to respect as significant and influential the everyday experiences and actions of human individuals when it comes to the professional practice of psychology. The way in which psychology has historically positioned itself with respect to other disciplines and professions requires success in both of these ventures. Yet, it is difficult to understand how disciplinary psychology can have it both ways. For, if all of our decisions and actions are fully determined by conditions and factors outside of ourselves, in what coherent sense might we be said to initiate our own actions? Even if strict origination of actions is replaced by the lesser requirement of mere voluntariness in desiring and acting as we do, the requirements of deterministic psychological science and agentic psychological practice are not easily reconciled. For example, even if I act in accordance with my desire not to become upset by the political views of my colleague, in what sense is either my desire or my action free if both are located in a strictly causal sequence of events that prevent me from desiring and acting otherwise?

For the most part, psychologists and organized psychology have opted for an approach to psychological research that has disavowed human agency in order to identify itself with natural science and the latter's use of reductive methods and explanatory systems. Moreover by inventing what organized psychology has termed the "scientist–practitioner model," it also has pretended that this reductive approach to psychological science can undergird both personally and socially effective professional psychological practices, despite the fact that the concerns for which most individuals seek psychological assistance are mostly agentic, reflecting difficulties in deciding, choosing, and acting. At first glance, this combination of reductive, deterministic psychological science and professional practice targeted at goals such as self-empowerment, problem solving, and personal coping seems incomprehensible. This is especially so when it is realized that, if successful, reductive psychological science actually would do away with the very phenomena it purports to explain, and on which professional psychology is based: agentic phenomena such as human choice and intentional action. The paradoxical key to unlocking this irony lies in the recognition that the devaluing of agency through reductive psychological science actually serves the purposes of agency-enhancing professional psychology as well. The crucial insight is that agency, once devalued by the science thought to undergird psychological practice, becomes a detached, facile thing that seems readily pliable through the frequently and grossly oversimplified manipulations of professional psychology.

The aim of this book is to provide a coherent conception and approach to the question of agency that does not disparage serious scholarly and scientific work in psychology and related areas, but which resists the kind of reductive science upon which so much contemporary psychology rests. In particular, it is argued that human agency cannot be reduced to purely biological and/or cultural determinants, yet must be understood as arising nonmysteriously within appropriate developmental, historical, and sociocultural context. Resolutions to two seemingly paradoxical ideas are critical to the success of this enterprise. First is the idea that agency can arise from biology and culture, without being reducible to any combination of biological and cultural determinants. Second is the idea that humans can be both determined and free, and not merely in the sense of demonstrating voluntariness in their activities.

However, before presenting and arguing for particular approaches to these ideas as resolutions to the very paradoxes they appear to contain, the topics of agency and the reduction of agency within psychology require further introduction. This task exhausts the rest of this first chapter and the chapter that follows. With such an introduction in place, chapters 3 and 4 present arguments for the nature, necessity, and irreducibility of agency in human affairs. Chapter 5 is then devoted to a detailed theoretical and practical explication of human agency, its development, and its indispensable role in human life. More specifically, in chapter 5, our own conception of situated, emergent, and deliberative agency is clarified and illustrated, both developmentally and theoretically. Finally, in the last chapter (chapter 6), psychological research, practice, and the societal impact (socioculturally, politically, and ethically) of psychology are reinterpreted in light of the conception of agency developed herein. In this final chapter, detailed examples are provided concerning what transpires when a historically and socioculturally constituted, situated, and deliberative agency (one that emerges developmentally within necessary physical and biological requirements) is assumed rather than disavowed and devalued. We believe that the resultant, interpretive reconfiguring of psychological research, practice, and societal impact provides a strong rationale for the theoretical work we undertake in this volume.

SOME RELEVANT BACKGROUND FOR WHAT FOLLOWS

The issue of freedom of choice and action has taken a variety of forms since first broached by Chrysippus, Aristotle (384–322 B.C.E.), and other classical Greek philosophers. It lies at the very center of human existence, both personally and socially. It is what imbues personal being with significance, and social being with virtue. For, if human individuals have no agency, no freedom to choose and act, personal life loses its possibilities and social life loses its responsibilities. If there is no agency, there is no praiseworthy accomplishment—no personal triumph, no service to a common good. In a very real sense, the assumption of agency is a metaphorical cornerstone to Western culture. It is difficult to understate the enormous impact of this assumption, even if seldom articulated explicitly, on our personal and collective existence.

And yet, at least since the Enlightenment, many philosophers, scientists, and social scientists have toiled to disavow or "downgrade" agency because it does not fit easily within a particular scientific viewpoint. They have taken the perspective that everything is caused in such a way that it can be reduced to a basic physical, microparticulate level of reality. The ambition of this scientific program is that we will discover that agency really is nothing more than the firing of neurons and fibers, and related neurophysiological activity of our bodies and brains made possible by our particular evolutionary history as a species. In the same way that water is composed of molecules consisting of two atoms of hydrogen joined to one atom of oxygen, that temperature is mean kinetic energy, and that light is electromagnetic radiation, we will learn that our choices and actions are reducible to physical states and processes of our biological brains and bodies. Moreover, these physical states and processes determine, sometimes in interaction with our physical and social environments, all that passes for our experiences of agentic freedom and responsibility to ourselves and to others. Our conventional phenomenology and morality are revealed as mere epiphenomena, without causal influence or real significance. Even though we may wish to retain our folksy way of talking as if we make choices about how to act based on our own sense of what is appropriate, practical, reasonable, and moral according to our beliefs and desires, all such talk really is beside the point. It is merely a kind of window dressing that could just as easily be eliminated with no resultant alteration in the real, correct, underlying scientific picture of how we are in the world.

The human genome project, advances in artificial intelligence and robotics, cloning, and reproductive and other biological technologies, we consistently are told, are converging in a way that soon will reveal how insignificant, almost childish, our everyday agentic assumptions and aspirations really are. The mere fact that such possibilities strike us at once as both so startling and so seemingly inevitable indicates the extent to which we have accepted a scientific and technological worldview, and the progressive, inexorable march of progress through which it manifests and confirms itself. Some envision a time when our languages and cultural practices will dissolve into a universal, more sophisticated, and scientifically correct way of speaking about our experiences and actions in ways that have little place for agency and associated ideas. Just as science has eclipsed other forms of superstition, our agency also will be eclipsed in ways that we now only can glimpse, but which soon will congeal into an efficient, parsimonious scientific discourse more consistent with our material, atomistically constituted being.

Thus, it is hardly surprising to learn that contemporary disciplinary psychology as a research enterprise has been, at least for most of its history, not much concerned with agency, understood as choosing and acting on the basis of one's own desires, beliefs, and reasons. Prior to the 1980s and 1990s, the number of articles in journals of psychology that contained any refer- ence to human agency was almost negligible when set against the vast number of articles produced within disciplinary psychology as a whole. As a science in the contemporary mode, psychology has been more concerned with the reductive explanation of agentic phenomena in terms of their supposed biological, neurophysiological, and environmental determinants. As most undergraduate university students can attest, for the most part the experiences, choices, and actions of everyday life have been redefined, resituated, reduced, and reinterpreted by scientific psychology to fit the language of variables, stimuli, factors, and conditions. Much of the modest increase in psychological work on aspects of human agency that has oc- curred since 1980 remains couched in such terms.

Of course, many (although certainly not all) psychologists admit to a gap between their research and theorizing and the understandings of the lay public. Indeed, some psychologists apparently regard such distance as evi- dence of the scientific status of their discipline. After all, how many auto- mobile drivers understand the physical mechanics of their vehicles? How many recipients of medical care know anything about the neurophysiologi- cal, chemical, and biological mechanisms and functions of their bodies? The descriptions and explanations of science and its technical applications fre- quently differ from and exceed the understandings of nonscientists. Many psychologists believe that scientific psychology is capable of penetrating the everyday actions and experiences of human subjects in ways, and with results, that should not be expected to relate to lay impressions. After all, the methods and findings of psychological science are superior to those available to nonpsychologists. Although ordinary humans in their everyday lives be- lieve that they make choices about what to do today and tomorrow, and sometimes act on these choices in ways that affect their lives, research psychologists expect that behind all of this agentic facade lies the real realm of their scientific aspirations: an underlying level of physical, material microparticulate entities and inanimate causal processes that determine all of what goes on above.

And yet, the attachment of disciplinary psychology to this reductively deterministic viewpoint is not complete, for contemporary psychology is a profession as well as a research enterprise. While the assumed scientific status of research psychology serves to support societal acceptance of the expert interventions of psychologists in many areas of contemporary life, such interventions and their practitioners cannot afford to be quite so dismissive of agency as experienced in everyday life. After all, those clients and com- munities who request the professional services of psychologists make their requests for assistance in mostly agentic form. Difficulties for which psycho- logical services are sought are expressed in terms of alienation, depression, angst, uncertainty, and bewilderment, not in terms of biological and neuro- physiological features of the brain and body. Moreover, such difficulties are understood by clients and other consumers of psychological services to relate to their relationships, aspirations, work, and emotional states in ways that can best be captured in ordinary, everyday language, not in a scientific, materialistic vocabulary that seems mostly unrelated to relevant personal concerns and difficulties.

The obvious gap between what disciplinary psychology has to offer and what the clients of professional psychologists are seeking, may, in part, explain the drift of most psychological practitioners from the research traditions and theoretical orientations in which they were trained (e.g., Jensen, Bergin, & Greaves, 1990; Morrow-Bradley & Elliot, 1986). Practitioners, who are faced daily with the agentic, meaningful, and morally laden questions and concerns of their clients, surely must feel that they are dealing with subject matter that is entirely different from what they read about in the texts and research articles that populated their education. Whereas the psychological research literature aims at prediction using inferential statistical techniques and large samples, professional psychologists and their clients engage together in quests for idiographic, reflexive, narrative, practical, and evaluative self-understandings and meanings (Woolfolk, 1998). Researchers isolate variables of interest and statistically control others, while practitioners and their clients must deal with problems as they are lived, in complex, changing, and meaning-laden contexts.

Unfortunately, turning to the practice-oriented, clinical literature in psychology also is unlikely to assist professional psychologists, reflecting, as it does, a different, yet still unsituated, stance toward human agency. Humanistic psychotherapies, for example, with their Romantic roots, invest individuals with an innate, natural form of agency that, if unfettered, allows them to be radically "free agents" in determining their own behavior on the basis of access to immediate, inner, true experiencing. As Louis Sass (1988) has pointed out, the humanist view of human nature is deficient in that its valuing of privacy, freedom, and uniqueness, as defining and desirable human qualities, leads to a devaluation of and blindness to the potential importance of cultural practices, social structures, tradition, history, and even biology. From the humanistic perspective, culture and tradition, for example, are seen mostly as external barriers to individual freedom and uniqueness. The pursuit of a radical freedom "to follow true feelings" ignores the socially constructed, value-laden nature of emotions, and necessary and inevitable historical, sociocultural constraints on possibilities for action. For example, imagine an individual in psychotherapy deciding whether to end a marriage solely on the basis of accessing and acting on "true" feelings about the marriage, feelings that are completely free of personal history and sociocultural background, of what is right, good, responsible, acceptable, traditional, or practically possible. Clients' feelings and possible actions in such circumstances are not unconstrained by sociocultural, historical, and personal factors, conditions, and contexts. Clients and psychological therapists cannot help but realize that psychological agency and change involve much more than discovering true feelings and acting on them.

Yet, despite such obvious shortcomings in its agentic attachments, disciplinary psychology continues to hold simultaneously to the idea of psychology as a kind of deterministic, reductive science and to the idea that psychology somehow can contribute to the empowerment of human beings with respect to attaining goals they set for themselves in their everyday lives. For example, in a recent volume entitled, "On the Self-Regulation of Behavior," Charles Carver and Michael Scheier (1998) cling tenaciously to a conception of self-regulation in terms of a cybernetic system of input functions, reference values, and output functions that they claim operates equally well in machines or animals (including human animals). At the same time, they repetitively claim that it is human beings who experience personal growth through "decisions made by the self" (p. 315) and who "live life by identifying goals and moving toward them, and by identifying anti-goals and staying away from them" (p. 346). Such unsettling juxtapositionings have become so common in the writings of contemporary psychologists that they frequently escape close scrutiny. However, even a modestly critical sensibility must regard the partnering of such claims as jarring. What possibly viable, coherent conception of agency might fit deterministically and reductively within a nonhuman animal without language or a machine, yet also fit with a human individual's free pursuit of self-set decisions and goals? Perhaps such writings reflect a misunderstanding of the conventional meanings associated with the idea of agency, or perhaps their authors have developed an unarticulated theory of agency that somehow transcends and transforms those conventional meanings in convincingly coherent ways. However, it seems more likely that the joint concerns of disciplinary psychology for a foundation in deterministic, reductive science coupled with a marketable set of self-empowering methods and practices simply have deflected the usual kinds of critical attention found in most branches of scholarly activity. And, moreover, it seems that many psychologists have been caught up unthinkingly in this disciplinary background within which they work.

As will become clear in chapter 2, our own view is that psychologists' conflicting "double take" on agency has avoided critical scrutiny within psychology for the simple reason that it works for both psychological scientists and practitioners. The reductive disavowal of agency within psychological science serves to devalue and simplify it in ways that allow it to be picked up by psychological practitioners as an easily malleable thing, one that can be readily detached from its complex human context and probed and serviced by psychological professionals. Of course, we do not believe that such a connection between psychological science and practice has been strategically preplanned by disciplinary psychology and the psychological establishment. Ours is not a conspiracy theory. Rather, over the course of the twentieth century, a host of influential cultural, historical, social, and institutional events have come together in ways that have made it sensible and practical for psychology and psychologists to adopt the stance that psychology constitutes a seamless, progressive program for the scientific understanding of human experience and action that can be placed in the service of bettering human kind through the ministrations of its practitioners.

Whatever the reasons for disciplinary psychology's failure to come to grips with the issue of human agency and its implications for psychological research and practice, it seems appropriate to call for greater critical attention to these matters. We hope that the arguments attempted herein will contribute in some small measure to such critical study. What we will argue is that psychology, if it is truly to be about human agents, must give up its pretensions of being a highly deterministic, reductive science. This is not to say that psychology should cease attempts to attain a rigorous scholarly standing, even one based on an appropriate model of science, only that its subject matter should not be misconstrued or inappropriately transformed to fit the methods and models extant in areas of scholarship and science that do not encompass human agency as a central aspect of their subject matter. However, before arguing for the necessity of nonreductive agency in human affairs and for a viable conception of agency in appropriate developmental, historical, and sociocultural context, a brief overview of reductive programs within the history of psychology will serve to set the stage more completely for what will follow. For it is important to understand the extent to which disciplinary psychology has attempted to avoid the implications of agency for psychological science by different means of reducing agency to biology, behavior, neurophysiology, computational and other machine mechanisms, and even to disembodied systems of language and social practice.

PSYCHOLOGY'S DISAVOWAL OF AGENCY

To understand why disciplinary psychology has attempted so consistently to reduce agency to nonagentic determinants, it helps to recapture something of the enthrallment with the natural sciences that typified the latter part of the nineteenth century. At the time of the founding of psychology as an independent discipline, all theoretically inclined studies were in considerable turmoil. The natural sciences were in full swing, piling up success after success, in a way that was widely accepted as far outstripping the more uncertain, debatable output typically associated with work in philosophy and the humanities. This was a time when a newly born attachment to positivism and empiricism, which were thought to explain the success of the natural sciences, was stifling speculation about what things were and how they might be understood. The triumphant march of the natural sciences in industry and medicine seemed based on an exact knowledge of, and technical command over, nature. Moreover, all of this seemed to have been achieved by shelving traditional metaphysical concerns and focusing on how things functioned. Hypothesis, experiment, and verification made up a new and better logic of inquiry that was accepted unquestioningly as capable of penetrating all of nature, including human nature.

This was the intellectual climate in which disciplinary psychology emerged. In fact, given the persistent scientific temper of our times, it is no accident that the birth of psychology usually is marked by the establishment of a scientific laboratory devoted to psychological experimentation by Wilhelm Wundt in 1879 at the University of Leipzig, despite the fact that formal university courses in applied areas of psychology had been offered in the United States as early as 1839 (Glover & Ronning, 1987). In association with certain branches of physiology and brain chemistry, the new laboratory psychology claimed to be a kind of natural science of the psyche. The guiding idea was that the new experimental psychology would explore and understand the psyche on a mostly inductive, mechanistic basis. By employing what then were understood to be the methods of natural science, psychology would keep the psyche in front of psychological researchers in neat isolation. From the very beginning, there was a strong tendency to treat the psyche as an aseptic object, whose functioning could be formulated in causal, mechanistic laws. Questions of reason and meaning were converted into physiological stimuli, empirical regularities, and idea images and complexes.

From these beginnings, the idea of psychology as a natural, experimental science committed to the functional explanation of a natural psyche persisted across what commonly is perceived as a steady march of scientific and technological progress throughout the twentieth century. Models and metaphors drawn from computer and biotechnology gradually have gained ascendance over previously favored models and metaphors drawn from mechanics and the study of physical systems and lower organisms. However, the core commitment to psychology as natural science has continued to dominate disciplinary psychology in both its research and clinical practices.

Thus, throughout the history of disciplinary psychology, the lofty idea of "psychological science" looms large. By equating human action and experience with the inanimate phenomena of physics and the involuntary phenomena of biology, psychologists have aligned themselves with the methods and explanations of natural, physical science. In so doing, they have bestowed upon themselves (with society's apparent blessing, or at least little demur) all of the prestige and privilege of modern science and technology. So powerful a move has psychology's identification with natural science proven to be, that a steady stream of well-reasoned criticism has done little to deter it. Such criticism has consistently attended the steady march of psychological science throughout the twentieth century, but just as consistently has failed to capture the attention of most psychologists and nonpsychologists. When occasional notice has been taken, it is to dismiss the critics as uninformed, antiscientific, and/or emotional, even though many critics have themselves been prominent scientists, philosophers of science, and not infrequently, prominent psychologists. Seldom has organized psychology felt the need to mount any serious defense of its natural scientific practices and identifications.

THE BASIC ERROR

And yet, the basic assumption that undergirds the idea of psychology as a natural science is in error. Human actions and experiences are not the same kinds of things as are rocks, chemicals, plants, and brain tissue. Psychological kinds differ from natural kinds and other "indifferent" kinds of things in rather obvious ways. Moreover, these differences matter a great deal when it comes to understanding psychological kinds. When these differences are clarified, it makes little sense to conduct psychological inquiry using only the methods and strategies that have proven to be so very successful and undeniably powerful with respect to the description and explanation of physical and strictly biological phenomena.

The phenomena of psychology—human action and experience—are not indifferent to the ways in which they are classified by researchers and others, but interact with these classifications in ways that must be considered if they are to be understood. Ian Hacking (1995) uses the term *human kinds* to refer to kinds of people, kinds of human action, and varieties of human behavior. For Hacking, the important feature of human kinds is that they can exert effects on themselves. Human kinds are affected by their classifications and can interact with their classifications in ways that affect the classifications themselves. For example, if a person is aware that she is upsetting her friends because she is unhappy, she might make a special effort to "put on a good face," in their company.

On the other hand, chemicals, inanimate physical entities, and even nonhuman species, forests, and ecosystems exhibit no ability to exert such effects. These are natural kinds. Natural kinds are unaware of how they are classified and do not interact with their classifications. Unlike people, water, salt, horse, lemon, influenza, heat, and the color green are indifferent to their classifications. Even though, for example, horses may interact with people, horses are no different for being classified as pintos or thoroughbreds. Even though it may make a difference to a horse if it is considered by its owners to be mean-spirited or not, any such difference is not because the horse knows how it is considered or classified.

People are self-conscious and capable of self-knowledge. They are agents, for whom autonomy (at least since the days of Jean-Jacques Rousseau and Immanuel Kant) is a central Western value. Humans can become aware of how they are classified within their groups, societies, and cultures and can experience themselves in particular ways as a consequence of these classifications. They also can act to alter their classifications. Because human psychological beings are agents who are aware and reflective, their courses of action and ways of being are affected not only by the classifications of societies and cultures but also by their own conceptions of, and reactions to, such classifications.

Having drawn the foregoing distinction between human and natural kinds, Hacking (1995) also is quick to point out that just because they are not natural does not mean that human kinds are not real. Human kinds definitely are real, but it is a reality in which they themselves are deeply involved. It is a reality of which they are a part. Hacking's point here is that just because human psychological beings are contingently molded by the practices and classifications of their cultures and societies does not mean that they are not real entities or that they can be construed in any way whatsoever. Human psychological being may be mostly a matter of social construction, and as psychological beings, humans may have no fixed essence outside of their particular sociocultural constitution. However, once evolved as self-referring, self-knowing individuals, humans can exert real influence on their societies and cultures through their informed actions and activities. Human psychological beings require sociocultural, biological, and physical reality for their existence, but they are not entirely determined by, nor reducible to, these other levels of reality (Hacking, 1999; Martin & Sugarman, 1999).

More recently, Hacking (1999) has referred to "human kinds" as interactive kinds and natural kinds as indifferent kinds. We mostly have retained his earlier use of natural kinds and use the term *psychological kinds* to refer to what he previously called human kinds. Nonetheless, at times we use the terms *interactive* or *indifferent kinds* or add them to the terms *psychological kinds* or *natural kinds,* respectively, so as to capture more precisely particular distinctions we wish to draw. Of course, the important point to emphasize in all of this is that human or psychological or interactive kinds are as they are because they are the beliefs, desires, reasons, imaginings, memories, experiences, and actions of human agents. They are agentic phenomena in a way that the inanimate phenomena of physics and the animate, but nonagentic, phenomena of biology are not.

Hacking's (1995, 1999) views on human psychological beings are consistent with those expressed in our own previously espoused theory of human psychological development (Martin & Sugarman, 1999). We have argued that human psychological being is emergent within particular sociocultural contexts but, once emergent, is not reducible to these sociocultural contexts, even while continuing to be affected by them. Given the biological makeup of humans, it is inevitable that they will develop some kind of psychological being by virtue of being embedded from birth in sociocultural contexts and practices that constitute particular forms of personhood and identity. The claim is that if this basic premise is accepted there is no need to resort to anything further in the way of natural or essential arguments concerning the nature of human psychology. In short, human psychology issues from the developmental embeddedness of biological humans within established cultures and societies, but once emergent within sociocultural contexts that include practices of self-reflective agency, human psychological beings and their actions and experiences are not entirely determined nor constrained by such contexts. As Hacking (1995) claims, human psychological beings are human kinds capable of affecting the very classifications that enable and identify them.

Psychological individuals, and their memories, imaginings, beliefs, and goals, are possessed and reflective of human agency. Human or psychological kinds are agentic. They interact with their classifications in ways that natural, indifferent kinds do not precisely because they are self-interpretive and self-determining, reflecting the human capacity to choose and decide with respect to purpose and action. In other words, they are encased in the life projects and understandings of intentional, reflective beings.

This broad understanding of human psychological being has important consequences for psychology and psychological inquiry. With such an understanding in place, it becomes difficult to accept the naturalistic, essentialistic, ahistorical, and reductionistic assumptions that have attended most psychological inquiry since the formal establishment of psychology as an independent scientific discipline in the late 1800s. Psychologists have, for the most part, failed to recognize that their subject matter consists of human kinds that are historically and socioculturally constituted but capable of agentically influencing how they are classified and understood. This failure has led to an uncritical infatuation with psychological research as a natural science and with psychological practice as a technologically related form of human psychological engineering. Moreover, as hinted at earlier, the social consequences of all of this are far from benign in that the words and work of psychological scientists and expert practitioners increasingly are invading our everyday interpersonal interactions and practices. Ironically, such debatable consequences are possible precisely because human individuals are interactive agents, even if such agency is mostly unrecognized by psychology and psychologists.

METHOD OVER SUBSTANCE

One of the most remarkable hallmarks of the natural science approach to psychology is to pretend ignorance, in the sense of acting as if one knows nothing whatsoever, about the psyche. Such pretense is, of course, consistent with the desire for scientific objectivity, understood as indifference or neutrality with respect to one's subject matter, and explanation. The aim of natural science is to explain in causal, functional terms not to understand. The search is for empirical regularities not for meaning. In this spirit, the everyday understandings of the psychologist are to be left at the laboratory door. Under no circumstances is the psychological researcher to turn into an accomplice of the subjects under study.

One of the most startling examples of the implications of this attitude for the development of psychology can be found in the early-twentieth-century turn to behaviorism in American psychology. At this time, the study of behavior largely replaced the earlier study of consciousness for reasons expressed by Harold S. Jennings in his early text *Behavior of the Lower Organisms* (1906/1962): "[A]ssertions regarding consciousness in animals, whether affirmative or negative, are not susceptible of verification" (p. v). For purposes of scientific study, Jennings proclaimed that one must turn elsewhere, namely, to behavior. Jennings was discussing the behavior of lower animals, but the comparative psychology of the time drew a sharp line between the study of consciousness and other psychological phenomena and the conduct of science. Over time, the subsequent experimental work and logic of an entire generation of American psychological behaviorists from John Watson to Burrhus F. Skinner succeeded in expanding the category of behavior to include almost everything from washing a dish to learning a second language, including the supposedly epiphenomenal thoughts and sensations accompanying all of the action. A scientific method of detached objectivity could now prevail over an entire range of psychological phenomena reduced to behavioral form.

Sigmund Koch (1981) described the scientistic "methodology" that has enveloped psychological science, in the most colorful of language, as

> a view of all aspects of the cognitive enterprise as so thoroughly rule-regulated as to make the role of the cognizer superfluous . . . [the] tendency to persist so rigidly, blindly, patiently in the application of rules . . . despite fulsome indications of the disutility—that the behavior would have to be characterized as schizophrenic in any other context. . . . It presumes that knowledge is an almost automatic result of a gimmickry, an assembly line, a "methodology." It assumes that inquiring action is so rigidly and fully regulated by rule that in its conception of inquiry it often allows the rules totally to displace their human users. (pp. 258–259)

One of the great ironies of this methodological fetishism is that even in physical science there is considerable evidence that researchers do not engage in atheoretical, value-free, rule-bounded inquiry. Many important insights and discoveries in natural science reflect the broad cultural competence, everyday understanding, and speculative theorizing of researchers (cf. Hanson, 1958). In psychology, such scientistic methodologism is even more suspect, given the highly contextualized, historically and socioculturally situated nature of human psychological kinds. It seems almost inconceivable that generations of experimental and other psychologists could be so convinced about the everyday relevance of their greatly simplified, highly controlled, and artificially induced results. A large part of the answer to this conundrum concerns the powerful influence on psychololgists' inquiry and clinical practices that has been exerted by various kinds of reductionism. It is a deeply rooted commitment to a scientistic, reductionistic strategy that more than anything else has convinced psychologists that they can, and should, mistrust and dismiss their everyday understanding of themselves as agents, rather than use it as a basis for their inquiries. To summarize, the methodolatry of disciplinary psychology, by which it has pretended to the status of natural science, has ensured that psychologists consistently have put their methodological cart ahead of their substantive horse, even when such confusion disavows that which is most uniquely and importantly human, that is, agency.

ASPIRATIONS

In concluding this first, introductory chapter, we want to give the reader a more direct sense of the aspirations that lie behind what we attempt herein. To do this, we reproduce excerpts from the later-twentieth-century writings of three prominent psychologists who have called for a different kind of psychology, one which recognizes that psychological kinds are interactive and agentic, not indifferent and natural. In presenting the following quotations, we hope to indicate that the work in this book is embedded in a considerable history of related aspirations and works of many others, from many of whom we have drawn directly in the pages to follow, but from all of whom we have benefited. It is this legacy that constitutes an important part of the relevant context of this current undertaking.

> Characteristically, psychological events . . . are multiply determined, ambiguous in their human meaning, polymorphous, contextually environed or embedded in complex and vaguely bounded ways, evanescent and labile in the extreme. . . . One is tempted to laugh off the ludicrous prescriptionism of self-anointed visionaries like Watson, Skinner, and even certain infinitely confident prophets of the theory of finite automata, but their actual impact on history is no laughing matter. . . . [P]sychologists must finally accept the circumstance that extensive and important sectors of psychological study require modes of inquiry rather more like those of the humanities than the sciences. (Koch, 1981, pp. 268–269)

> Human kinds . . . are not natural kinds, but neither are they mere legends. They do refer to features that are real. But it is a reality in which they are themselves heavily implicated, a reality of which they are a part. The reality to which human kinds refer

is a cultural reality, and that in several senses: first, because the phenomena depicted are ones which exist only in some cultural context; secondly, because these phenomena commonly depend on a certain social technology for their visibility and their production; thirdly... because the categories used in their representation are culturally grounded. (Danziger, 1997, pp. 191–192)

[P]sychologists should study the people around them. More than this, ... we should scrutinize our work; our social, political, and cultural loyalties; the lives we live in the privacy of our own homes; and the lives we live in the privacy of our own heads. Psychology students have for generations been encouraged to see themselves as taking ruler and stopwatch to the world, measuring people with all the dispassion that they might show in recording the orbit of Jupiter, or the structure of a fruit fly's wing. This self-image has been strengthened by our need for academic respectability, as a fledgling profession; but it has led us to overlook the intuitive processes whereby we decide to collect one set of evidence rather than another, and to place upon it one interpretation rather than another. ... [E]vidence about people is less determinate than evidence about animals or about inanimate objects. If we are in the least interested in the rigor of what we do, we are forced to abandon the conception of ourselves as impersonal measurers, and to see ourselves more modestly as interpreters. ...

If we disavow the false objectivity that scientifically minded psychologists have claimed for themselves, we are under no obligation to plunge to the other extreme. We can analyze and explore the elements of uncertainty that psychological knowledge contains without committing ourselves to a complete relativism of judgment, in which all interpretations of human thought or deed are ultimately of equal value. An interpreter works with evidence: he deals not in black or white, but in the subtly shifting and graduated shades of gray that reasoned doubt entails. His search, in practice, is always for the best reading that his evidence permits. (Hudson, 1975, pp. 8–9)

We very much hope that the perspective and arguments we offer in the pages that follow are worthy of this heritage. What we want to do is convince you that psychology cannot avoid the fact that human beings are embodied agents active in the world. Moreover, such agency goes beyond mere voluntariness (acting consistently with one's desires) by encompassing a modest capability to "originate" courses of action, at least in the sense of imagining and selecting possibilities for acting that are broadly within or suggested by one's historical, sociocultural situation. In our view, this is the kind of agency that cannot be ignored by disciplinary psychology, in either its research or professional arms.

We will argue that human agency arises nonmysteriously from biology and culture but cannot be reduced back to these origins. We also will argue that human beings are both determined and free. These two central theses are connected in that while the kind of agentic emergence we champion is determined by physical and biological requirements and sociocultural constituents, once emergent the agent's own self-determination always may figure into the determination of her or his choices and actions. Together these theses make possible a perspective on agency that fits coherently within a nonreductive scientific and scholarly framework, on the one hand, and a professional orientation toward practical understanding, on the other hand.

However, before turning to these matters, we first, in the very next chapter, offer a more complete historical sketch of reductionism in disciplinary psychology, indicating why we believe that such reductionism has been central to psychology's traditional disavowal and/or devaluation of human agency. Chapter 3 then provides a brief history of various debates and positions within both philosophy and psychology with respect to the question of human agency. Such a history allows us to locate our work within those broader traditions of scholarly writing and inquiry that relate to our topic. It also sets the stage for chapter 4, in which we offer arguments for the kind of agency we wish to champion in this volume and provide a critical reading of various reductionist, competitor programs in contemporary cognitive science, neuroscience, and philosophy of mind. Finally, in chapters 5 and 6 we turn, respectively, to a detailed consideration of the core theses mentioned in the preceding paragraph and to their implications for psychological inquiry, practice, and social impact.

CHAPTER TWO

REDUCTIONISM IN PSYCHOLOGY

THE NATURALISTIC PROJECT that attempts to explain psychological kinds (human experience, understanding, thought, and action) according to empirical regularities and causal laws, is possible only if one holds the belief that psychological phenomena can be reduced to what are thought to be more basic, constitutive phenomena amenable to the methods of natural science. Psychologists have primarily employed five reductive strategies: (a) biological, (b) psychometric, (c) behavioral, (d) neurophysiological, and (e) computational. Various combinations of these have been attempted as well. All of these reductive strategies, as employed in programs of psychological research, attempt to remove psychological kinds from the everyday historical, sociocultural contexts that, in large part, create and maintain them. Once everyday psychological phenomena are reduced, whatever remains is placed in highly controlled, idealized laboratory settings and/or formal psychometric–statistical or logical systems. By the time research psychologists set to work, they no longer are dealing with human psychological activity in its usual historical, sociocultural surroundings; instead, they are dealing with reflexes, personality factors, operant classes, patterns of cerebral excitation and inhibition, semantic and procedural networks, and so forth. As we shall see in chapter 3, such language contrasts sharply with an agentic discourse of beliefs, understanding, reasons, purposes, choices, and actions.

In commenting on the history of reductionism in the human sciences in general, Rüdiger Safranski (1998) recently has remarked:

> It is astonishing how, ever since the middle of the nineteenth century. . . there has suddenly been a universal desire to make Man "small." That is when the thought pattern of "Man is nothing other than ___" began to advance. . . . This [reductionism] of the second half of the nineteenth century would achieve the trick of thinking of Man as "little" but doing great things with him—provided one wishes to describe the scientized civilization, from which we are all benefiting, as "great." (p. 29)

Without necessarily joining in Safranski's implied diminution of the successes of natural science in areas such as physics, chemistry, and some branches of biology, it is indeed remarkable the extent to which psychologists have chosen to reduce their subject matter so that they can view themselves as "natural scientists of the psyche." If one is committed to what one regards as scientific methodology above and beyond any concern with understanding focal phenomena as they really are, the seductive power of reductionism comes into focus. What we are calling scientism includes both the misunderstanding, and misapplication of the methods of natural science to phenomena that are not indifferent natural kinds. To make such scientism plausible to psychologists requires a reduction of interactive, psychological kinds to indifferent, natural kinds. This maneuver involves stripping psychological kinds of the historical, sociocultural contexts in which they arise and are constituted and ignoring their agentic capacity to interact with the ways in which they are classified and studied.

A HISTORICAL SKETCH

Perhaps the first major program of reductionism in disciplinary psychology was the attempt, at the end of the nineteenth century, and the beginning of the twentieth century, to erect a psychological science on a biological basis. As previously mentioned, comparative psychology provided the required link to biology. By using terms such as *reflex, instinct, habit,* and *behavior* to refer equally to either the involuntary activity of frogs and rats or to the reflections and intentional actions of adult humans, comparative and other psychologists constructed what they regarded as a seamless continuum spanning the activity of all organisms. For example, early functionalists like James Angell (1913) described the general direction of their work as promoting a "sympathetic acceptance of the behavior concept as a general term under which to subsume minor distinctions in modes of action whether conscious or unconscious" (pp. 258–259).

Thus, by the time that Watson began his program of full-scale behavioral reduction, the ground already had been prepared for assuming a common set of concepts and principles that would span biological, social, and psychological levels of human and subhuman activity. In a very short time after Wundt's early advocacy of a kind of social psychology based on the analysis of human cultural products and his championing of introspection as a method for experimental psychology, anything mental, historical, social, or cultural was allowed to enter the world of psychological experimentation and research only as a stimulus external to a basic organism, much like any other. The only conceptions of sociocultural collectivity or community that were allowed took the form of statistical aggregations. Throughout the first half of the twentieth century, the twin reductions of psychological phenomena to behavior and to statistical–psychometric variables ensured that psychologists would never get close to the everyday phenomena in which they continued to claim interest. Such reductions also guaranteed an ever widening gap between psychological researchers and practitioners, the latter of whom found little use for conclusions about averages, groups, and relations among variables when confronted with particular clients and their circumstances.

The addition of statistical–psychometric reductionism to existing biological and behavioral reductionisms has had especially far-reaching consequences for psychology because it has allowed psychologists to continue to reduce their focal phenomena even while moving outside of formal experimental settings. So long as one has one's "tool kit" of variables, operational definitions, and psychological measures or instruments in hand, there no longer is any reason to be content with the sterile surroundings of the laboratory. Even though experimental work (although certainly not its extensively generalized applications) in reflex and stimulus-response psychology was mostly confined to the laboratory, the language of statistics seemed capable of traveling beyond such confines. Moreover, talk about independent and dependent variables appeared to fit neatly within the lawful, causal ambitions of psychological science.

One of the many ironies concerning psychologists' adoption of what they have understood as the methods of the natural sciences occurs in the realm of statistical reductionism. In what must stand as one of the best extant examples of critical historical scholarship in psychology, Koch (1992) documented how the inquiry practices of research psychologists at Harvard University during much of the first half of the twentieth century were dramatically influenced by a misunderstanding of Percy Bridgman's (1952) notions of operational analysis and definition and how such confusion quickly became the norm in American experimental psychology. Whereas Bridgman suggested that operational definitions are cues or indicators that help investigators locate and perceive the meaning of a concept, psychologists began to treat such definitions as exhaustive of the very conceptual meanings to which they are intended, under Bridgman's construal, only to point. As a consequence of the continued, widespread adoption of this misconceived practice, contemporary psychologists' conceptualizations of complex psychological phenomena continue to be afflicted with a kind of statistical reductionism that most often goes unremarked. In this manner, human motivation is equated with sets of responses to rating scales on which individuals indicate the extent to which they attribute their actions to a small number of predetermined factors such as effort, ability, luck, and task difficulty. In similar fashion, human confidence is taken to consist of ratings of one's judged capability of coming within various distances of feared objects and situations such as snakes, airplanes, and members of the opposite sex.

While statistical reductionism continues to be popular, much recent work in experimental psychology and contemporary cognitive science has adopted seemingly sophisticated, state-of-the-art, neurophysiological or computational reductionisms. Here, we are told that human experience, thought, and action can be understood scientifically by attaining an exacting knowledge of either the chemical, neurological activity of the brain, senses, and nervous system or (by more metaphorical extension) the mechanical operations and architecture of computers and computer programs. Once again, any consideration of historical, sociocultural contexts or truly agentic capabilities is removed so thoroughly in the reductionistic strategy that resultant scientific models and findings are not troubled by the real nature of the psychological phenomena they are intended to explain.

Again, what is quite amazing about psychologists' historical and continuing penchant for various kinds of reductionism in the service of psychological science is that it has survived the kind and amount of critical scrutiny to which it has been subjected for much of the twentieth century (cf. Robinson, 1985). In fact, so strong has been the attachment of disciplinary psychology to its scientistic pretensions that, for the most part, psychologists have simply ignored such criticism. Nonetheless, to anyone not already committed irrevocably to the mantras of psychological science, such critiques provide clear indications that everything is far from right in the reductionistic inquiry practices of psychologists.

IDENTITY VERSUS REQUIREMENT

One way to comprehend the impossibility of reductionism in psychology is to clarify the distinction between *identity* and *requirement*. To say that something is identical to something else is to claim that the two things are the same and, that for the purposes under consideration, they may be substituted, one for the other. In natural science and engineering, identity relations of this kind are quite common because of the atomistic constitution of many focal phenomena. Machines really are identical to their various parts, appropriately connected. Water, at least in chemical terms, is identical to a particular arrangement of hydrogen and oxygen atoms. Nuclear energy is the product of a given mass and the square of the speed of light.

However, in psychology, phenomena of interest are not constituted atomistically, rather, they consist in relations among historical, sociocultural, and linguistic practices in interaction with physical entities and biological bodies. Under these conditions, identity relations are impossible to achieve. In fact, it is precisely because of this impossibility that the various reduction-istic strategies employed in psychology really do not employ identity rela-tions at all. Rather, they are based on relations of requirement. For example, an emotional experience such as joy cannot be reduced to its biological, behavioral, or neurophysiological components, even though it requires any or all of such contributions. Joy is not identical to any combination of these components. Joy, like other psychological kinds, must be understood within particular historically effected, sociocultural practices that contribute both to its constitution and interpretation as a psychological kind. All psychological kinds (human actions, experiences, and understandings) are partially, even mostly, constituted by human practices. Unlike natural kinds, psychological kinds exist only because of relevant human sociocultural and linguistic practices.

To say that something requires something else, for example in the way that psychological behaviorists state that human action is a function of various environmental stimuli, is not sufficient to satisfy the identity require-ments of a true reduction. Musical performance requires a musical instru-ment but is not identical with the musical instrument and its constitutive, properly arranged mechanical components. Similarly, human experience and action require brains, biological bodies, and behavior but are not identical to cerebral activity, biological processes and functions, or bodily movements. Nor are human psychological kinds identical to the ways in which they have been represented in statistical or computational models, even when these are instantiated in operational computer environments. What needs to be appre-ciated with respect to various attempts to reduce psychological kinds to biological, behavioral, statistical–psychometric, neurophysiological, and com-putational entities is this: When all is said and done, human action, experi-ence, and understanding are not identical with any of these other phenomena, even though they may require them and/or have been construed by psy-chologists and others as analogous to them.

OMISSIONS

In addition to understanding why the various reductionistic strategies em-ployed by psychologists will not work, it is equally important to understand what they attempt to eliminate or disavow. By treating psychological kinds as if they were natural or indifferent kinds, reductionism in psychology assumes erroneously that the atomistic constitution of the latter applies equally to the former. What is ruled out or ignored by this strategy is human agency—the fact that psychological kinds are not indifferent but interactive with the sociocultural practices and systems of classification within which they develop and emerge. Psychological kinds like human action, experi-ence, and understanding make use of the linguistic, relational, symbolic practices of societies and cultures. They are not constituted atomistically from within but relationally from without. Moreover, once emergent in historical, sociocultural context, agentic, psychological kinds (such as desires, beliefs, reasons, goals, and actions) are capable of influencing the very historical, sociocultural contexts from which they spring.

For example, the ways in which individuals in Western societies understand themselves as autonomous, responsible selves require immersion in communal ways of talking and acting that assume and endow a particular sense of personhood—one in which moral accountability and will are seen to reside in the capacity of individuals for rationality and considered action. In this way, psychological kinds, like the self (in this case, as an experiential center and related set of descriptive attributes), actually are formed by the particular sociocultural practices into which biological humans are born and develop as psychological beings. If there were no societies or cultures to engage biological human infants in relevant practices of selfhood, biological humans maturing in isolation would not develop to experience, understand, and act as psychological beings, even if they somehow were to survive physically. Psychological kinds require biological bodies, but they are specifically constituted by sociocultural practices. We will have much more to say about the nature and development of agentic, psychological beings and kinds later in this book.

To recap, human agency and the sociocultural constitution of psychological beings are mostly ignored in reductionistic programs in disciplinary psychology. And, the way in which both agency and the sociocultural are discounted is through the conflation of psychological kinds with natural kinds. In the case of biological and neurophysiological reductions, the script goes much like this: Physicians and neurosurgeons occasionally encounter individuals (casualties of war, accident, or disease) whose memories, actions, and/or emotions are impaired in identifiable ways associated with the nature and location of injury. In such instances, it is clear that the injured area is required for full memorial, activity, or emotional functioning. This being so, it is not only tempting to conclude that memories, actions, or emotions require the injured areas in uninjured state but to conclude further that memories, actions, or emotions actually reside in the injured sites, or, more accurately, can be equated to the neurophysiological and biological processes and functions that occur in those and related areas.

Conversely, there is no corresponding, readily identifiable cultural or social injury that can be associated easily with specific psychological impairment or dysfunction. The ways in which sociocultural practices constitute psychological kinds are more difficult to comprehend, not only because they are less dramatically obvious and present but because they are not emphasized in our scientifically minded culture. Consequently, the necessary presence of relevant sociocultural practices for psychological functioning go relatively unnoticed in comparison with the more obvious biological, neurophysiological requirements for psychological functioning. And yet, the idea of human psychological functioning outside of requisite sociocultural embeddedness should be as ridiculous as the idea of human psychological functioning in the absence of intact, functioning physical–biological brains and bodies. The fact that the former situation is not as transparently non-sensical as the latter to most Westerners says a great deal about our continuing enthrallment with natural science and the unquestioning ways in which we have accepted psychologists' extension of its reign to the domain of psychological kinds. To illustrate the point, just imagine trying to formulate problem solving or coping strategies with no reference to, or reliance on, relevant, conventional social practices. For example, how would one approach marital difficulties without any reference to sociocultural practices, institutions, conventions, and expectations of marriage?

Disciplinary psychology has pursued its reductionistic programs within a culture deeply committed to natural science and technology. By simply ignoring the sociocultural constitution of psychological kinds and appealing to more obvious biological and neuophysiological requirements for psychological functioning, disciplinary psychology has mostly succeeded in drawing attention entirely to these latter requirements in a way that makes reductionistic strategies appear much more viable than they possibly can be. As we already have seen, the exceedingly broad use that psychologists have made of key terms and categories, such as behavior or learning, also has figured large in this overall reductionistic scenario. If all of human activity is understood as a kind of behavior independent of the intentions and circumstances of psychological individuals, then such behavior can be more easily equated with the nonintentional activity of say, for example, rats in mazes. The activity of rats in mazes requires relatively little in the way of sociocultural constitution, and the scientifically sanctioned infliction of biological, anatomical injury in such contexts can be seen to be almost fully determining of maze behavior.

But the practice of eliminating or ignoring sociocultural context in psychological experimentation has gone far beyond the biological reductionism of early comparative psychology (cf. Danziger, 1990). Having become accustomed to ignoring sociocultural context, experimental psychologists mostly have failed to recognize that the experimental settings they employ in collecting their data are social settings that are embedded within larger social and cultural contexts. To recognize such contexts makes things considerably more complicated than the tenets of reductionistic psychology can tolerate.

A final feature of psychology's traditional sociocultural blindness may be seen in the by now well-known penchant of many clinical psychologists to relocate what most reasonably might be understood as economic, political, and/or social difficulties in the minds, psyches, and personalities of individual clients. Thus, there is a tendency in the literature of clinical psychology to assume that particular events and experiences (often described as "traumatic") lead more or less directly and automatically to particular psychological symptoms and syndromes (e.g., posttraumatic stress disorder). Paradoxically, not only does such a maneuver place the problem to be treated within the client (and therefore within the realm of psychological intervention and expertise), but the assumed lawfulness of the connection between traumatic event and resultant psychological condition also leaves little room for the possible exercise of agency on the part of the individual client (cf. Bowman, 1997). And, of course, the administration of individual treatments by expert psychological practitioners directs both attention and resources from the possible alleviation of larger political, economic, and social problems.

SUMMARY AND IMPLICATIONS

Reductionism in psychology, thus, goes hand in hand with the false identification of psychological kinds with their physical and biological requirements and the ignoring of their sociocultural constitution and agentic character. From the mechanistic model of the reflex to stimulus–response psychology to statistical talk of independent and dependent variables to more recent computational analogies of input and output, the reductionistic models and metaphors employed in traditional psychology have attempted to remove what is most defining of psychological development and functioning (i.e., the sociocultural context) and to replace it with mere biological and physical requirements. However, the various reductionistic programs in psychology all fail because requirement is not identity, and the sociocultural constitution of psychological kinds cannot be ignored without failing to address the reality of psychological kinds per se.

What are the implications for psychology of the impossibility of the various psychological reductions proposed and practiced by psychologists? The methods of natural science assume identity reductions that can be understood in terms of general, causal laws. If psychological kinds are resistant to identity reductions, does this mean that they are impervious to the methods of natural science? In a word, yes. However, this conclusion needs additional clarification, and we will return to it in chapter 5. Then, we will present a detailed discussion of psychological reality as nested within other levels of reality: the sociocultural, biological, and physical. In anticipation of this forthcoming discussion, we want to be clear that our rejection of natural scientific reductionism in psychology does not mean that we reject natural science and its contributions at physical and biological levels of reality or as components in an overall understanding of human existence and experience. We certainly are not against natural science, nor do we wish to challenge the necessity, for a full account of human activity, of natural scientific understandings of the physical and biological world in which we exist as human beings. What we are against is what we regard as wrongheaded attempts to reduce psychological reality, in the sense of claiming that it is identical to and nothing more than physical and biological entities and processes, for no better reason than that the scientific pretensions and related methodological and professional commitments of disciplinary psychology are based on a confusion of requirement with identity.

Of course, psychologists' attempts to reduce human psychological kinds to their own statistical–psychometric and computational measures, methods, and models are also problematic. These kinds of reduction are parasitic on the inquiry practices of psychologists and tend to confuse everyday psychological actions and experiences with psychologists' favored methods of studying them. In the following section, we argue that such practices are far from benign and actually can succeed in yielding an impoverished, flattened picture of human psychology that may come to masquerade as the real thing. In this sense, the conflation of manufactured statistical and computational reality for everyday psychological reality is a difficulty unique to the twentieth, and presumably twenty-first, centuries. But, here again, a caution is appropriate. By offering the following critique of much traditional research practice in psychology, we do not wish to suggest that such methods have produced absolutely nothing of value or use. However, as we shall see in chapter 6, the possible value and utility of much psychological research and findings may be apparent only after a certain amount of reconfiguration that involves the reinterpretation of results under assumptions and critical understandings that may differ quite radically from those under which the research was conducted.

RESEARCH PRACTICES AND THE CONSTRUCTION OF PSEUDO-PSYCHOLOGICAL KINDS

In their efforts to reduce psychological kinds to natural kinds so that they might employ what they have understood as the proper methods of physical science, psychologists have displayed a penchant for empiricism that far outstrips their concern with conceptual issues pertaining to the phenomena they have chosen to investigate. Often, they have failed to recognize differences between near logical necessity and empirical contingency. Many of the propositions that psychologists have treated as matters of empirical contingency turn out to be logical and noncontingent (cf. Smedslund, 1988). It really is not necessary to conduct empirical research to determine that individuals who are confident that they can do something are more likely to attempt to do so, that individuals are surprised when they encounter the unexpected, or that young children who have no conception of one-to-one identity respond incorrectly to questions concerning whether differing arrangements of the same number of items contain more or fewer items relative to each other. Nor is it surprising to learn from empirical research that people prefer to look at attractive individuals, or that we experience stress in situations that we find stressful. These and many other supposed discoveries of psychological science are matters of reasonably direct semantic and logical analysis that require almost nothing in the way of the time, energy, and resources of psychological researchers.

The fact that many logical, noncontingent relationships that have stimulated the empiricist penchants of psychologists seldom are expressed as clearly or directly in the psychological literature as in the preceding paragraph should not be allowed to conceal their nonempirical character. It takes a relatively modest amount of conceptual work to determine that research support for, or "discovery" of, many empirical regularities in psychology is simply not required. For example, the proposition that "mothers who hold autonomous representations of their attachments with their infants form more secure attachments with their infants," should come as no surprise, given that the study purporting to test this proposition operationally categorizes mothers as autonomous if, and only if, they are responsive to the attachment cues of their infants (Fonagy, Steele, & Steele, 1991). The empirical literature of psychology is replete with examples of how psychologists' mistaken practices of operationalization interact with their empiricist worldview to yield "significant results" such as this.

Some commentators (e.g., Wallach & Wallach, 1998) even have gone so far as to suggest that the kind of hypothesis testing practiced in psychology results in almost all of psychologists' hypotheses being unfalsifiable. This is so, they claim, because any test of psychological hypotheses "requires reliance on conceptualizations that imply the hypotheses themselves. . . . If manipulations or observations are to serve as operationalizations of a variable, they must instantiate factors already recognized as relating to that variable as it is currently and commonly understood" (p. 186). Although we agree that much psychological inquiry may be criticized appropriately in this manner, we are not willing to accept some kind of Popperian falsificationism as an ultimate justification strategy for psychological inquiry. In fact, as we will attempt to argue in chapter 5, it is precisely the recognition that all psychological inquiry is interpretive in the manner implied by Michael Wallach and Lise Wallach (1998) that makes it possible to warrant at all, albeit never conclusively, the more sensible claims of psychological researchers. However, both the critical point made by the Wallachs and our own use of this insight in justifying some of the more sensible conclusions that might be drawn from some psychological research mostly have escaped the attention of psychological researchers.

At any rate, as we already have hinted, the empirical research practices of psychologists frequently do much more than restate what already might reside in everyday language and understanding. More often, they actively displace and redefine everyday psychological phenomena. The historical and sociocultural constitution of psychological kinds is a formidable challenge for psychological inquiry conceived as natural science. Whereas physical phenomena are constituted atomistically, psychological phenomena are constituted relationally in sociocultural context. By failing to recognize and conceptualize adequately the historical, sociocultural character of psychological kinds and the ways in which psychological individuals are capable of actively construing their actions and experiences, psychologists frequently "misplace" the objects of their inquiries.

Experiences such as pleasure, despair, and uncertainty and actions such as rewarding others, exacting vengeance, or striving for love and acceptance cannot be conceptualized adequately if relevant social–collective or individual–personal constituents are ignored. Such experiences and actions consist of the interpretations of psychological beings of the contexts they inhabit, historically and currently, and reflect their intentions with respect to existing and future possibilities. Experiences like humiliation, and related actions devoted to "saving face," require individual interpretations of collective sociocultural practices and forms, interpretations which themselves are embedded in the sociocultural life of communities of psychological beings.

When psychologists study such phenomena as if they were akin to plants, rocks, and planets, they pretend that our ways of knowing people and their experiences and activities are the same as our ways of knowing these inanimate objects. When psychological subjects are placed in psychological research settings, they are removed from the everyday sociocultural contexts that constitute much of their psychological actions and experiences. When standard psychological measures are used to determine human personality and functioning, the psychological subject is treated as if the personality characteristics and action tendencies supposedly evident in her or his paper-and-pencil responses exist in isolation from the everyday circumstances that give rise to, are caught up in, and make sense of them.

As early as 1894, the dislocation of psychological phenomena, and the distancing of psychologists from that which they were investigating, already was receiving strong criticism from prominent scholars like Wilhelm Dilthey (1894/1977). Moreover, such criticism was accompanied by positive proposals for the conduct of psychological inquiry. Eschewing the machinelike recording and analysis of laboratory observations by investigators who actively suppressed their everyday understandings, Dilthey, for example, proposed that psychologists use their everyday experience as a basis for interpreting the psychological meaning that could be directly sensed in peoples' actions. Such injunctions went almost completely unheeded by mainstream psychologists, who drew a sharp line between the activities of psychological science and those of everyday understanding and who conveniently chose mostly to disregard the context of the latter in preference to their reductionistic practices.

CAUSAL WOES

One of the most interesting consequences of psychologists' attempts to adopt what they regard as the research practices of natural science to the study of human behavior concerns the difficulties they have experienced in establishing the kinds of causal claims that natural science demands. Because of the atomistic constitution of physical phenomena, many focal phenomena in physics and chemistry can be isolated in idealized laboratory situations without undue distortion. Physical science takes advantage of this characteristic of physical phenomena in establishing general causal laws. By isolating phenomena of interest and by manipulating and/or controlling forces acting upon them, in idealized settings (e.g., total vacuums, particle accelerators, computer simulations, frictionless planes, etc.), causal regularities can be observed that likely would avoid precise detection in everyday circumstances outside of the physical laboratory.

However, such isolation and manipulation under idealized conditions is not available to the psychologist attempting to understand human experience and action. When human kinds are uprooted from their everyday contexts of occurrence, they are altered. Grief at the loss of a loved one or exhilaration following a victorious performance on the playing field cannot be captured "as they really are" in the research settings and/or on the research instruments of the psychologist. Without the ability to isolate and manipulate focal phenomena in ideal settings, psychologists are without any known method of establishing and warranting the causal claims they frequently make.

But the issue of causality in human affairs cuts deeper than this. The meanings, interpretations, and reasons that must be used to account for psychological kinds do not lend themselves easily to causal determinism. Even if human psychology requires, at different levels, the operation of biochemical and neurophysiological causes (which we do not doubt at all), such underlying causal patterns hardly can be appealed to, at least in any sensible way, as satisfactory explanations for human aspirations, plans, commitments, values, and emotional experience. All genuinely psychological kinds are historically and socioculturally situated in ways that escape the investigative and explanatory modes of natural science. Their understanding requires interpretation of meanings and reasoned argument. The possible fact that one's hostility might be associated with neural state X2P is not a satisfactory answer to one's concern about it. If phenomena can be accounted for entirely and satisfactorily on the basis of physical causation alone, such phenomena are not psychological kinds.

The foregoing observations and arguments seldom make a dent in psychologists' penchant for drawing and advancing causal claims and psychological prescriptions based on their mostly correlational data that better represent psychologists' measures and operational definitions than the real phenomena of interest. After all, the entire point of psychological science modeled after physical science is to establish and promote causal relations that must pertain (by analogy) in the realm of human psychology. Fees as reimbursement for psychological services and taxpayers' dollars in support of psychological research are not likely to be attracted, at least in contemporary social and political arenas, by explicit acknowledgment of psychologists' inability to warrant the causal assertions they insist on making. In passing, it might be noted that one of the more fascinating chapters in the history of psychology concerns the early enlisting of psychologists and psychological research by the military–industrial and educational sectors of American society in the interest of advancing their own agendas under the banner of psychological science (cf. Danziger, 1990). Given the disciplinary and personal opportunities they perceived in such associations, many psychologists were enthusiastic in offering themselves and their fledgling science to such service.

Variability and Its Statistical Treatment

A related, yet distinct, difficulty with psychological research practice concerns the variability of psychologists' data across individual subjects and settings. Of course, this is exactly what would be expected if the historical, sociocultural constitution of psychological phenomena were understood. In fact, data from most psychological research that are not directly or indirectly logically predetermined (see previous discussion) differ considerably in kind, pattern, and direction. Recently, some psychologists (e.g., Sohn, 1999) have coined the term *effect constancy* to connote the extent to which the overall experimental effects discussed in reports of psychological research actually pertain across individual participants in the studies reported. The coining and use of such a term acknowledges growing concern with the observed variability of experimental effects across individuals and contexts. After more than one hundred years of mostly assuming uncritically such constancy of effects, such concern is welcome indeed.

The characteristic inconsistency of complex human activity, across individuals, settings, and time always has presented a huge difficulty for psychologists. Since Sir Francis Galton's (1908) early work in anthropometry and William Winch's (1908) pioneering use of the treatment group in educational psychology, psychologists' most common pseudo-solution to this problem has been to pool data from large numbers of individuals and to use aggregated statistical averages and regularities to mask, and actually to take advantage of, individual, situational, and temporal variability. Through statistical manipulation and treatment, psychological data are given an appearance of regularity and predictability that they do not possess on their own, even in the already operationalized world of psychological research. In fact, it is this statistical "laundering" of psychological data that does much to support the interpretation of psychological findings in ways that take on a quasi-lawful appearance. However, statistical generalizations alone are not laws and statistical regularities only masquerade as psychological regularities.

In some programs of psychological inquiry, reported statistical regularities fail to correspond precisely to the actual actions or experiences of most individual contributors to the reported statistics. In short, much extant psychological inquiry testifies to a triumph of statistical method over substantive psychological conceptualization—a substitution (but not a bona fide reduction) of statistical for psychological reality (cf. Danziger, 1990). Even the arguable ancient adage to the effect that science does not deal with individual cases *(scientia non est individuorum)* cannot reasonably be interpreted to mean that science and its applications can ignore individual cases and instances altogether, especially if psychological interventions, supposedly tied to psychological science, are targeted primarily at individuals.

Probing further into the statistical applications favored by psychologists reveals yet another way in which psychologists' mimicking of natural science differs from the real thing. Over the years, some of psychology's foremost statisticians, methodologists, and theoreticians have recognized that the use of statistical methods and tests in established areas of natural science differs from the use of statistical methods and tests in psychology (cf. Cohen, 1994; Meehl, 1967). In developed areas of natural science, statistics are often used in attempts to determine the likelihood that the physical world is as it is theorized to be. Here, statistics are tools that do not substitute for, or conceal, focal phenomena. In properly conducted natural science, statistical methods are employed only after clearly conceptualized, and mathematically modeled "point" predictions have been made that adequately reflect well-formulated, competing theoretical possibilities.

By comparison, in psychology, hypothesis testing tends to be much more atheoretically and generously open-ended. Psychologists frequently aspire to discover from their research "nothing more precise than that some independent variable has an effect on some dependent variable. . . . What *exactly* is meant by the finding or proposition that a treatment works or that a treatment affects some dependent measure is virtually never specified" (Sohn, 1999, p. 637). Add to this a typically overly generous setting of statistical probability levels and we are left with what amount to very general appeals to any kind of difference between two or more conditions, treatments, or other levels of quasi-experimental variables. Given the high likelihood that any two levels of such factors will differ in some unspecified way and given the fact that most such differences detected through psychological testing account for somewhere between only five and thirty percent of the variation in the dependent or criterion measure of interest (even with formal levels of statistical probability as low as $p < .01$), research psychologists are almost guaranteed of finding something to report as significant, at least in statistical terms. When commonly pursued post hoc search strategies are added to this already liberal mix, as they frequently are (sometimes at the urging of journal editors and granting agencies anxious to report "positive" results, and with the acquiescence of researchers in consideration of their career aspirations), it is fair to say, in Will Rogers fashion, that research psychologists seldom meet an hypothesis they can't advance. The price of such imprecision is high. In fact, it amounts to an inability to enhance our understanding of the matters under consideration.

In short, psychologists' use of statistical methodology and language departs dramatically from the use of such tools in established areas of natural science. In psychology, variability owing to differences among individuals and across settings is treated statistically in ways that actually take advantage of it. Witness, for example, attempts by psychological researchers to inflate the variability displayed in their questionnaire data by using an even number of response options without a middle position, or by subsequently (during data preparation) systematically eliminating middle-range or neutral responses. Not only do these so-called good research practices artificially manipulate patterns and trends in the data, but they actually go a considerable way toward creating results with respect to particular research hypotheses and purposes—presumably not at all the kind of thing that natural scientific methodology would condone. By confusing explanations of focal phenomena with explanations of their (sometimes forced) variability, psychologists' use of statistical procedures typically "papers over" the general absence of consistent, powerful, and precise effects in the experimental, quasi-experimental, and correlational research conducted under the rubric of psychological science.

The general absence of lawful relations that has been revealed by psychological research contrasts sharply with the many such relations evident in physical science in which empirical regularities allow applied scientists and engineers to make exacting and routine use of mathematical tools such as applied differential calculus. In contrast, applied psychologists can point only in a vague way to what might be construed as relevant, statistical findings.

MANUFACTURING AND GENERALIZING PSYCHOLOGICAL ENTITIES

However, the problems created by psychologists' peculiar adaptations of reductionism, operationism, causal determinism, and statistical methods go much further than the creation of a highly debatable psychological science modeled after misunderstandings of natural science. Over time, after inappropriately reductive, operational indicators are entertained in psychological research in the form of statistical variables, such research-manufactured, statistical entities come to be thought of as real psychological factors with important causal influence. In this way, we gradually come to confuse such overly simplified, unidimensional, pale imitations with the everyday, full-blooded actions, experiences, and understandings of human psychological individuals. In this sense, not only has disciplinary psychology, through its research practices, consistently put methodological concerns ahead of more substantive concerns about the nature of its subject matter, but it has begun to succeed in replacing that subject matter with watered-down, flattened, and highly imperfect clones invented through the practices of psychological research. The fact that this invented reality is more tractable with respect to the scientific aspirations of disciplinary psychology often is considered as adequate warrant for the success of the enterprise of psychological science conceived as natural science. However, a closer look at what actually is going on is much less reassuring, for as we argue throughout this book, human psychological kinds are not indifferent natural kinds, and should not be construed as if they were.

Unlike physical objects in idealized laboratory settings, humans do not respond predictably to circumstances they encounter in their lives. Not only are psychological phenomena constituted by their historical and sociocultural contexts, they also reflect individual representations and constructions of these contexts that can vary greatly across individuals, settings, and time. Consequently, human experience and action are uncertain in a way that is not true of physical phenomena.

The uncertainty of psychological kinds makes it extremely difficult to generalize from information gathered about such phenomena at times and contexts in the past to times and contexts in the present and future. Although all generalizations run headlong into well-known problems of induction and skepticism, generalizations concerning psychological kinds, unlike those concerning natural kinds, are rendered even more uncertain by the fact that psychological kinds are doubly interpretive in both their existence and manner of study. As stated earlier, the real role of statistical tests and procedures in psychology often is to hide highly variable patterns of empirical results across individuals and contexts.

Of course, matters become even more disquieting when psychologists offer prescriptions supposedly based on their findings, which they almost invariably do. When this happens, psychologists not only court difficulties of generalizing from what was to what is and what will be, they also take on the added burden of generalizing from what was or what is to what ought to be. Of course, such moral injunctions are seldom recognized explicitly for what they are, and the fact that they cannot be justified on empirical grounds alone is mostly ignored, even in the highly proceduralized ethical guidelines routinely issued by various professional associations of psychologists.

The overgeneralization, manufacture, and prescription of psychological findings has had a considerable cumulative effect on our everyday understandings of psychological kinds, including our selves and others. Moreover, this effect has been extremely conservative, despite the attempts of organizations like the American Psychological Association to attend to and promote social diversity and justice. The core problem is that the overly simplified, overly generalized, and overly tame version of human psychological functioning demanded by psychological science in its naturalistic posture has consistently demonstrated a general lack of interest and indifference to differences in human actions and experiences across historical, sociocultural, and political contexts. Moral issues, including questions pertaining to issues of race, gender, ethnicity, and other sources and manifestations of difference, generally have been ignored in psychological science. However, even though questions of meaning and moral significance do not constitute the indifferent kinds of physical, natural science, they lie at the very center of all psychological kinds. But before turning to more extended examples of the possible social consequences of organized psychology, it is important to consider the complicity of professional psychology in the furtherance of psychology's attachment to natural science and engineering as models for psychological research and practice.

THE ROLE OF PROFESSIONAL PSYCHOLOGY

To understand why organized psychology has shown relatively little concern about the various matters discussed in this chapter, one must understand the demands of professional psychology for a scientific foundation for its practices of personal and social intervention. As indicated in chapter 1, we believe that while many have commented on the reductive excesses of scientific psychology (including many disgruntled psychological practitioners), the unintentional complicity of professional psychology in this reductive exercise mostly has been overlooked. For somewhat paradoxically, and despite frequent protests about the practical irrelevance of psychological science, one of the primary benefactors of reductive psychological science has been professional psychology. Where scientific psychology has reductively disavowed human agency by removing it from its historical, sociocultural context and treating "isolated atoms" of it as natural kinds, professional psychology has been happy to receive these detached fruits as readily malleable entities that can be instrumentally measured and theorized to provide a scientific basis for their "helping" practices.

Professional psychology has been one of the growth industries of the twentieth century. It takes little imagination to appreciate the high value and utility for professional psychology, especially in North America, of a relatively uncritical acceptance and promotion of professional psychological practice based on presumably solid psychological science. The scientist–practitioner rhetoric of organized psychology consistently trumpets the virtues of this fantasy. And the fantasy continues, for the most part, even in the presence of increasingly frequent, eloquent, and well-argued suggestions that psychology would do well to cease its pseudoscientific pretensions and rejoin the tradition of serious scholarship (e.g., Koch, 1993).

Historians of psychology (e.g., Cushman, 1995; Danziger, 1998) are fully aware of the extent to which professional psychology, especially in North America but increasingly worldwide, has both fueled and traded on the seemingly unfettered fetish of contemporary individuals for self-enhancing commodities and services. In many ways, this addiction may be considered one of the primary exports of what sometimes is deridingly referred to as American cultural imperialism. From the time of Plato (ca. 428–347 B.C.E.) and Socrates (ca. 470–399 B.C.E.), the Western intellectual tradition, for the most part, has claimed a unique "self" for each human being. Moreover, it has been assumed that these individual "selves" can be known. Indeed, as Miguel de Cervantes (1547–1616) proclaimed, it is our business to know ourselves. Contemporary people have taken the Socratic and Quixotic injunction to know our selves very literally. Self studies have become a major scholarly, therapeutic, publishing, and commercial enterprise, even as some postmodernists declare and celebrate the alleged death of the self to a growing market of the self-absorbed.

In contemporary Western life, individuals are viewed as responsible for their own success and failure. At the same time, some of their heightened sense of self-empowerment and entitlement frequently takes the form of blaming others (often with the help of the law, the media, and organized psychology) for circumstances that fall short of their self-assessed rights as autonomous, free persons. Self-centeredness and widespread social anomie have emerged as common modes of contemporary life. More and more, our identities are molded by what Wolfgang Haug (1986) refers to as commodity aesthetics. Commodities no longer are viewed as means of survival but as means of valorization. The use value of commodities has been replaced to a great extent by image and appearance, especially associated with the promise of enhancement to buyers' selves. The appearance of a commodity always promises more than it can deliver. What is necessary no longer can be distinguished from that which is not, but which now is perceived as something one cannot do without. In short, the ideal of commodity aesthetics is to deliver the absolute minimum, disguised by the maximum in seductive illusion.

An important part of contemporary commodity aesthetics is an over-reliance on expert knowers, and it is here where professional psychology figures large. In a world increasingly committed to appearance, no pain or suffering (physical or psychological) need be tolerated. Experts promise to remove all problems that beset us, even as the refinement of supposed expert skill rebounds in a multiplication of problems for which expert assistance is thought to be necessary. Of particular importance in such a world is the marketing of tools of identity making. Here, professional psychological services appear to offer both practical and aesthetic value to contemporary selves and to be capable of removing impediments to self-promotion (now accepted as a moral good).

The demand for professional psychology fits well with a commodity aesthetics in which appearance is everything, whatever the reality behind the upbeat front. In such times, it makes good sense to market psychological services as if they are saturated with scientific merit. What matters is the maintenance of a steady stream of individuals seeking expert psychological assistance. On this measure, psychology in its professional guise, undergirded by its purported scientific foundation, has been one of the major success stories of the last half of the twentieth century. Contemporary Westerners now seek psychological counseling, therapy, and consultation for problems and concerns they previously would have dealt with themselves, with the free assistance of family, friends, and the clergy.

Today, a real danger exists that professional psychology will continue its cult of scientistic professionalism for increasingly self-serving economic and political motives (Wertz, 1995). For the first time in many years, reimbursements for professional services and grants for applied psychological investigation appear to be in decline, as governments at all levels strive to gain control over their budgets. Because funding for psychological research and practice tends to be predicated on the kinds of misplaced assumptions and confusions that psychologists themselves have perpetrated through their past practices of inquiry and service provision, the most likely bet is that we now will see a new wave of scientistic and professional strategies and promises by the psychological establishment. Therefore, it comes as no surprise to witness current attempts on the part of many psychologists to align themselves with computer science, cognitive neuroscience, and evolutionary biology. The conception and image of psychology as trading expertly in natural kinds remains constant, even as strategic fashions change.

Psychological professionalism in combination with scientistic psychology has had a dramatic impact on our selves and our actions and experiences. To a considerable extent, contemporary Western people seem to have adopted the language and conventions of organized psychology as the means for identifying, experiencing, and acting. To understand such a replacement as an authentic advance in self-understanding is commonplace now. In this sense, organized psychology may be seen as a set of social practices engaged mostly by psychological experts, but increasingly by the rest of us, that has succeeded in playing a major role in the formation of our individual and collective identities. Nowhere is this trend more evident than in the wildly popular area of self-esteem and personal development, a facet of contemporary life mostly unknown to those who lived before the Second World War.

THE EXAMPLE OF SELF-CONCEPT

One of the most elastic of all those terms and categories employed by psychologists is that of *attitude*. By the 1930s, American psychologists had begun to explain everything from changing fashions to swings in public opinion and declines in traditional moral standards to the attitudes of individual citizens (e.g., Allport, 1935). For these psychologists, attitude went well beyond a disposition to act. In a move consistent with the rampant individualism of American culture between the First and Second World Wars and since, psychologists gradually began to talk as if attitudes were real entities interior to, and possessed by, every functioning person. Once developed, the attitudes of a person were considered to be relatively permanent, interior possessions that exerted a causal influence on what a person believed, thought, and did.

The "natural reality" of psychologists' conception of attitudes was confirmed in the minds of most psychologists and many others when L. L. Thurstone and his student Rensis Likert developed various methods of measuring the attitudes of individuals (cf. Danziger, 1997). The most popular of these consisted of simply asking people to rate the extent to which they agreed or disagreed with a variety of statements concerning whatever it was that was being measured. Of course, such a method was indistinguishable from many of those then in use for purposes of opinion polling. Nonetheless, when coupled with psychologists' conviction that attitudes were semipermanent, individual entities, it became widely accepted that the attitude measures of psychologists constituted an important scientific achievement. Psychology seemed to have succeeded in advancing itself in ways reminiscent of how increasingly sophisticated methods of physical measurement were associated with advances in the natural sciences.

With the practical use of psychological attitude research during and after the Second World War, the measurement of soldiers' and civilians' attitudes became widely accepted as a scientific practice in areas such as recruitment, personnel selection, and vocational and educational guidance. With popular use, the assumption that attitudes were natural possessions of individuals rather than disciplinary enhancing creations of psychologists was mostly forgotten. Psychological research on attitudes consisted simply of obtaining agree–disagree responses from a large number of individuals (typically and most conveniently groups of students) and subjecting seemingly meticulous quantifications of these responses to a variety of statistical procedures. Of particular interest here is the way in which psychometric and statistical reductionism in psychology has come more and more to reflect the applied "scientific" interests of professional psychology. Although basic experimental psychology has employed biological, neurophysiological, and computational strategies of reduction in quasi-laboratory settings, professional psychology has made use of psychological measurement and statistics to extend the constructions of psychologists to the world outside the laboratory.

Research on almost any attitude proposed by psychologists as worthy of scientific or practical consideration now could be unproblematically undertaken, including research on those attitudes individuals have about themselves. Within the historical tradition of psychological research on attitudes, self-concept is understood by psychologists to consist of a causally efficacious property of an individual that is implicated in a wide variety of personal actions and experiences and which can be measured by individual responses to an appropriately constructed psychological measure. By creating numerous items on many measures that claim to reveal a person's self-concept, generations of psychologists have operationalized the self. For many psychologists and others, an individual's ratings of the extent to which statements such as "I feel good about myself most of the time" are more or less like me, not only describe, but actually constitute, the self.

The self as operationalized self-concept certainly renders the self more accessible but only at the obvious cost of reducing the human agency it connotes to a set of ratings on the attitude questionnaires of psychologists. In effect, the entire exercise converts an important set of metaphysical and ontological issues concerning the nature of human existence and agency to a grossly simplified exercise in methodology. For many scientific and practical purposes, the self has become a collection of self-ratings on a particular instrument at a specific time and place. Psychologists have obtained what they consider to be a scientifically respectable method of measuring the self and have not been shy about advancing the professional implications of their technical achievement.

Because the self has been made readily accessible to psychological measurement, it has become a tractable focus for the applications of professional psychology in education, psychotherapy, vocational counseling, and industrial–organizational psychology. In all of these areas, professional psychologists now routinely engage in, and talk about, how their interventions positively affect the self-esteem of students, clients, job seekers, and employees. The fact that it now is possible to walk into many elementary school classrooms in North America and find posters advertising all those things that students like about themselves and that make them special is only one minor example of the pervasive impact of psychologists' "self" research and practice. The obvious fact that one is not especially unique because one can ride a bicycle or has a brother is of little consequence in a world of facile descriptions masquerading as genuine self-consideration and reflection. Agency has been reduced to checking the "most of the time" box at the end of a written description of mostly uninteresting and uninspired dispositions and actions.

Of course, many psychologists would regard such facile application as unmitigated nonsense. Nonetheless, it seems clear that this particular kind of nonsense would not exist were it not for psychology's mostly unwavering commitment to the idea that supposedly substantive agentic entities like self-concept can be measured successfully by the descriptions and rating scales employed in much applied psychological research and intervention. By reducing the question of self to a mere description of how one currently is doing (as seen through the instruments of professional psychology), it becomes possible to achieve seemingly amazing results through rather straightforward psychological interventions purporting to enhance the self-esteem and self-worth of students, clients, and others. In the individualistic, self-concerned cultural context of America, these interventions of professional psychology, aided and abetted by the ostensible scientific foundation of psychology as a whole, are now accepted as both efficacious and appropriate. Professional psychological helpers now appear on almost every horizon of human accomplishment or tragedy as it unfolds within the North American landscape.

In a simplified "natural" psychological world, all the understanding or intervention that is required is one capable of measuring and altering individual responses to psychological measures and expert assessment. Because such understanding and change can be achieved relatively easily in the psychological laboratory, the classroom, or the psychologist's office, there is no need to deal directly with the everyday psychological and sociocultural world in which most complex human difficulties and challenges reside. In a world constituted primarily by disciplinary psychology, it is possible to publish an incredible number of journals and books each year that provide empirical support for psychologists' practices in an ever expanding panoply of areas.

In this world, nothing is too difficult to attempt, and very few things fail to yield to a psychological "fix." All that is required is that individuals understand themselves and change according to the ways and means that psychologists have fashioned through their research and clinical practices. And when the inevitable difficulties arise (all of which might be expected to attend the export of this idealized psychological world to the real world of human experience in sociocultural context), psychologists lament the extent to which many members of the public at large obstinately refuse to join in their scientistic fantasy. Nonetheless, as organized psychology gradually broadens its public venues and promotes its message with enhanced media "know-how," contemporary society is becoming more and more saturated with what might be regarded as some of the worst excesses of psychological scientism and professionalism.

For our purposes in this book, the biggest casualty in all of this is a viable conception of human agency, one that adequately reflects the human condition as historical and sociocultural, as well as physical and biological. For human agency, understood as the human capacity to choose and act in ways that are not fully determined by factors other than an agent's own self-determination, cannot arise and emerge from physics and biology alone. History, culture, and society also are required, and these are not atomisticallly constituted, natural kinds, even if they may yield to intelligible understanding. The human context of psychological, agentic kinds has not been captured adequately by reductive psychological science or its professional handmaiden.

ANOTHER KIND OF REDUCTIONISM IN PSYCHOLOGY

Despite most psychologists' historical and continuing commitment to psychology modeled after physics (cf. Dawda & Martin, 2001), there always have been dissenting voices to the tradition of psychology as natural science. In fact, a considerable effort by the psychological establishment has been devoted to ensuring that these various alternatives have stayed on the margins of mainstream experimental psychology, so as not to challenge the ever optimistic promise of a scientifically grounded psychological practice (cf. Koch, 1981). Psychoanalytic psychology has been granted mostly peripheral status in clinical and developmental psychology, and the long-standing alternatives of gestalt psychology (e.g., Köhler, 1947), symbolic interactionism (e.g., Mead, 1934), and humanistic psychology (e.g., Rogers, 1961) have been pushed far from the scientific center of the discipline.

Nonetheless, in more recent years an increasingly diverse set of alternatives has been proposed, all of which challenge the core idea of psychology as natural science. Phenomenological (e.g., Giorgi, 1985), narrative (e.g., Polkinghorne, 1988), rigorous humanistic (e.g., Rychlak, 1988), cultural (e.g., Marsella, DeVos, & Hsu, 1985), feminist (e.g., Hare-Mustin & Marecek, 1990), critical (e.g., Tolman, 1994), pragmatic (e.g., Barone, Maddux, & Snyder, 1997), and discursive (e.g., Harré & Gillet, 1994) approaches to psychological inquiry are now much discussed. Sustained programs of research that adopt these perspectives are increasingly visible, even if they remain as yet little attended by the majority of psychologists. Given the obvious growth of interest in these various alternatives among psychologists and others, it seems reasonable to assume that the next twenty years will see an ever greater representation in the published literature of psychology, of work conducted from these perspectives. Indeed, many of the ideas championed in such work may be seen to be consistent with the overall aim of this current volume in promoting a more agency-friendly psychology. However, there are some trends within this body of work that contain a slightly different threat to a full recognition of human agency within psychological research and practice.

Of particular interest in this regard are more radical challenges to psychology by some versions of postmodernism and social constructionism. These critical approaches go well beyond concerns about psychology as a physical science and challenge psychology's status as a discipline concerned with the study of the individual psyche, with the promised yield of warrantable psychological knowledge. As Kenneth Gergen (1991) has said, "Under postmodernism, processes of individual reason, intention, moral decision making, and the like—all central to the ideology of individualism—lose their status as realities" (p. 241). The gravity and radicalness of such postmodern proposals has led some psychologists (e.g., Sass, 1992; Smith, 1994) to wonder if the postmodern cure for psychological scientism and detached individualism might not be an equally insidious sociocultural reductionism that once again rules out human agency and the possibility of bona fide psychological understanding. Given the current prominence of Gergen's views as an alternative to psychological scientism, we believe that they deserve particular, critical attention.

By offering a critique of Gergen's social constructionism in psychology, we hope to succeed in creating an opening between the extremes of traditional scientistic psychology, on the one hand, and what we regard as too radical postmodern reactions to psychological scientism, on the other hand. It is in this clearing that we subsequently will envision a genuinely agentic psychology that does not reduce human agency to either biological or cultural phenomena, even though both kinds of phenomena are required in the formation of agency itself.

Gergen's (1991, 1994, 1997) rejection of essentialist realism and objectivity takes a strongly antisubjectivist and relativistic, even anarchistic, turn. His postmodern social constructionism favors a strong sociocultural reduction of individualistic psychological phenomena. The aim of Gergen's approach is "to reconstitute [the psychological world] as a domain of the social" (1997, p. 736)—"we can envision the elimination of psychological states and conditions as explanations for action, and the reconstitution of psychological predicates within the sphere of social process" (p. 740). Moreover, because social constructionism "traces ontological posits to language, and language to processes of relationships" (p. 740), there are "no transcendent grounds for eliminating any theoretical formulation. To eradicate a theoretical perspective would be not only tantamount to losing a mode of human intelligibility (along with related social practices), but to silence a community of meaning making" (p. 724). For Gergen, this relativistic conclusion is warranted because "there can be no canonical slate of criteria for evaluating [perspectives or accounts or appraisals] . . . with respect to 'the real'" (p. 725).

Again, the aim of Gergen's social constructionism is "to press beyond the individual performance to consider the patterns of interchange within which the performance is embedded" (1997, p. 741). To this end, "[t]he goal of truth is eschewed, and objectivity as the research desideratum is replaced with intelligibility" (p. 741). "The attempt, then, is to extend the use-value of the theoretical discourse to patterns of daily life" (p. 741). "And while much . . . discursive work is politically neutral, the present account is explicitly set against individualist ideology and related practices" (p. 741).

Commentary on Gergen's social constructionism, especially as joined to his stated postmodern agenda for the social empowering of marginalized voices and perspectives, has focused on his elision of crucial distinctions, the absence of coherent justification of his own epistemic and moral conclusions, his inappropriate reduction of psychological to sociocultural phenomena, and his rejection of possibly necessary practical, physical, and biological limits to constructionism (see Harré & Krausz, 1996; Richardson, 1998; Taylor, 1988). For example, Rom Harré and Michael Krausz (1996) claim that Gergen "elides two ontologically utterly different notions; the set of attributes that can be ascribed to a subject, and the subject to which they are ascribed" (p. 197). According to Harré and Krausz, Gergen only establishes successfully the already widely shared view among psychologists that identities of persons are constituted relative to languages and cultural practices. In no way does he show that one's sense of self is "threatened or eroded or in any way compromised by the fact that we must adapt to many diverse contexts in our everyday lives" (p. 197). By failing to take seriously the idea that there is a private self as well as a public discourse, "Gergen quite omits to consider whether there may be necessary conditions for the possibility of language as a human practice that undermine the alleged moral openness of the postmodern condition" (p. 198). As Anthony Holiday (1988) has argued, there may be certain requirements for language practices in any community of language users—for example, that there be a certain kind of attitude of respect that interlocutors must extend to each other to make any conversation possible. Or as H. J. G. Kempen (1996) more recently has urged, the human physical, biological body is itself an evolutionary given that all cultures somehow must sustain within a real physical world that places some basic constraints on such sustenance.

Gergen's social constructionism, while pointing to important limitations on psychological theorizing and inquiry, seems to go too far in combating unfettered individualism and epistemic certainty, to the point where some obvious constraints on, and distinctions concerning, human experience and action are ignored or elided, respectively. One important consequence is that Gergen ultimately has no means available to justify or argue coherently for his own anti-ontological and anti-epistemological conclusions nor to support his favored moral, political agenda.

However, Gergen, is very familiar with such criticisms and seems to accept them as a necessary cost of resisting the allure of foundationalist essentialism. In responding to his critics, Gergen (1994) defends his antisubjectivism after admitting freely that his constructionism forces us "to confront the loss of what, for many, is the central ingredient of personal existence: private experience" (p. 70). He then goes on to promote his constructionist project as follows. "Given the difficulty in locating a referent for the term 'experience,' let us adopt a constructionist standpoint and attend to *discourse about experience*. In considering such discourse, the paramount question is one of social consequence" (p. 70). However, Gergen eventually tempers his rejection not only of "experience talk," but of experience itself "Yet it is important to stress that there is nothing about such explorations [discursive studies of language in use] that militates against either a scholarly concern with the nature of experience or the common use of the term in everyday life" (p. 71). If an acceptable social consequence of Gergen's espousal of constructionist antisubjectivism is continued scholarly focus on the nature of human experience, one might well wonder about its intended point. Having rejected the possibility of human intentionality, while simultaneously respecting talk about intentionality as a form of collective human social activity, Gergen seems to accept such seeming incoherence as a necessary price for resisting any kind of ontological claim concerning human essence.

In defending his antirealism and related strong relativism, Gergen (1994) displays a similar willingness to accept what appear to be troubling consequences of his resistance to foundationalist claims. Initially concerning himself with commonly encountered objections to these core commitments of social constructionism, he states, "Constructionism makes no denial concerning explosions, poverty, death, or "the world out there" more generally. Neither does it make any affirmation" (p. 72). It is difficult to know exactly what to make of this statement, but Gergen once again moves quickly past questions of ontology to discourse: "Once we attempt to articulate 'what there is,' however, we enter the world of discourse. At that moment the process of construction commences, and this effort is inextricably woven into processes of social interchange and into history and culture" (p. 72). For Gergen, the fact that discourse is necessarily contingent in this way means that "[t]he adequacy of any word or arrangement of words to 'capture reality as it is' is a matter of local convention" (p. 73). It also is clear that Gergen attaches a decidedly moral significance to this strongly relativistic conclusion: "And why, from a constructionist standpoint, should we press toward closure of all intelligibilities save one? Why set out to impoverish the landscape of language as opposed to enriching it?" (p. 76). And later, "there is no single value, moral idea, or social good that, when fully pursued, will not trammel upon the alternatives and obliterate the social patterns these alternatives support" (p. 81).

Gergen's (1994) defense of his antirealism thus consists of a rapid move from ontology to discourse, culminating in the conclusion that because discursive practices are necessarily contingent they neither reflect nor are constrained by any necessary state of the world. Further, because all that is at stake is contingent discursive practice, there exists no rational basis on which to judge the relative merits of any such practices that might emerge. The obvious fact that such a conclusion must include the discursive practices of social constructionism is not lost on Gergen, who claims to regard "the process of dismantling constructionist 'rhetoric' [as] an end much to be valued" (p. 77). The upshot is that there apparently is no basis either for Gergen's own project or for the values of pluralism and tolerance for diversity that it wishes to champion, all of which seems a very high price to pay for resisting any kind of psychological essentialism, realist foundationalism, or epistemic certainty.

We sympathize with Gergen's attempt to combat the scientistic pretensions, ethnocentrically assumed foundationalism, naive realism, and runaway individualism of much North American and European psychology.

What may previously have been considered to be universal, ahistorical essentials of a single human psyche are, in Gergen's perspective, revealed as necessarily and inescapably embedded in historical, sociocultural contexts—our seeming certainty about them and their status is a matter of contingency rather than transcendental necessity. We psychologists would do well always to remember that we inhabit times, societies, and cultures that construct us as subjects through our participation in them, a participation that is mostly inarticulate and taken for granted. In our attempts to reflect on and articulate our lives and work, we are forever embedded in the particulars of our locations in historical, sociocultural time and space, from which we never can escape. Our insights, generalizations, and understandings arise within this contingency and, consequently, are necessarily incomplete, power-infused, limited, and open to revision—points that have been developed in many important ways by feminist and postcolonial theorists (e.g., Butler, 1997; Spivak, 1996).

Against this background of inescapable context, construction, and contingency, it is the height of presumption to herald our inquiries and conclusions as if they mattered more generally across times and contexts and, imperialistically, to ignore that which differs from our own necessarily limited practices and perspectives. When understood in this way, even our best attempts at critical reflection on our work and our selves are revealed as ritualistic and self-advancing, serving mostly to promote our own interests and positions of relative power and advantage. Insofar as Gergen's social constructionism challenges, shocks, and occasionally "jollies" us out of our complacently nonreflective mythologies of purely rational and empirical, unproblematically progressive, and widely generalizable psychological inquiry, good!

However, in our opinion Gergen's antiscientism and antifoundationalism fail to preserve the very human kinds they claim to address. He reduces human agency too radically and irretrievably to its sociocultural and historical origins and places insufficient importance on the practical and moral significance with which we humans endow our interpretations. As Hacking (1995, 1999) and Martin and Sugarman (1999) make clear, just because human psychological kinds are constituted within historical, sociocultural context and practice does not mean that they are ultimately reducible to these contexts and practices. Once emergent within societies and cultures, psychological beings not only continue to be affected by sociocultural practices but also are affected by their own interpretations and conceptions of, and reactions to, such practices. Moreover, human psychological agents invest activities and practices with differential practical and moral significance in ways that may alter the sociocultural conventions within which they exist and act. By denying the possibility of even a limited and constrained (yet nonetheless real and irreducible) psychological agency, Gergen leaves too little space for the possibility of a kind of psychology that might navigate between the Scylla of scientism, on the one hand, and the Charybdis of postmodern anarchism, on the other hand.

AN ANTIDOTE IN BRIEF

What we propose as an antidote for the foregoing kinds of reductive scientistic and constructionistic excess is an unequivocal recognition that psychological kinds are not natural, biological kinds, nor purely cultural kinds, but agentic kinds, and that psychological inquiry cannot be modeled on reductive natural science or sociology. What psychologists choose to study depends on what they find to be significant in human affairs. The finding of significance is, at heart, about values, and values have a historical and sociocultural constitution, but they also matter to individual human beings. The topics, categories, procedures, and explanations employed in psychological research and practice reflect historically established and culturally sanctioned positions with respect to the legitimacy of existing and assumed relations of interaction, power, affiliation, rights, and responsibilities. Recent inquiries into the priorities of academic and professional psychology unfortunately reveal that concerns for human welfare may be overshadowed by concerns for professional self-interest and the pursuit of knowledge as a source of expert power, often to the particular detriment of the more marginalized and vulnerable members of society (e.g., Prilleltensky, 1994).

Everyday psychological phenomena are agentic. They are the experiences and actions of irreducible, embodied human agents located in a real world of sociocultural practices and conventions, which in turn are constrained by physical and biological reality. Humans experience and act out of caring about things, ideas, objects, themselves, and others. Caring is not a sole function of our physical, biological makeup or of our physical surroundings. Only by understanding the constitution of psychological agents in historical, sociocultural, political, and developmental context can caring and other central values of human psychology be approached. As it stands, for the most part psychology construed as natural science and professional technology, or alternately as agentless social constructionism, is silent about what matters to us most. As embodied agents in the world, humans care about their existence by choosing to act in particular ways and not to act in others. Agency, understood as the freedom of individual human beings to make choices and to act on these choices in ways that make a difference in their lives, is an unavoidable fact about human psychology—one that cannot be ignored or disposed of through engaging the various kinds of reductive exercises that have been all too prominent in the history of psychology to date.

At this point, the reader may well wonder about the exact kind of agency we have in mind and how it requires but is not reducible to both biology and culture. Moreover, at this point, it is far from clear why we are so insistent on the existence of such an irreducible agency. To begin to clarify these matters requires a critical understanding of historical and contemporary conceptions of human agency. It is to the cultivation of such an understanding that we turn in the very next chapter.

CHAPTER THREE

BETWEEN HARD DETERMINISM AND RADICAL FREEDOM

HAVING PROVIDED a historical overview of reductionism in psychology, with the aim of indicating the extent to which agency has been reduced, disavowed, simplified, and thus devalued in disciplinary scientific and professional psychology, it now is appropriate and necessary to focus more directly on agency itself. As recently noted by the psychologist, Joseph Rychlak (1999), "human agency is a difficult topic to discuss due to the innumerable approaches that have been proposed for centuries in its explanation" (p. 386). Since any attempt at exhaustively reviewing such a voluminous outpouring inevitably would fail, it is possible only to point to some useful set of organizing distinctions and then to consider ideas and works that relate most directly to matters of immediate concern. In this case, of course, the concern is to move toward a conception of agency that might steer psychology between a scientistically reductive determinism, on the one hand, and a too facile, unrealistic interventionism, on the other hand.

In this chapter, the question of agency is addressed initially in the way in which it has been treated in much past and contemporary philosophy, including moral philosophy and philosophy of mind. Later in the chapter, some recent, nonreductive psychological work on agency is examined and critiqued. Finally, hermeneutic conceptions of agency are considered, with a view to conceptualizing agency as a kind of deliberative, emergent self-determination embedded inextricably within human existence in the world. As we will see, such a view requires a rather radical rethinking of the agent as an embodied actor within the physical and biological world who is constituted developmentally by historical, socio-cultural practices and conventions.

In the initial part of this chapter, we describe how most philosophical debate in this area has been mired in two competing traditions that have shared a common perspective on agency but have diverged dramatically with respect to its existence and ontological status. One of these positions—libertarianism—champions our everyday sense of ourselves as persons who make our own way in life through exercise of our capacities for freedom of choice and action. The other—hard determinism—considers persons to be nothing more than large aggregations of very small units (e.g., cells or atoms) that are completely determined by genetic and environmental factors. Debates between hard determinists and libertarians seldom advance beyond a basic disagreement concerning the implications of agency for a scientific understanding of human beings. In short, hard determinists and libertarians disagree from the start in that they hold different premises concerning the admissibility of agency to a scientific or other scholarly discourse.

Of course, there always have been attempts to forge middle-ground positions between hard determinism and libertarianism. Most often such middle positions go under the rubric of compatibilism or soft determinism. Compatibilists most often conceive of agency somewhat differently than do libertarians or hard determinists, and mostly because of this difference they attempt to reconcile the seemingly irreconcilable options of freedom of choice and deterministic science and social science. However, as we shall see, these soft determinists have been hampered in their efforts to date by two outstanding difficulties: (a) The lack of a nonquestion-begging argument for agency that is not entirely determined by biology and/or culture, and (b) a conceptualization of agency adequate to the demand that agency can somehow be both determined and not determined. As hinted in chapter 1, the major aims of this volume are to propose resolutions to precisely these difficulties and to explore the implications of the resultant arguments and perspective on agency for psychology.

DEFINITIONS AND DISTINCTIONS

Libertarian defenders of free choice typically understand such choice as a decision that could have been different up to the moment it was made by the person making it (e.g., Kane, 1998). It means having alternatives such that until the decision is made the person deciding is not limited to only one of the available alternatives. As mentioned at the outset of this book, the matter of free choice lies at the very heart of our personal freedom and social responsibility. If a person could not possibly have done otherwise, the person cannot be held responsible for what has been done. The principle that our actions are the result of free choice, unless proven otherwise, is a fundamental principle of Western law, governance, and interpersonal relationships. In fact, this same principle, the assumption that we have the power to make free choices and to act on these choices, is basic to Western life in general.

But do we really have freedom of choice? And exactly of what does this capability consist? It is one of the most revealing aspects of the entire historical and contemporary debate about freedom of choice and action that so much attention has been paid to the first of the questions with so little attention devoted to the latter. Consequently, before turning to a more detailed consideration of libertarianism, hard determinism, and compatibilism, it is worth taking a moment to consider exactly what freedom of choice involves.

We already have defined freedom of choice as having a choice between alternatives right up to the moment that a decision is made. Freedom of action can be defined as being able to do that which one chooses to do. Where freedom of choice is about decisions or choices, freedom of action is about actions. What is important here is to note that freedom of choice need not be linked to freedom of action or vice versa. You can have one without the other. For example, a person may decide to move his car, only to find it unexpectedly hemmed in by other cars in a crowded parking lot. Or he may unthinkingly swerve his car around a cyclist, rather than slowing to allow the cyclist to get clear of his path. Full agency in a psychological sense implies both freedom of choice and freedom of action. However, it is important to recognize that these two freedoms need not necessarily imply each other. Moreover, it is important to keep in mind that one may exercise either or both freedom of choice and freedom of action at certain times in one's life and exercise neither at other times in one's life. In other words, it is extremely important that agency, considered as freedom of choice and action, not be assumed to be a once and forever union of these two freedoms—one which if present and exercised on one occasion need necessarily be present and exercised on another.

For the most part, the classic positions of libertarianism and hard determinism have been developed in relation to the question of freedom of choice, understood along the lines presented thus far. So, for the time being, let us consider these positions in this way. As already noted, the everyday picture of persons is of them as free choosers, while the scientific picture is one of persons as causally determined. Libertarians accept the everyday picture, and hard determinists accept the scientific picture. Both libertarians and hard determinists invoke a principle of contradiction, to the effect that something cannot be both what it is and what it is not, to argue their cases. Libertarians argue from the premises that (a) free choice exists and that (b) if this is so, assuming that free choice and determinism are in logical opposition, complete causal determinism is false, to the conclusion that complete causal determinism is false. Hard determinists argue from the premises that (a) complete causal determinism is true and that (b) if this is so, again by the principle of noncontradiction, free choice does not exist, to the conclusion that free choice does not exist. Notice two things about these classic arguments. First, their premises do not permit conclusions other than those just stated. And second, the implication of the resultant impasse is that we are asked either to give up a crucial aspect of our everyday conception of ourselves or to reject a scientific account of ourselves. Therefore, it is not surprising that many past and present philosophers and some psychologists and social scientists have attempted to reconcile these two classic perspectives by insisting that the two pictures they paint are entirely compatible with each other.

On the face of it, compatibilism seems impossible to get off the ground. Obviously, to take flight, compatibilists must challenge some part of the traditional arguments of libertarians and hard determinists, both of whom assume strict incompatibility between determinism and agency. The most usual compatibilist move is to deny the second premises in the arguments stated in the previous paragraph. Thus, for the compatibilist, free choice is not ruled out by virtue of a decision being causally determined. What the compatibilist wants to assert is that freedom of choice is itself a kind of causally determined sequence of events. The typical manner of this assertion is to employ a strategy that might be called "self-determination." What the compatibilist asserts is that a decision or choice can be causally determined by oneself. Self-determination occurs when the factors that cause a choice are aspects (e.g., desires, beliefs, reasons) of the person who makes it. Although there has been much debate in philosophy concerning the nature of causality and causal determinism, all that matters to the compatibilist is that causal determinism, however construed, must not rule out self-determination as just defined.

Moreover, compatibilists are quick to point out that the libertarian's notion of freedom of choice requires walking a very fine line between the possibly viable and the totally mysterious. If a decision is to be more than a completely random occurrence, it must be connected in some way with the person making it. True decisions do not just happen, they are made by agents. Even if the connection between agents and decisions is not the causal connection favored by hard determinists, there still must be some such connection. Consequently, if the libertarian insists on too much indeterminism, the resultant chaos would make it impossible to attach any decision or action to any agent. This surely is not what the libertarian has in mind, and therefore it might seem as if the libertarian actually also requires some defensible notion of self-determination. If so, the compatibilist position, as differentiated from the libertarian position, may be the only way to oppose hard determinism in human affairs, and the kind of reductionism that we already have seen is so frequently associated with it, especially in psychology.

But there is much more to the compatibilist option than what has been said thus far, and compatibilism has taken on many different guises throughout its long history. One important matter concerns an additional way in which compatibilist conceptions of agency have tended to differ from those of incompatibilists. Incompatibilists (whether libertarians or hard determinists) understand free choice as a decision that could have been made otherwise up to the very point it was made. Such a view assumes that the initiation of action involves both voluntariness (acting in accordance with one's desires) and origination (being the ultimate source of one's actions). Even though compatibilism comes in many forms, for the most part, compatibilists' conceptions of agency with respect to the initiation of actions require only voluntariness.

A major part of the compatibilist challenge is to ask why freedom of choice cannot be considered to be self-determination in the sense of the exercising of voluntary control over one's actions, such that these actions are in accordance with one's genuine desires. What more is there to free choice than this kind of voluntary self-determination? Of course, compatibilists or soft determinists suspect strongly that there is nothing more, and that when libertarian incompatibilists insist that human actors be the ultimate originators of their own actions, outside of determined causal sequences and right up to the point at which an action is undertaken, they really are arguing about nothing. Or, worse, they are invoking some mysterious metaphysical source of freedom that lacks both definition and substance. Nonetheless, this commonly employed combative strategy of compatibilists is not really an argument, let alone a theory, so much as it is a rhetorical question and challenge. Compatibilism, or soft determinism, still requires a theory of agency understood as self-determination—one that might succeed in positioning a compatibilist-like middle position between hard determinism and the kind of mysterious freedom apparently sponsored by radical libertarians. It is to some notable attempts to engage this project that we now turn.

A CRITICAL CONSIDERATION OF SOME NOTABLE ATTEMPTS AT SOFT DETERMINISM

Many ancient (e.g., Chrysippus and other Stoics), enlightenment (e.g., Thomas Hobbes, John Locke, Baruch Spinoza, David Hume), and modern (e.g., Arthur Schopenhauer, James Mill, Peter Strawson) compatibilists have employed dissolutionist strategies of various kinds to claim that the freedoms we embrace in everyday life are really not ruled out by hard determinism, and that complete freedom of the will is unintelligible. For example, Strawson (1959) argued that reactive attitudes, such as gratitude, that assume the possibility of morally praiseworthy freedom of action are so deeply embedded in our form of life that it would be impossible for us to abandon them even if determinism were true. Such dissolutionist stratagems certainly qualify as compatibilist (in opposition to the incompatibilist positions of libertarianism and hard determinism). However, some more contemporary compatibilists (e.g., the philosopher Harry Frankfurt and the psychologist Joseph Rychlak) have not so much treated incompatibilism as a pseudo-problem that should be dissolved but have attempted to provide alternative conceptions of freedom that do not deny, although they do "soften," determinism. Thus, Frankfurt (1971) talks about the uniquely human capacity to form "higher-order desires," and Rychlak (1997) speaks about a kind of "transpredication" rooted in the use of language that allows humans to respond antithetically to their determination. In what follows, no exhaustive attempt will be made to survey past and present compatibilist theorizing in either philosophy or psychology. Nonetheless, the works and ideas that are mentioned certainly represent many of the major theoretical ideas that have contributed to attempts to reconcile agency with a determinism permissive of the idea of self-determination.

PHILOSOPHICAL CONSIDERATIONS

In the Nicomachean Ethics, Aristotle (ca. 350 B.C.E./1953), argues that it is when actions are voluntary that moral issues arise. He provides one of the first conceptual clarifications of voluntariness to be found in recorded Western thought: "By a voluntary action, let me repeat, I mean one which (a) it was in the agent's power to do or not to do, (b) he performs not in ignorance but with full knowledge of the person affected by his action, the instrument he is using, the object he seeks to attain, (c) in no particular is determined by accident or *force majeure*" (p. 159). By coupling voluntariness with an agent's ability to do otherwise than what he did and by tying agency to the deliberative rationality of human beings, which for Aristotle separated humans from the brute world of nonrational powers, Aristotle set the course for much of the debate between libertarians and determinists within the Western tradition. For compatibilists, exactly what is entailed by the notions of alternative possibility ("could have done otherwise"), compulsion (e.g., versus determinism), and rational deliberation emerged as central matters of philosophical concern.

As previously noted, compatibilists typically have proceeded by denying the second premises in the basic libertarian and deterministic arguments, arguing, in various ways, that free will and determinism are not directly oppositional. In the manner of Hobbes's (1962) famous seventeenth-century debate with Bishop Bramwell, traditional compatibilist arguments point out that our ordinary sense of freedom, as an absence of coercion or compulsion or constraint, is not at all incompatible with determinism. This is because we are free when we are self-determining, and we are self-determining when nothing prevents us from doing what we will. Consequently, we can be free in the sense of intending and doing what we will even if our intentions and actions are necessitated by antecedent circumstances. Moreover, Hobbes declared that determinism actually is required in order to make coherent sense of the idea of freedom as self-determination. For, in the absence of determination, resultant conditions of chaos hardly could be viewed as an adequate context for purposeful self-determination. He therefore concluded that any kind of mysterious freedom that might be incompatible with determinism was simply unintelligible, a point of view iterated ever since by various compatibilists in response to a succession of allegedly mysterious libertarian conceptions such as noumenal selves (e.g., Immanuel Kant), nonoccurrent causes (e.g., Thomas Reid), transempirical egos (e.g., Henry James), and the like. Thus, for the traditional compatibilist, freedom of choice is not ruled out by virtue of a decision being causally determined. The law of contradiction is not seen to apply. And, for many compatibilists, freedom of choice is itself a kind of causally determined sequence of events.

After Hobbes, libertarians like Reid, Kant, and, more recently, F. H. Bradley provided strongly worded arguments and assertions in favor of agency as necessarily assuming both voluntariness and origination. Bradley, for example, was outraged by what he saw as the indignity of subjecting human action to rational, empirical forms of explanation that eschewed any doctrine of uniquely human origination. In replying to expressions of such explanation by Mill, Bradley (1927) states, "When you speak to us plainly, you have to say that you really understand a man to be free in no other sense than a falling stone, or than running water. In the one case there is as little necessity as in the other, and just as much freedom" (p. 25). The broader target of such criticisms was, of course, the compatibilist theorizing of a succession of British philosophers including Hume, Locke, and Mill, all of whom were anxious to fit human agency seamlessly into the larger tapestry of an emerging scientific and, therefore, deterministic worldview.

In the 1900s, the British philosophical tradition had evolved to the conceptual clarifications of ordinary language philosophers such as George Moore, John L. Austin, and Sir Alfred Ayers. Adopting the traditional compatibilist construal of freedom as the absence of constraints or impediments preventing agents from doing what they will, these philosophers offered a variety of conditional analyses of everyday expressions such as "You could have done otherwise," by interpreting them as more formally stated conditional expressions such as "You *would* (or, alternatively, *could*) have done otherwise, *if* you had willed or chosen or wanted to do otherwise." Thus, Austin (1966) is able to conclude that it would be entirely consistent to say that a golfer standing over a three-foot putt could have made the putt even though he might have missed it. Such arguments and examples subsequently have been much debated by contemporary compatibilists, despite seeming to offer the kind of wedge between determinism and agency that they appear to require in order to maintain that the two are not inconsistent with each other.

Like Hobbes, many contemporary compatibilists also claim that a decision or choice can be causally determined by oneself (i.e., self-determination). But, as previously hinted, for this sort of contemporary compatibilist, self-determination occurs when the factors that cause a choice are aspects (e.g., desires, beliefs, reasons) of the person who makes it. Although not necessarily compatibilist in and of itself, Frankfurt's (1971) analysis of agency has been adopted by many contemporary compatibilists. He asserts that not only must a choice be self-determined, but it must be in accord with, if not actually caused by, a person's higher-order desires. Higher-order desires take first-order desires as their objects and are uniquely human. Thus, a first-order desire for a cigarette is governed by a second-order desire not to give in to the first-order desire to smoke. Because desires exist in great variety, different higher-order desires also may relate to, and/or compete with, second-order desires such as not to desire smoking (e.g., one might also desire not to appear agitated and believe that smoking helps to maintain this impression). This implies that freedom of choice must involve a process of deliberation through which the agent considers and assesses relevant first-order desires in relation to higher-order desires, eventually arriving at a decision. Moreover, the implication is that such deliberation must be effective in that it is connected to the resulting action in a way that alternative deliberations would not be so connected. What Frankfurt's model succeeds in doing is providing a conceptualization of what it is to be an agent, who self-determines through deliberation involving desires that take other desires as their objects. According to Frankfurt, such deliberative self-determination is unique to humans in that higher-order desires lie in the realm of values, goals, and life projects, all of which are distinctively human. Nonhuman animals and machines do not possess such higher-order desires or engage in deliberations with respect to them. Only human agents are so possessed and engaged.

Even though, as we have seen, some compatibilists and most libertarians hold that freedom of choice requires alternative possibilities of action, such that were an agent's deliberations to differ, the resulting action would also differ, Frankfurt actually disagrees, or at least restricts, the range of application of this kind of thinking. Through a series of so-called Frankfurt-style cases, he argues that even in situations in which alternative courses of action are somehow blocked or otherwise made unavailable a choice is agentic and responsible so long as the resulting action accords with the person's higher-order desires and context-specific deliberations. (See Fischer [1994] for an extended discussion of Frankfurt's cases and examples.) So long as we choose in relation to our higher-order desires, even if unbeknownst to us we could not have done otherwise, we are agents. Frankfurt wants to convince us that it is our happiness in such cases, not our total freedom, that is critical and makes us both agents and responsible. Frankfurt's account goes beyond the traditional Hobbesian strategy of dissolutionism, in that it attempts to make intelligible a limited kind of agency that seems compatible with determinism, but which is recognizable as a kind of capability that is uniquely human and worth having. However, it still leaves intact the possibility that agency, because it no longer requires ultimate origination, is nothing more than a possibly epiphenomenal, experiential link in a causal chain of otherwise nonagentic factors.

Against Hobbesian dissolutionism and Frankfurt-style deliberative voluntariness are arrayed a formidable set of historical and contemporary incompatibilist arguments. Kant (1781/1949) called such compatibilist maneuvers a "wretched subterfuge," while James (1909) used the phrase "a quagmire of evasion" in response to the compatibilist attempt to remove the requirement of ultimate origination from our everyday sense of free will, and to leave only the mere shadow of voluntariness. Contemporary incompatibilists such as the libertarian Robert Kane (1998) and the hard determinist Ted Honderich (1988) are no less scathing in their reactions, regarding the compatibilist dismissal of ultimate origination as a significant departure from both common truth and usage. They argue, albeit for quite different reasons, that compatibilist voluntariness is a kind of agency that is not worth having because it is not that which is assumed when agency is employed as essential for moral responsibility, personal autonomy, human creativity and accomplishment, and meaningful interpersonal relationships of friendship and love.

In response, contemporary compatibilists (e.g., Dennett, 1995) continue to regard past and present libertarian proposals for "agency as origination" as unacceptably mysterious. And it is easy to understand why when one considers that traditional libertarians like Kant had to invent a highly improbable "two-world account" in an attempt to establish such an agency as issuing from an in-principle unknowable, noumenal self. Moreover, the compatibilist concern with respect to mystery also seems warranted when contemporary libertarians like Kane (1998) rely on a mostly unspecified kind of "brain-event indeterminacy" to support their cases for ultimate origination and responsibility: "I think that a full understanding of how actions outflow from agents would require a better understanding . . . [I]t may be that both the unity of conscious experience and the unity of the self-network are somehow related to the quantum character of reality" (p. 195).

In opposition to such speculative "mysteries," Daniel Dennett (1995) and other contemporary compatibilists like Alfred Mele (1995) have offered a variety of models of agentic decision making and action that not only maintain the traditional compatibilist idea of voluntariness but also seem to hint at a modest, yet highly constrained, capability of origination. For example, Dennett (1995) proposes that when faced with an important decision

> a consideration generator whose output is to some degree un-
> determined produces a series of considerations, some of which

may of course be immediately rejected as irrelevant by the agent (consciously or unconsciously). Those considerations that are selected by the agent as having a more than negligible bearing on the decision then figure in a reasoning process, and if the agent is in the main reasonable, those considerations ultimately serve as predictors and explicators of the agent's final decision. (p. 51)

Although containing currently fashionable terms with a decidedly cognitive scientific ring, it is interesting to note the extent to which Dennett's (1995) compatibilist proposals retain such Aristotelian concerns as reason and alternative possibility. Of course, in these contemporary models, the actual generation of alternative possibilities is somewhat removed from the subsequently conscious deliberative reasoning of the agent. (As we shall see later in this volume, the source of alternative possibilities is a potentially fruitful area for innovative theorizing with respect to the question of agency. In particular, in the theory of agency we present, the origination of such possibilities is drawn from the agent's existence as a being inseparable from the physical–biological, historical, and sociocultural world that constitutes her personhood.)

One of Mele's (1995) suggestions for going a bit beyond compatibilist voluntariness to a limited capability of origination takes a developmental turn mostly absent in traditional philosophical treatments of agency. In responding to Strawson's challenge to explain how neonates who do not act intentionally, let alone freely, develop into free agents, Mele offers the following comment.

> If there is a free, responsible (ordinary) human being at some deterministic world, he *developed* into such a being, and his so doing was the result of a deterministic process. Free agency if some ordinary human being has it at a deterministic world, emerges in the being in a way explained by the laws of nature together with some earlier states of the world. (p. 227)

Thus, Mele speculates about a kind of developmentally emergent agency that might have important implications for a revamped compatibilist thesis that might not be restricted to mere voluntariness alone. Of course, Mele recognizes fully that any such emergent agency still would not give libertarians like Kane (1998) the ultimate origination they seek.

In summary, even though the traditional compatibilist idea of agentic initiation as mere voluntariness may seem insufficient, most available explanations of agentic initiation as origination seem highly implausible, speculative, or unconvincing. And yet, it remains the case that to remove all traces of origination from our conception of agency understood as the initiation of action seems not to capture our everyday sense of our freedom to choose and act. As Isaiah Berlin (1970), a staunch defender of libertarian free will, has attested

> [i]f social and psychological determinism were established as an accepted truth, our world would be transformed . . . in literally unimaginable ways: the notions of choice, of responsibility, of freedom, are so deeply embedded in our outlook that our new life, as creatures in a world genuinely lacking in these concepts, can, I should maintain, be conceived by us only with the greatest difficulty. (p. 113)

Thus, past and present debates within moral philosophy and philosophy of mind between compatibilists and incompatibilists with respect to free will and determinism, while informative and clarifying in many ways, fall far short of resolving those matters with which we are most concerned. The possibility of a determined and a determining agency understood as self-determination still seems elusive, especially if what we want is something more than mere voluntariness of action.

Most philosophical accounts of agency are more concerned with what it means to be an agent than with how agency, however it is conceived, might be acquired or with how agents might develop. In fact, traditionally, philosophy has tended to assume that entities in the world have an essential character that distinguishes them from other entities and defines them as the kinds of things they are. When considering human agents, such essentialism has manifested in a kind of "ontologically prior" view of personhood. For example, Hobbes (to whom we already have referred with respect to his dissolutionist approach to compatibilism) also held that basic human needs, capabilities, desires, and motivations are all formed within each individual independently of social interactions and historical traditions: "[The] causes of the social compound reside in men as if but even now sprung out of the earth and suddenly, like mushrooms, come to full maturity without all kinds of engagement to each other" (1962, vol. 1, p. 109). Anyone familiar with the reductive functionalism currently favored in contemporary cognitive and neuroscience will recognize the persistence of the Hobbesian legacy in today's mainstream psychology (a matter taken up in the next chapter).

Nonetheless, Hobbes and his successors have not been unopposed. Since neoliberals like Thomas Hill Green and Leonard Trelawny Hobhouse first renounced atomistic conceptions of the person during the latter part of the nineteenth century, a wide variety of scholars (including many Marxists, sociologists, cultural anthropologists, hermeneuts, feminists, narrativists, poststructuralists, and postmodernists) have eschewed the ontologically prior self. In its place, they have offered various versions of a socioculturally contingent self wherein both the conception and actuality of personhood are understood to be constituted by human sociocultural (especially relational and linguistic) practices. A prototypic statement of socioculturally contingent personhood is E. A. Tiryakian's (1962) summary of Émile Durkheim's view that

> instead of collective life arising from the individual, the individual personality is a product of society. If there is nothing in social life which is not found in the minds of individuals, it is because almost everything found in the latter has its source in social life. Collective beliefs are manifestations of an underlying reality which transcends and yet is immanent in the individual. It transcends him because society does not depend on any particular individual for reality, and because its temporal span is greater than that of any individual. At the same time, society is immanent because it is the individual who is the ultimate vehicle of social life. (p. 22–23)

Many scholars who have forsaken the ontologically prior person also have jettisoned commitments to fixed, natural, and essential components of human nature. The new socioculturally contingent person is held to be highly mutable, artifactual, and without a recognizable center that holds across diverse societies and cultural traditions. Interestingly, as noted toward the end of the previous chapter, while adamantly refusing reductions of socioculturally contingent personhood to biology, neurophysiology, or other natural kinds, several of these more recent perspectives (e.g., some versions of Marxism and postmodern social constructionism) have come surprisingly close to eliminating individual personhood by reducing it to its supposed societal and cultural determinants and constituents.

At any rate, what the foregoing consideration of philosophical versions of compatibilism or soft determinism offers are two distinctive versions of compatibilism, neither of which is adequate for our purposes herein. The first, Hobbesian dissolutionism, is mostly unconcerned with theorizing about agency per se; it is merely content to assert its compatibility with determinism, at least insofar as agency can be equated with voluntariness and little more. The second, Frankfurtian voluntarism, does offer a specific account of agency as self-determination, considered as acting in accordance with one's higher-order desires, but says little about the ultimate source of such desires and the alternative possibilities that may be (although on Frankfurt's account are not necessarily) associated with them. Contemporary compatibilists, like Dennett and Mele, seem to address the absence of origination evident in traditional compatibilist accounts but do so in ways that seem to assert generative mechanisms or volitional entities, the origins of which are sketched in only the most meager and broadest of ways. Given that much traditional philosophical work on human agency has tended to assume an ontologically prior conception of personhood, wherein persons either possess relatively fixed capacities or they do not, such limitations are perhaps to be expected. In this sense, philosophy, at least for the most part, has shown little concern with developmental theorizing.

Given this state of affairs, it is not unreasonable to turn for inspiration to that branch of human activity supposedly concerned with human action and experience and its development and manifestation in the world—that is, psychology. Although we already have examined in some detail the ways in which traditional psychological science and practice have eschewed and devalued human agency, at least some work in mainstream and critical, theoretical psychology during the 1980s and 1990s has begun to take agency seriously and to focus specifically on it. In what follows, we turn to various recent programs of work within psychology that might offer us something of what we find absent in the philosophical literature just discussed. That is, we turn to contemporary agentic psychology with the hope of finding traces of the development of agentic capability in human individuals and societies. In particular, we seek indications of how agency might originate, develop, and emerge within a mostly deterministic (including self-determination), yet nonreductive, approach to the understanding and study of psychological kinds.

The need for such a developmental, more psychological perspective on agency is critical to the project of this book for the following reason. Recall that soft determinism requires self-determination—the idea that decisions and actions are determined, at least in part, by one's own deliberations. If we are to succeed in our desire to move toward a middle-ground position between hard determinism and mysterious freedom, we must be able to furnish a viable account of how such self-determination is possible. Where does it come from? This is the critical developmental question for our purposes. Why is it so critical? Because if it is possible to explain how human agents acquire self-determination from genetic–biological and cultural–environmental factors, we then might still distinguish between how human agents acquire self-determination and how they use it in any given situation. If such a distinction is viable, we will be in a position to argue that self-determination itself is nonmysteriously acquired through genetic and environmental influences, but once acquired, its actual use in any given situation requires the kind of reasoned, intentional deliberation we have found in accounts like that of Frankfurt (1971). Thus, our strategy for the rest of this chapter will be to consider additional work in social cognitive, developmental, and theoretical psychology and hermeneutics that might provide the bases for a developmental approach to the acquisition of agency that will make possible the kind of argument just outlined. Our full developmental account of agency will appear in chapter 5.

PSYCHOLOGICAL CONSIDERATIONS

The recent work within psychology with which we will be concerned in this section, unlike the majority of work described in chapter 2, treats agency in a nonreductive manner. Before discussing a representative cross section of this work, it is important to note that a great deal of writing in psychology has appeared under headings like self-determination (e.g., self-regulation, self-efficacy, self-control) during the last three decades of the twentieth century. Unfortunately, much of this work has tended to assert and assume a kind of agentic self-determination in the absence of explicit theoretical arguments in support of its assertions and assumptions. Just as frequently, it has displayed the kind of ambivalence described in chapter 1 by employing reductive methods of inquiry in attempts to study empirically the core phenomena of interest. In contrast, the programs of theory and research about to be described have at least some explicit theoretical components that translate into serious attempts to study agentic phenomena without reducing them to nonagentic, natural kinds that demonstrate the kind of indifference to their classifications described by Hacking (1999).

At least two programs of work in mainstream psychology have adopted, at least in the more recent publications of some of their leading proponents, mostly nonreductive approaches to the study of human agency. The first of these is social cognitive psychology (mostly through the efforts of Albert Bandura [1986, 2001]). The second is cognitive developmental psychology (including some interesting recent work in the theory of mind and intentional self-development, much of which is conveniently summarized in a recent volume by Jochen Brandtstädter and Richard Lerner, [1999]). In addition to these mainstream efforts, a small number of theoretical and philosophical psychologists has attempted to provide more complete theoretical and developmental frameworks for agency understood as self-determination. For example, Rychlak (1988, 1997) has produced an important body of work on human agency that contains extremely innovative treatments of the roles of language and reasoned understanding in the development and maintenance of agentic capability. The works of John Greenwood (1991) and of Rom Harré and Grant Gillett (1994) also provide important and, for our purposes, useful perspectives on agency as an irreducible aspect of human psychology. Even though such works certainly do not exhaust important recent theorizing about human agency in theoretical psychology (see, for example, Howard, 1994; Williams, 1992), they do raise most of the matters with which we will concern ourselves in the remainder of this volume. (Readers also should be aware that, in addition to the recent work reviewed here on agency in psychology, there is a growing body of applied psychological research [mostly in personality, clinical, social, and family psychology] that has been concerned with the measurement of agency [e.g., Skinner, Chapman, & Baltes, 1988], particularly in relation to the measurement of communion [e.g., Hegelson, 1994; McAdams, Hoffman, Mansfield, & Day, 1996]. Much of this work finds its immediate origins in the suggestion of David Bakan [1966] that agency and communion represent the "two fundamental modalities in the existence of living forms" [pp. 14-15]. Although potentially valuable in many ways, this program of psychological research typically does not concern itself, at least directly and focally, with the kinds of theoretical matters on which the current discussions converge. Finally, those readers interested in surveying earlier psychological work on agency, some of which led directly and indirectly to the relatively recent work discussed in what follows, might wish to consult relevant reviews by Malcolm Westcott [1988] and A. A. Sappington [1990].)

Bandura's Social Cognitive Theory
Probably no single, contemporary individual has exerted the widespread influence on different branches of psychology that reasonably can be attributed to Albert Bandura. Throughout his long and illustrious career, Bandura has struggled against the reductive tendencies of mainstream psychology, while attempting to develop research methodologies that would be accepted by many of his more micro-deterministic colleagues. Since the mid-1970s, Bandura has devoted the majority of his energies to the study of human agency as mediated by beliefs of personal efficacy. More recently (e.g., Bandura, 1997, 2001), he has attempted to offer explicitly theoretical summaries of his work on efficacy and agency. Bandura's definition of agency includes as a core feature that agency is "the power to originate actions for given purposes" (p. 3). And, as already indicated, "beliefs of personal efficacy constitute the key factor of human agency" (p. 3). Bandura further understands such beliefs as propositional and embedded in networks of functional relationships with other propositions and schemata.

Bandura explicitly recognizes and discusses some of the philosophical issues that arise from his treatment and description of beliefs in contemporary, psychological "language of mind." For him, mental events, such as propositional networks, are brain activities not immaterial entities somehow existing apart from neural systems. However, such physicality does not imply reductionism because Bandura regards processes of thought as "emergent brain activities that are not ontologically reducible" (1997, p. 4). Following Roger Sperry (1993), Bandura asserts that mental states, as emergent properties generated by brain processes, differ in novel respects from those elements that feature in their creation. Further, such novelty is not merely a matter of increased complexity of the same properties, just as emergent properties of water, such as viscosity and transparency, are not merely aggregates of the properties of oxygen and hydrogen.

But not only are thought processes (involved in reasoned deliberation, choice, and beliefs such as efficacy beliefs) emergent brain activities, they also exert determining influence. For example, with respect to efficacy beliefs, such beliefs require and are made possible by "a host of microsensory, perceptual, and information processing activities" but "once formed . . . efficacy beliefs regulate aspirations, choice of behavioral courses, mobilization and maintenance of effort, and affective reactions" (Bandura, 1997, p. 4).

Throughout all of this, Bandura (1997) is adamant that the fact that belief, thought, and reason are cerebral occurrences does not imply that functional relationships expressed in psychological theories are reducible to those in neurophysiological theories. The psychosocial subject matter of psychology has no counterpart in neurobiological theory, and one cannot possibly derive the former from the latter because psychosocial subject matter inevitably involves "the construction and organization of events external to the organism" (p. 4). Such events are inescapably social and cultural and have no direct counterpart at an intra-individual level. Nonetheless, the human agency that emerges with the formation of efficacy beliefs (i.e., beliefs in one's capability to perform particular actions) is generative and creative, not simply reactive to either its neurophysiological requirements or to its sociocultural influences. In fact, "through their intentional acts, people shape the functional structure of their neurobiological systems" (p. 5).

With respect to how the self is understood and functions, Bandura rejects any dualism that might separate self as agent from self as object. Maintaining that social cognitive theory is committed to a holistic conception of selfhood, Bandura maintains that one is just as much an agent when reflecting on one's experience as when executing a particular course of action.

At a more macroscopic level of analysis, Bandura's conception of agency operates within an interdependent causal model that he calls "triadic reciprocal causation" (Bandura, 1986). In this model of self and society, internal personal factors (cognitive, affective, biological events), behavior, and environmental factors operate as interacting determinants that influence each other bidirectionally. What this broader model makes clear is that

> people are both producers and products of social systems. Social structures . . . do not arise by immaculate conception; they are created by human activity. Social structures, in turn, impose constraints and provide resources for personal development and everyday functioning. But neither structural constraints nor enabling resources foreordain what individuals become and do in given situations. (Bandura, 1997, p. 6)

For Bandura, determinism signifies the production of effects by events, including events controlled and influenced by individuals. Further, because most action is codetermined by many factors, psychological events produce their effects in a probabilistic manner. Consequently, Bandura endorses a compatibilist sense of self-determination as partial influence.

> [T]here is no incompatibility between freedom and determin-
> ism. Freedom is not conceived negatively as exemption from
> social influences or situational constraints. Rather, it is defined
> positively as the exercise of self-influence to bring about desired
> results. This agentic causation relies heavily on cognitive self-
> regulation. It is achieved through reflective thought, generative
> use of the knowledge and skills at one's command, and other
> tools of self-influence, which choice and execution of action
> require. . . . It is because self-influence operates deterministically
> on action that some measure of freedom is possible. (Bandura,
> 1997, p. 7).

And, of course, much of Bandura's career has been devoted to the provision
of empirical demonstrations and examples of precisely the kind of self-
determination assumed in his compatibilist psychology (see Bandura, 1986,
1997 for extensive summaries of such work).

A final aspect of Bandura's recent efforts to promote his conception
of human agency is that he has begun to speculate about mechanisms and
organizations of "collective efficacy" (1995). Although open to some ambiguity, what Bandura wishes to connote by his use of this term is people's
shared beliefs in their capabilities to produce effects collectively. Moreover,
such effects are understood by Bandura not as the simple sum of the efficacy
beliefs of various individuals but as an emergent group-level attribute of a
coordinated and interactive collective. Such recent theorizing takes Bandura's
work into broader social and political contexts than typically are recognized,
at least explicitly, by most psychologists.

In addition to offering this summation of Bandura's work on human
agency, we want to voice a few criticisms that might be leveled at Bandura's
ideas. We do this not only to bring closure to our consideration of Bandura's
perspective but also to point to difficulties with which we believe the theory
of agency that we will advance, in chapter 5, may be better equipped to
confront. Nonetheless, many features of Bandura's nonreductive, compatibilist
approach are ones that we also will champion, but within a broadened
perspective on sociocultural influence that includes much more in the way
of historical and linguistic perspectives than anything to be found in Bandura's
work alone.

Perhaps the most obvious difficulty is that despite his attempted dis-
solution of various, potentially unhelpful dualities Bandura remains wedded
to what might be regarded as a too strict separation between the social and
the cognitive and between behavior and intention. The former separation is
reflected in the very term *social cognitive theory;* the latter in the separation
of behavior from personal factors such as purpose, in his model of triadic
reciprocal causation. The latter might suggest what we believe is an unin-
tended association with behavioristic theorizing in psychology in that it

appears to imply that it somehow is possible to conceptualize behavior as an object of study apart from the intentions, deliberations, reasons, and purposes of agents. In this same vein, it seems to imply that behavior somehow is not personal in the manner of cognitive, affective, and biological factors and events. The former separation raises questions concerning the exact nature of the relationships between mind–brain and society, which are not fully developed in Bandura's theoretical work.

In our view, too great a separation of mind and society in Bandura's social cognitive theory flows from what we regard as his too narrow conceptualization of sociocultural factors. In the vast majority of Bandura's research and writing, these factors are restricted to such obviously and immediately present social conditions as the actions of models, verbal instructions, demographic characteristics of learners and models, and the presence or absence of varying levels of social stimuli. It seems clear that Bandura intends such empirical demonstrations, and his discussions of them, to generalize to broader social contexts and circumstances. However, he provides little explicit theorizing, outside of various broad recommendations for societal improvement and for the enhancement of collective efficacy (e.g., Bandura, 1995), that goes beyond the social enablers and constraints of an immediate situation. Thus, there is little said about what we regard as the importance of historically established and enacted, sociocultural traditions of living. Such traditions include the complex manifold of linguistic and social practices, regulations, and conventions that we believe to be so critical with respect to bequeathing conceptions of personhood and agency to individual members of societies. We will have much more to say about such matters toward the end of this chapter when we discuss the contributions of hermeneutic thinkers to the question of agency in human affairs.

At this point however, it is useful to distinguish clearly between the sociocultural constitution of psychological phenomena, like mind and self, and sociocultural influence on such psychological phenomena (or on biological–genetic potentials for psychological phenomena). For the most part (see Bandura [2001] for a slightly more constitutive account), Bandura conceptualizes sociocultural contexts and practices as influential not constitutive. His reciprocal determinism posits a dynamic interaction between the social and the cognitive that mostly stops short of suggesting that the psychological cognitive is cut initially from the sociocultural fabric. But culture is more than influential communications and interactions. It consists in conceptual and symbolic systems that furnish routines, frames, and other resources for thought and action—resources that once appropriated and internalized help to constitute psychological persons. (Note: To hold that the sociocultural is constitutive of the psychological in this way does not imply that psychological phenomena, once emergent from their sociocultural origins, cannot develop beyond these origins—but, more of this in chapter 5.)

To end this commentary on Bandura's work on a more positive note, we believe that the philosopher William Rottschaefer (1991) provides an important summary of what many see as most valuable in Bandura's work on agency when he expressed the following sentiment with respect to intentionalistic, social cognitive psychological theories.

> [Such] theories may themselves provide a level of scientific discourse that is both explanatory and predictive of human agency. At the same time this level of discourse may itself be the object of explanation and prediction at another level by a nonintentionalistic cognitive psychology of the connectionist sort. Besides avoiding elimination of intentional states, such a relationship between levels would imply neither reduction in the sense of ontological identification nor epistemological and methodological superfluousness. (p. 155)

Although sympathetic to some of what Rottschaefer suggests here, we have reservations concerning his reliance on the warrant of prediction and on the kind of connectionist, functional theorizing currently popular in some areas of philosophy of mind and cognitive science. Indeed, we will have more to say about such matters in the latter part of chapter 4. Nonetheless, the idea of levels of discourse (and reality) that might support other such levels in a nonreductive manner is one of which we make considerable use later in this book.

Theory of Mind and Intentional Self-Development

Several strands of contemporary cognitive developmental psychology recently have converged on a picture of the developing human agent that includes several suggestive lines of theorizing of direct relevance to our project herein. Richard Kegan (1983) provides a useful summary of important developmental markers that enable the child to develop conceptions of self and mind that eventually can be employed for intentional self-development and for the understanding of others. Four lines of development appear to enable the child to distinguish between self and nonself during the early stages of sensorimotor development. These include (a) the emergent capability of recognizing action outcome contingencies so that the consequences of actions might be anticipated; (b) the emergence of a semantically structured self-concept that captures one's distinctive features and facilitates comparisons with others; (c) the development of self-regulatory capabilities (sometimes referred to as "metavolitional skills") that can be used to evaluate, control, and correct one's intentional actions; and (d) the integration of these various self-processes and capabilities into an identity structure concerned with longer-term life projects and aspirations.

Notice that the various self-related capabilities described here in the language of contemporary developmental psychology may be interpreted as roughly synonymous with the kind of reasoned deliberation with respect to choices and actions, with which philosophers of agency have been traditionally concerned. What is unique to this particular psychological perspective is the idea that these agentic capabilities are emergent developmentally, that they seemingly arise as a consequence of activity in the sociocultural world, and that they are intimately bound up with our self-understandings.

Additionally, the critical importance of language for the acquisition of agentic capability is highlighted when a developmental perspective is adopted. It is the acquisition of semantic rules as a consequence of immersion in the practices of a language community that guides the ascription of attributes to oneself and others. At about the age of three, children have a sense of appropriateness and competence as enshrined in the language rules and practices in which they have been embedded, and they begin to evaluate their actions and themselves in these terms (Kagan, 1984). Such self-guides (Higgins, 1988), derived from sociolinguistic standards, are used to adjust one's own behavior and are thought to correlate with the emergence of self-evaluative emotions such as shame, guilt, and so forth.

Also tied to the development of linguistic, symbolic competence is the capability of reflecting on the mental states of other individuals. The emergence of such a "theory of mind" gives a qualitative boost to intentional action and self-regulation. Now, developing individuals not only can anticipate likely consequences of their actions on their physical surroundings but also are able to begin to deliberate with respect to the likely social, interpersonal consequences of their actions. Over time, with the gradual evolution of increasingly complex and hierarchically structured understanding of themselves and their sociocultural contexts, individuals become able to coordinate their everyday activities not only in relation to immediate circumstances but also in relation to lifelong projects and aspirations.

Recently, Brandtstädter and Lerner (1999) elaborated a theory of "intentional self-development" that draws heavily on the kind of developmental theorizing and empirical research just summarized. Moreover, while retaining a decidedly cognitive emphasis in their work, they make a serious attempt also to emphasize the sociocultural origins of much cognition. Thus, they endeavor to straddle the long-standing divide in developmental psychology between more individualistic conceptions of relations between agency and culture (e.g., Bruner, 1986; Valsiner, 1998) and social, communal conceptions of these same relations (e.g., Ratner, 1991; Wertsch, 1998). The core idea of intentional self-development is "the proposition that individuals are both the products and active producers of their ontogeny and personal development over the life span" (p. ix). They also contend that this uniquely human characteristic of being both determined and determining arises developmentally in the following way:

Through action, and through experiencing the effects and limitations of goal-related activities, we construe representations and
internal working models of ourselves and of the physical, social,
and symbolic environments in which we are situated. These representations in turn guide and motivate activities through which
we shape the further course of personal development. (p. ix)

Recognizing some of the philosophical implications of their "determined and determining" perspective, Brandtstädter and Lerner (1999) admit
that their "action perspective" might "necessarily involve a disavowal of the
classical nomothetical ideal of developmental research [in psychology], which
aims at universality and lawful connectedness" (p. x). For, despite their strong
cognitivism, they also recognize explicitly the plasticity and contextual variation in development attributable to sociocultural context, as well as to personal agency, and provide numerous references to psychological research in
support of these recognitions. They go on to elaborate the relationship they
envision between sociocultural context and agency in the following terms:

It is only when both sides of this circular relationship are heeded
that the central contours of a new developmental paradigm emerge.
From early transactions with the environment, and by initiation
into social networks of knowledge and practice, children form the
primordial representations of self and personal development from
which the processes of intentional self-development evolve. These
lines of development eventually merge in the formation of
knowledge systems, identity goals, and self-regulatory skills that
are basic to intentional self-development. Typically, the skills and
intentional contents involved in self-regulation become more
articulate in adolescence and early adulthood, that is, during a
transitional period when developmental tasks of identity formation and of an autonomous, self-reliant life planning become
salient concerns. The emergence of processes of intentional self-
development marks a dialectic shift in the relation between action and development. To the extent that development gradually
forms intentionality and the self, intentional action comes to
form development. (pp. xi–xii)

Thus, at the same time as they emphasize self-regulation and personal
control over development, and despite their strong cognitivist leanings,
Brandtstädter and Lerner (1999) continue also to emphasize the contextual
embeddedness and sociohistorical specificity of developmental patterns.
Further, they also suggest that both psychological (agentic) and sociocultural
contributions to development might be integrated with certain biological
and evolutionary points of view.

Among the biological and evolutionary factors that enforce, and at the same time make possible, intentional self-regulation, the great openness and plasticity of human development must be mentioned as of primary importance. . . . Anthropologists and biologists have recognized that culture, and the functional potentials to create culture and cultivate personal development, to a large extent compensates for a lack of adaptive specialization in the human species. . . . Biology does not impose rigid constraints on development, but rather establishes norms of reaction that involve a range of developmental outcomes over a range of environmental conditions. . . . Epigenetic environmental influences, however, are structured and temporarily organized through interactions of the developing individual with his or her environment. Phenotypic and genotypic conditions are thus linked in a circular, co-constructive relationship; the influence and expression of genetic factors in ontogeny are interactively moderated, as well as mediated, by activities through which individuals select and construct their developmental ecology. . . . In this view, traditional splits between "nature" and "culture," as well as attempts to establish a causal priority between these categories, are rendered obsolete. (pp. xiv–xv)

In summation, the work of Brandtstädter and Lerner (1999) begins to braid together action theoretical, developmental, cultural, and historical perspectives on the development and evolution of human agency. Clearly, intentional action cannot be isolated from the sociocultural forces and developmental sequences that structure goal-related human activity in the world. Across settings and developmental phases, the development of human agency is shaped and canalized by culturally enacted patterns of stimulation, information, beliefs, and practices with respect to what constitutes optimal development and successful aging. It is through their transactions with their sociocultural contexts that individuals come to understand themselves as persons, to sense the possibilities available to them with respect to their development, and to acquire the tools to select and pursue such understandings and possibilities. These are all themes that will be repeated in our own theorizing about agency. Nonetheless, we believe that many contemporary developmental psychologists, like Brandstädter and Lerner, who adopt the kind of developmentally emergent compatibilism we also seek, remain too literally wedded to certain aspects of cognitive psychology (e.g., information processing and schema models). (A potentially more promising line of developmental theorizing that features an emergentist epigenesis within a more broadly systemic account of the overall developmental context may be found in Thomas Bidell and Kurt Fischer [1997]. Bidell and Fischer, following George Edelman [1987], claim that emergent neurological structures required for agentic self-organization and coordination are stimulated and pruned differentially through engagement in particular forms of sociocultural activity. Nonetheless, there remains the strong suggestion in Bidell and Fischer that the cognitive–behavioral system [not the sociocultural system] leads the emergent epigenesis of agentic capability.) Our concern is that such "mental hypotheses" ultimately can detract from what we wish to regard as the basic reality of human being-in-the-world. This is a theme that we will explore in much greater depth later in this chapter. In the meantime, we turn to a brief examination of the work of a handful of theoretical psychologists who also have made important contributions to the contemporary psychology of human agency.

Theoretical Psychology of Agency
Rychlak's (1988, 1997) psychology of rigorous humanism contains a unique approach to the question of human agency—one that serves to introduce additional and important functions of purpose and language with respect to the acquisition of agentic capability. For Rychlak, the agent is "an organism that behaves or believes in conformance with, in contradiction to, in addition to, or without regard for environmental or biological determinants" (1997, p. 7). In this construal, agency is the capacity to influence one's behavior intentionally, and such a capacity cannot be explained reductively in terms of material and efficient causation; instead it requires the admission of formal and telic causal processes appropriate to the study of human language, logic, and reason. The most important aspect of human language, reason, and logic is the process of predication that refers to the purposeful affirmation, denial, or qualification of patterns of meaning. To behave intentionally or agentically is to behave with the goal of affirming certain understandings rather than others. Free will is defined "as this capacity to frame the predication for the sake of which behavior will be intentionally carried out" (p. 61). "The very meaning of free will is to transpredicate, to reply to theses with antitheses, to negate and redirect the course of events according to purpose" (p. 279).

   In this way, Rychlak (1997) and others working within his orbit (e.g., Howard, 1993; Jenkins, 1997; Slife, 1994) firmly place agency within human language, culture, and projects of understanding and insist that such a realm is not reducible to physical elements or patterns of causation but must be approached through processes of reason that necessarily involve the interpretation of meaning and purpose. In our opinion, in addition to capturing the Aristotelian agentic idea of dialectical (or oppositional) reasoning, Rychlak's core idea of transpredication highlights the possibly important role of imagination in the development and enactment of human agency. What Rychlak proposes is that human possibilities for action are not restricted to the actual or "factual" experiences of particular individuals but may include imaginative, even "counterfactual," extensions or alterations that are based on actual

experiences. The human capabilities of imagining based on actual experience, and of projecting such imaginings into the future as goals or models
for action from which human deliberators might select and choose, provides
yet another potentially important piece to the puzzle of human agency.

It is of critical importance to emphasize that neither the oppositional
deliberations nor the imaginative projections highlighted in Rychlak's account of agency are easily captured in models of agency and/or determinism
that assume only efficient causation as an adequate basis of explanation.
Thus, in his recent critique of computer models of human reasoning, Rychlak
(1999) emphasizes that

> there is no hope for true agency in a computer explanation
> because without the capacity to break free of the "given" input
> and look to its opposite implications, an agential explanation
> makes no sense . . . people [must be] seen as predicators who
> affirm meanings even as they grasp the opposite of these mean-
> ings and therefore can bring them into play without further
> input or feedback! When "A" is input they can move to "non-
> A" at will, for they are dialectical as well as demonstrative reasoners
> just as Aristotle claimed. (pp. 387–388)

Finally, for our purposes, it is important to note that Rychlak appears
to regard a capacity for dialectical–oppositional mentality as inherent in an
emergentist epigenesis. Like Bidell and Fischer (1997), Rychlak cites Edelman
(1987) and appears to suggest some sort of developmentally evolving, possibly socioculturally influenced, biological basis for the oppositional deliberation he considers central to the exercise of human agency. Nonetheless,
to us, he remains decidedly vague about the exact nature of such assumptions, and we again worry that they reflect a biological primacy that might
detract from what we regard (and will argue for) as a proper sociocultural,
historical, and developmental grounding of human agency.

Another theoretician who has challenged traditional conceptions of
causality with respect to human agency is Greenwood (1991), whose work
provides an excellent example of a theoretical account of agency and soft
determinism in the theory of social psychology. Although acknowledging
that certain causal explanations are inconsistent with certain construals of
agency, he maintains that "it is not the case that a commitment to the causal
explanation of human action precludes the recognition of human agency"
(p. 70). Greenwood accepts a compatibilist idea of agency as involving the
claim that actions are self-determined by an agent, rather than by other
conditions or factors, including the psychological states of the agent understood in nonvolitional terms. He also acknowledges that agents, at least
sometimes, have freedom of choice in deciding an action from a number of
possible actions. In short, to claim agency is to claim that an action is at least

partially generated by an agent in the absence of any conditions sufficient to cause the agent to do one thing rather than another.

Most important to Greenwood's (1991) acceptance of agency and soft determinism is his rejection of the principle of universal causal determinism (associated with the empiricist account of causality in terms of the invariant conjunction of events). This principle, which states that for every physical event or human action there is a set of conditions that is ontologically sufficient for the event or action, is inconsistent with agency and agency explanations. After recounting a number of telling arguments against the principle of universal causal determinism and the empiricist account of causality, Greenwood rejects both in favor of his own realist account of causality which allows for the possibility of agency and agency explanations. This is so because such a realist account understands causality in terms of the powers of particulars (particular physical events or properties or particular persons). This account maintains that to attribute a causal power to such particulars is to say nothing more than that it can generate a certain effect, not necessarily that it will or must.

Greenwood's (1991) argument here resonates to a point frequently raised by soft determinists in issuing their compatibilist challenge to libertarians and hard determinists. For many soft determinists, being able to make choices is an ability or power. Whether someone is writing does not affect his ability to write, even if at any given moment of not writing, his not writing is causally determined. When he is not writing, he nonetheless retains his capability of writing, a capability that might be demonstrated on any number of subsequent occasions when not writing is not determined, but writing is. We do not lose abilities or powers if we are causally determined; and the ability to make choices is no different from other powers such as writing. No powers are lost, including agency, because of causal determinism. What this argument also suggests is that the same or similar actions may be causally or agentically (self-)determined at different times. (Of course, as we shall see in chapter 4, it also is the case that a particular action might be partially self-determined and partially determined by factors and conditions outside of or not under an agent's control.)

Having argued for a realist account of causality that will admit agency explanations, Greenwood (1991) nonetheless maintains that there is a critical difference between natural and human powers, in that the exercise of human power lies within the control of an agent. Thus, it makes no sense to talk about the power of metal conductors as within the control of those metals. However, it makes complete sense to talk about the power of an agent to speak a language or play a musical instrument as entirely within the control of the agent who has such powers or capacities. Given opportunity, an agent can act or refrain from action according to personal reasons.

None of this is intended by Greenwood to deny that some human actions may be determined outside of the exercise of agency understood as self-determination. Many human actions undoubtedly do not require agency explanations. Humans may be driven to aggression, betrayal, even suicide. However, it is entirely ungrounded to suppose that all human actions can be explained in such ways. In the final analysis, the extent to which agency is manifest and influential in any particular case requires careful empirical consideration and cannot be predetermined.

> The best explanation of intentionally directed acts of aggression may be that they are causally determined by specific brain states. The best explanation of socially located acts of conformity may be in terms of peer pressures that are sufficient to determine them. The best explanation of some acts of aggression or conformity may be in terms of determination by brain states or peer pressures, and other acts of aggression or conformity may be best explained as self-determined acts of revenge or expediency. (1991, p. 75)

Greenwood also disputes the assumption of many contemporary cognitive psychologists that the reasons that guide an agent's self-determination, when it occurs, are entirely private and personal. For Greenwood, rules, reasons, meanings, and values are intrinsically social entities—the historically located products of evolving social consensus and ongoing negotiation. Following Lev Vygotsky (1934/1986), Greenwood claims that an agent's reasons, rules, and values are appropriated from sociocultural conventions and practices during the course of individual development and further elaborated and adapted to cope with the particular exigencies of personal life experience. Thus, like theories in natural science, agents' reasons and beliefs are open to revision in the face of novel facts or features of reality. What this means is that social consensus is sufficient to handle standard situations and life experiences, but that agents themselves must decide how to act in nonstandard situations. Such an agentic decision inevitably involves interpreting social rules and applying such interpretations to novel and/or difficult situations, with a view to determining how best to act. In short, appropriated social rules and reasons are and must be developed by agents in accordance with their own personal experiences.

Thus, Greenwood's (1991) account of agency as self-determination allows for agent explanations within the framework of a realist social science that refuses to treat human actions as natural phenomena or to reduce agency to natural determinants. However, Greenwood also argues against what he regards as accounts of agency that are too psychological in that they are removed from necessary historical, sociocultural origins, constraints, and enablers. These key insights are developed further by Harré and Gillett (1994) in their attempt to forge a discursive psychology that recognizes agency and self-determination.

Harré and Gillett (1994) begin their account of agency by claiming that human freedom is a discursive activity, that it is something that humans do, and that they make manifest in what they say about their lives. The discursive study of agency aims to understand how individual humans come to understand themselves within those sociocultural, discursive conversations and practices into which they are born, and within which they participate and develop. Harré and Gillett argue that people tend to take normative, evaluative attitudes toward their own dispositions and actions, and that these are copied from the response that others make to their actions, just as the actions themselves are copied from others. Thus, individuals develop repertoires of actions and evaluations through their sociocultural participation with others. Through this developmental process, individuals come to structure their activity in light of meanings and prescriptive norms (or discursive validations) that are first social and public and then psychological and private (but always interactive with the social and the public), much in the way envisioned by Vygotsky (1986).

It is very important to emphasize that in Harré and Gillett's (1994) account, the recognition that social norms and conventional practices constitute the resources for an individual's intentional actions and evaluations does not imply that the active individual agent can be excluded from explanations of her actions. Even though an individual's reasons for, and evaluations of, her actions are socioculturally derived, it is these reasons and evaluations that are at the core of intentional action. Thus, when behaving intentionally, individuals are agents and not mere objects of social causation. It is an agent's decided commitment to a particular course of action, together with her implicit evaluations that define a given action as the action that it is, that produce that action. If an agent were to withdraw her commitment from a particular action, then that action would cease to be the action of an agent.

Nor does an agent's response to a given situation depend solely on a causally induced effect of physical features (either external or internal) on the agent. Human action is meaningful activity that is not subject to lawlike or scientific generalizations that do away with the need to make reference to an agent's reasons, intentions, commitments, and evaluations. The internalized and subjectively organized social norms and conventions that enable human activity in the world are not like those effects and forces at work in Newtonian mechanics. This is so because it is these features of a person's socioculturally spawned subjectivity that constitute them as situated agents. It is exactly these features of human agency that are "part and parcel of an understanding of events in which people think this and that and do this and that for reasons that they find worth acting on" (Harré & Gillett, 1994, p. 121). Social causation as it appears in human action creates the conditions and possibility of agency but does not exhaustively determine an agent's consent to follow or conform to socially shared, interpersonal rules governing meaning. Although humans "*ought* to judge and act thus and so, notoriously [they] do not always do so, even if almost nothing tells against it" (p. 123).

Against what they regard as overly determinist versions of social constructionism, Harré and Gillett (1994) champion the role of the person in adopting sociocultural meanings, norms, conventions, and practices. They explicitly counsel against merely replacing physical forces and causes with social and discursive practices that also negate the active agent in favor of extrapersonal explanations. Social causation serves to dispose agents to certain decisions, actions, and evaluations but does not determine that they will act in particular ways. An important implication for psychology of this crucial point is that while psychologists may be able to make statistical predictions of behavior on the basis of social variables they will not necessarily be able to make sense of the actions of individuals in particular situations. The latter requires an understanding of the particular ways in which agents construe, organize, decide, intend, and evaluate in specific context. Harré and Gillett thus give credence to the personal commitments of the subject in relation to the social meanings and practices he or she takes up. Ultimately, it is these features that are required for any adequate explanation of individual action. Thus, there always is the possibility of human freedom of decision and action.

Harré and Gillett (1994) provide a summary of their approach to agency that links it to both psychological life and psychological inquiry.

> People operate with the meanings available to them in discourse and fashion a psychological life by organizing their behavior in the light of these meanings and integrating them over time. The result of the integrative project is a personality or character that is, to the extent permitted by the discursive skills of the subject/ agent, coherent and creative. The ideal is a psychological life with the character of an artistic project and not merely a stream of experiences and responses to stimulation. Of such a life we might say that it has meaning in the same sense as a work of art has meaning. The meaning is no more summarizable in words than is a symphony or painting but it is discernible by those who are themselves well versed in discourses, their structures, and their interrelations. It is within this context that human behavior is able to be understood in terms of both breadth and depth (Taylor, 1964). A lesser conception of human beings and of psychology leaves us bereft of the components of such an understanding and fails to display the richness of the human mind and personality, which draw on meaning and value as determined within discursive contexts. (p. 143)

The works of Rychlak (1988, 1997), Greenwood (1991), and Harré and Gillett (1994) go a considerable way toward supplying a more complete and adequate theory of agency and its development within human societies and cultures. The conceptualization of agency evident in these accounts, together with those more mainstream psychological accounts summarized earlier, may be employed to support the kind of middle-ground agency hinted at, but not really developed, in the compatibilist arguments of philosophers like Frankfurt (1971). Recall that compatibilism or soft determinism requires an account of agency that indicates how agency can somehow be both determined and not determined, and that such a conception of agency, if possible, will need to differ from the agentic conceptions of both libertarians and hard determinists. For clearly, the classic positions of libertarians and hard determinists will admit to no such dual-aspect theorizing, requiring that human action is either determined or it is not, and that any such reality is fixed in the essential nature of human beings and the world. By suggesting that human beings themselves have an always developing, socioculturally and historically enabled, shifting, and relational nature in interaction with their situations, the psychological works we have considered provide a very different perspective on human agency. It is a perspective that views the agent as developmentally emergent within historical, sociocultural context but with intentional and evaluative features that cannot be reduced back to its sociocultural and biological origins. In the remainder of this chapter, we examine another tradition of scholarly work—Continental hermeneutics—which further advances this conception of agency, but does so in a way that understands human existence and "mind" as inseparable from the world in which humans are embedded and compelled to act.

HERMENEUTICS AND AGENCY

Wilhelm Dilthey, the father of contemporary hermeneutics, attempted to work out a general approach to the human sciences. In doing so, he drew a sharp distinction between the natural and human sciences. In the natural sciences, he said that it was possible to view objects externally as brute material things, without experience and intentionality. However, he viewed such objectification as entirely inappropriate for studying humans and their creations. The phenomena of the human sciences, especially psychological phenomena, not only require interpretation in their study (as do physical phenomena) but also are constituted by human interpretive practices (unlike physical phenomena). Dilthey's (1977) "descriptive and analytic psychology" begins with an examination of the totality of life-experience. Life-experience presents itself as a lived reality that precedes distinctions between mind and body and self and world. It is only against this ever-present, mostly unarticulated, background of lived experience (which includes the totality of historical and sociocultural practices and context) that we are able to perceive and comprehend things, including our selves. Psychology must, therefore, always consider the feeling, desiring agent within a shared, practical life-world. Human life involves a constant flow of interpretation and reinterpretation. Although our lives have a certain facticity in that we are located in a specific worldly milieu that limits what is possible, we also have the ability to take up this facticity in pursuing our goals.

After Wilhelm Dilthey, Martin Heidegger (1927/1962) and Hans-Georg Gadamer (1960/1995) continued the development of contemporary hermeneutics in similar, but also different, directions. Heidegger gave priority to ontological issues by asking, "What is the mode of being of the entity who understands?" For Heidegger, human existence has a hermeneutic structure, and humans are self-interpreting beings who care about their own lives. Through our care about our lives, things around us can be disclosed as meaningful. We human beings are always addressing and engaged with entities we find around ourselves in terms of those linguistic articulations accessible in our social world. For our purposes, Heidgger's ontology of human existence (or "Dasein") relates to human agency in at least four specific ways having to do with care, embeddedness (or "thrownness"), possibilities, and projection.

According to Heidegger, "care is the basic state of Dasein" (1962, p. 293). What it means to be human is to care deeply about one's life and how to live it. Because we care within the context of uncertain futures, the resultant combination of experienced significance in living coupled with future open-endedness puts our lives at stake for us. Our lives are our own precisely because we must choose what to make of them. For us, the meaning and worth of our lives always are issues. Whereas nonhuman objects are determined by their physical properties, humans are defined by their choices and actions that relate to possibilities they encounter in the course of living their lives.

For Heidegger (1962), possibilities for living are drawn from the familiar contexts of the world in which we act. These everyday contexts are shaped by broader, historically established, sociocultural conventions and practices that constitute a form of life. From birth, individual biological humans are "thrown" into their life contexts, within which they remain embedded for their entire lives. However, because we inevitably must draw possibilities for our actions and lives from the contexts in which we are embedded, does not mean that we are determined entirely by them and that we cannot develop as genuine agents. To the contrary, our embeddedness is an enabling condition that allows us to become human persons in the sense of developing substantive, meaningful identities.

It is because we are embedded in contexts of practice and meaning that we come to understand ourselves as persons. We are not condemned to follow mindlessly the dictates of our contexts and traditions, nor must we radically free ourselves from their influence. Both of these options are, in fact, impossible. Rather, we become fully human when we seize upon particular interpretations and possibilities for living that are available within those forms of life into which we are cast at birth and within which we develop into human persons. What this means is that we are self-interpreting beings who develop self-understanding in relation to those understandings available to us in the forms of life we inhabit. As such, our identities and our lives are never settled because additional possibilities for living and acting always may emerge as a consequence of our self-understanding and the agentic being-in-the-world that it enables. In sum, we appropriate certain possibilities for living from our historical culture, and in the process of interpreting and enacting these possibilities, we create more or less unique lives.

Notice that in Heidegger's ontology of being, humans are constantly choosing among available possibilities. They are self-interpreting agents.

> [O]n the one hand, the meaning of our lives can not be read entirely in terms of our own individual decisions and actions: they are intelligible only against the backdrop of our life-world. On the other hand, there are a great many possibilities available to us and our choice of which specific alternatives we seize and the manner in which we take them up cannot be reduced to any set of variables in our biological or social contexts. . . . Our actions are the basic interpretations we offer of the lifeworld in which we find ourselves. Charles Guignon (1983) notes that our lives are actually commentaries on that lifeworld. (cited in Blaine Fowers, 2000, p. 9–10)

Finally, as Heideggerian agents, we always orient toward the future by way of what might be thought of as life projects. This forward living comes about by projecting ourselves forward through the aims and activities associated with such projects. We make decisions in the present for the sake of those projects that define and give coherence to our lives. In doing so, we create "clearings" in which events and happenings in the world can be perceived and interpreted. Such projection is an important element in full-bodied human agency because it moves us to select one life stance over others in terms of future possibilities. Taking such stances always means making choices in relation to what we wish to become and the sort of life we wish to lead. (Interested readers also might wish to consult Richard Williams [1994] for a hermeneutic grounding of agency in an ethics of "living truthfully.")

Thus, the Heideggerian agent is both determined and determining in the developmental sense we are after. This is not a radically free agent nor an agent determined entirely apart from its own self-determination. For Heidegger, self-interpretation is self-determination, and such interpretation never could get off the ground outside of individual development within historically established practices and customs of living. Moreover, this is an agent that is not merely voluntary but seems to exert some mild origination through the selection of possibilities for action that are available in the culture at large but which inevitably must be tailored to the life projects and projections of self-interpreting persons. The understanding that enables such agency, an agency that originates in care for one's being-in-the-world receives extensive treatment in the work of Gadamer.

Gadamer's (1995) philosophical hermeneutics attempts to clarify the conditions in which understanding can take place and to uncover what is common to all forms of understanding. An important part of Gadamer's work is his grave concern about the uncritical acceptance of methodologism that he perceives in the human sciences. In particular, he suggests that the abstraction of natural science is counterproductive to human science. Gadamer's approach is to emphasize the role of the background of preunderstanding (including our prejudgments or prejudices) in which all of our understandings and interpretations inevitably are nested. In Gadamer's view, interpretation and reflection always are guided by this background and are understood as a frame of reference drawn from the shared understandings available in our historical culture. It is from this background that we identify things, pose questions, and know what kinds of answers make sense. Having such a "horizon" of intelligibility is what makes it possible for us to think and act. All of our thinking and acting is made possible by our historically mediated preunderstandings.

In inquiry in human science, there is a circularity between past and present. The past is understood as a tradition that is effective in providing us with possibilities for understanding, while our present interpretations of those possibilities rebound on the historically effective tradition by indicating how the past can make sense. It is in this way, Gadamer says, that understanding is achieved through a process of fusing horizons: "The present lets the voice of the other be heard as making a truth claim, while the claim of the other transforms the horizon of the present and compels us to rethink our prejudices" (cited in Richardson, Fowers, & Guignon, 1999, p. 230). It is through this fusion of horizons of intelligibility that understanding in human science is possible.

Although Gadamer discusses his concept of horizon fusion originally in the context of understanding historical texts, many philosophers and theoretical psychologists (Kögler, 1996; Martin & Sugarman, 1999; Richardson et al., 1999; Risser, 1997) have noted that "the concept applies quite generally to understanding others" (Richardson et al., 1999, p. 231). The critical insight is that reaching an understanding with another is not a matter of empathically reconstructing the other's mental processes and private experiences but of being open to, and integrating, another's horizon in such a way that one's own perspective is altered in the process. Inevitably, such a process also involves some greater degree of critical penetration of one's own background of preunderstanding and prejudice (cf. Kögler, 1996). In short, full-blooded understanding requires an agent capable of deliberating on conditions and events of interpretation. In this ongoing play, this open-ended dialogue, both the phenomena into which we are inquiring and our own understandings are transformed. Rather than undermining tradition, such inevitable dynamics actually constitute tradition as an ongoing process of transmitting and modifying what is understood.

Hermeneutic inquiry depends on our ability to recognize that our "truths" are made possible by a shared background of life into which we are initiated and to which we contribute through our dialogues and interactions with others (texts, cultures, interlocutors). Scientistic attachment to the methods of natural science is out of place in the human sciences. But so too is the sociocultural reductionism of some postmodern psychology (see chapter 2). Because humans simply are what they interpret themselves as being, within their historical and sociocultural contexts, the study of psychological phenomena cannot be conceived as a detached, neutral process of recording objective facts; nor can psychology ignore the agency reflected in human interpretive activity. Rather, psychological studies must seek to take advantage of our inevitable background of both insights and prejudices in an ongoing, dynamic process of interpretation that constantly and critically challenges our existing understanding, even as it makes use of it.

The specific relevance of hermeneutic thinking to the topic of agency is marked by Dilthey's assertion that any attempt to understand human psychology must consider the feeling, desiring agent embedded in a shared practical life-world. It is advanced further by Heidegger's recognition that human existence in the world is unique in that it exhibits care for itself, especially in relation to life projects that arise through the application of an agent's emergent self-understanding to possibilities available in the life-world. Finally, the manner of hermeneutic agency is further indicated through Gadamer's clarification of understanding as the principle basis upon which humans can act in ways that reflect the care for themselves that their existence bequeaths, and that their life projects demand. As already stated, these insights come together in a view of human life as involving a constant flow of interpretation and reinterpretation. While the particular being of any human individual within a particular worldly milieu both enables and limits what is possible, humans also can take up the facticity of their being by understanding it and using it to care for themselves and to pursue their goals.

In this vein, Maurice Merleau-Ponty (1962) describes a life-world in constant evolution and renovation, with the human agent as primarily responsible for this state of play. In living, humans constantly receive meanings that have been constituted previously within their life-world and, given the inevitable ambiguity of their lives, adapt and extend those meanings through their own worldly activity. In speaking words we have heard from others and engaging in open-ended relational activities with others, we simultaneously retrieve and creatively extend meanings in relation to what we find significant in our lives. In this way, humans constantly interpret and transform meanings in the life-world that are inextricably bound up with their own being and understanding. The articulations, understandings, and reasoning that partially determine their actions in the world and their very sense of themselves are constituted within, and serve to extend, the life-world of which they are a part. In this way, humans are agents of change, even, and sometimes especially, when they misunderstand and misinterpret those meanings and practices in which they are caught up, constituted, and transformed.

As "self-interpreting animals" (Taylor, 1985), we humans are intertwined with the world and with others. We are both products and producers of the world in which we live. *It is through us that what seems necessary and determined becomes free.* The claim here is that in addition to the ever-present, constitutive influence of the physical, biological, and sociocultural world "interpretation of ourselves and our experience is constitutive of what we are, and therefore cannot be considered as merely a view on reality, separable from reality, nor as an epiphenomenon, which can be by-passed in our understanding of reality" (p. 47). As well, "the human animal not only finds himself impelled from time to time to interpret himself and his goals, but [also finds] that he is always already in some interpretation, constituted as human by this fact. To be human is to be already engaged in living an answer to the question, an interpretation of oneself and one's aspirations" (p. 75).

In the work of hermeneutic philosophers like Wilhelm Dilthey, Martin Heidegger, Hans-Georg Gadamer, Maurice Merleau-Ponty, and Charles Taylor is an articulation of human agency that fits nicely with what seems to be required by the desire of soft determinists for a conceptualization of agency adequate to the demand that agency can somehow be both determined and determining. These hermeneutic perspectives allow a more complete glimpse of a conception of agency as embodied, historically and socioculturally situated, and both perspectival and intentional, in relation to the particular practical concerns of human individuals in their everyday lives. When added to the sociocultural, developmental, and theoretical insights of psychologists like Bandura, Brandtstädter, Gillett, Greenwood, Harré, Lerner, Rychlak, and others the resultant mix of ideas offers a fresh, alternative view of agency that departs sharply from the fixed, metaphysical agentic conceptions of libertarians and hard determinists and also diverges from many of the traditional and contemporary strategies of philosophical compatibilists.

The collection of ideas considered in the latter sections of this chapter open up a third compatibilist alternative that differs importantly from dissolutionism and mere voluntarism. In particular, with these ideas in place it becomes possible to think of agency as both determined (in the sense of acquired through our worldly participations as the kinds of biological beings we are within the kinds of societies and cultures we inhabit) and determining (in the sense of being self-determined at the point of decision and action by an agent's own commitments, choices, decisions, and evaluations). This is a developmentally emergent, yet always situated, deliberative agency that depends on nonmysterious processes of self-interpretation and self-determination, processes that themselves have a discernible developmental trajectory.

In the next chapter, we will argue more formally that the fact that human agency arises nonmysteriously in the context of a historical, sociocultural life-world of meanings and practices does not mean that agency is fully determined by this life-world. For human existence in the life-world is marked by inevitable ambiguity and complexity that require agents to interpret their situation and condition in ways that go beyond current sociocultural meanings and practices. From this perspective, it seems clear that biology and culture are not enough, even in combination, to account for the partially determined and partially transformative nature of human activity in the world; nor does it seem reasonable to conclude that such activity is only, though it often is, random and/or nonreflective (e.g., tacit or unconscious). Rather, it is human beings who frame, choose, and execute (at least some of the time) their own actions in relation to their own goals directed at what they find significant in their life-experience.

Here then, is an initial conception of the kind of human agency that a convincing compatibilism or soft determinism seems to require—one that will be developed further in subsequent chapters of this volume. It is a conception of agency that is very different from the reduced, decontextualized, simplified, and devalued agency so commonly apparent in much of the scientific and professional literature of disciplinary psychology. The next chapter takes up another outstanding difficulty posed by soft determinism. In so doing, it furthers our alternative conceptualization of agency as a truly psychological kind. This difficulty, as stated earlier, is the lack of a nonquestion-begging argument for agency that is not entirely determined by biology and/or culture.

CHAPTER FOUR

THE UNDERDETERMINATION AND IRREDUCIBILITY OF AGENCY

WE BELIEVE that an adequate conception of human agency requires a compatibilist notion of self-determination but one that goes beyond traditional dissolutionist or voluntarist arguments and proposals to include a limited aspect of origination. This is so because, as we will argue, some human actions, especially in nonstandard situations of uncertainty and ambiguity, are not explicable in terms of biological and/or cultural factors or conditions alone but also require the actor's own understanding and reasoning (including intentions, commitments, valuations, beliefs, and so forth). In this chapter, we present an argument for what we term *the underdetermination of agency* (cf. Martin & Sugarman, 1999). This is an argument that, unlike the classic arguments of libertarians, does not simply assert the existence of freedom of choice and/or action as an unassailable premise, thus begging the question of agency. Rather, we argue for agency, understood as a particular kind of self-determination, by eliminating possibilities other than self-determination as fully determinate of all of the choices and actions of a developed human being. Because our argument for agency is eliminative, it may not be as robust as more directly positive arguments, but in the absence of these, we believe it suffices for our purposes in this volume.

After presenting our argument for the underdetermination of agency by factors and conditions other than self-determination, we turn to a consideration of recent proposals in the philosophy of psychology and mind that attempt to rationalize various reductions of psychological (agentic) kinds to physical and biological factors in the interests of advancing a truly scientific psychology. Even though we already have indicated our general view of some such proposals in chapter 2 of this book, in the latter part of this chapter, we lay out the philosophical bases for several contemporary reductionist proposals in a more detailed manner. We then indicate what we believe to be their fatal flaws. These are flaws that, in our view, can be ameliorated only by abandoning the reductionist project and embracing the kind of nonmysterious, emergent, and irreducible agency that we began to describe in the previous chapter and will develop more fully in subsequent chapters of this book.

AN ARGUMENT FOR THE UNDERDETERMINATION OF AGENCY

As previously stated, our compatibilism is not a compatibilism of dissolutionism and/or voluntariness alone. Moreover, it issues in a kind of soft determinism that is not entailed by either of these more traditional compatibilisms. We begin our argument for agency as self-determination by offering a more detailed definition of agency than we have thus far advanced. For us, human agency is the deliberative, reflective activity of a human being in framing, choosing, and executing his or her actions in a way that is not fully determined by factors and conditions other than his or her own understanding and reasoning. Such other factors and conditions include external constraints and coercions, as well as internal constraints over which the person has no conscious control.

Note several things about this definition of agency. First, agency need not be unaffected by factors and conditions other than an agent's own reflective understanding and reasoning. It only must not be determined fully by such other factors, a state of affairs we refer to as underdetermination. Second, even if a given motive or desire may have been established initially by factors such as social conditioning or genetics, the actor (following Frankfurt, 1971) remains an agent so long as he or she has assimilated such motives or desires so as to make them objects of his or her own deliberation. Third, in saying that agency is underdetermined by "other factors," we do not mean that agency is necessarily undetermined, only that it must itself figure in its own determination. This is what we mean by self-determination.

We especially wish to emphasize the distinction we draw between undetermined and underdetermined because in our view the traditional Hobbesian framing of compatibilism is inadequate precisely because it fails to make this distinction. In the absence of the possibility of underdetermination, only two choices present themselves: strict determinism or randomness, either of which may be argued effectively to rule out a coherent sense of self-determination. The problem we see with the traditional Hobbesian dissolutionist argument is that, as Bishop Bramwell and many others have sensed, it reduces self-determination too radically to nothing more than a link in a chain of antecedent events, factors, and conditions. It leaves no room for the deliberation (reflective understanding and reasoning) of an agent that is not entirely determined by other factors and conditions—in other words, it rules out even a limited origination. From this, it should be obvious that our position is not intended to be compatibilist in the traditional sense of dissolving agency to determinism. Rather, it is intended to be compatibilist in the more radical sense of demonstrating how an agentic capability in deliberation and action is compatible with a deterministic, nonmysterious, and nonreductive account of the development of human agency within biological–physical, historical, and sociocultural context.

Finally, by avoiding the word *cause* in our definition of agency, we do not necessarily restrict determination to efficient causation. Given well-known difficulties with the concept of cause (e.g., problems of infinite regress, the question of reasons as causes, the difficulty in selecting specific causes from other conditions and factors in open systems, the satisfactory formulation of conditions of necessity and sufficiency), we feel justified in avoiding its use.

Nonetheless, our conception of determinism is broadly consistent with the folk psychological idea of antecedent events, factors, and conditions influencing subsequent events with varying degrees of completeness, such that when such influence is complete, full determinism results. This folk psychological idea of "fully determined" suggests a more formal doctrine of determinism which holds that for everything that ever happens at the level of human action there are factors and conditions such that, given them, nothing else could happen. Stating our thesis of determinism in this way rules out arguments for indeterminacy at the quantum level of physical entities. We believe that there is no good reason to believe that such arguments apply anywhere other than at the level of subatomic particles in interaction. Put most simply, for determinism to hold with respect to human agency, there must be determining conditions for human choices and actions. For us, the only viable option is a soft determinism that includes the kind of irreducible, agentic self-determination for which we will argue in this chapter.

STRUCTURE OF THE ARGUMENT

The only factors or conditions, other than agency (understood as self-determination), that might determine human choice and action, aside from explicit coercion that does not always exist, are (a) physical–biological (e.g., neurophysiological) states and processes, (b) sociocultural rules and practices, (c) unconscious processes over which an agent has no control, or (d) random events. (We omit theological speculation because in our opinion invoking an omniscient being or beings removes any rationale for human argument with respect to agency.) Assuming that these options exhaust plausible possibilities for explaining human choice and action (other than the positing of human agency understood as self-determination in the manner we have specified in our definition of agency), elimination of each and all of these options as fully determinate of human choice and action will establish the underdetermination of human agency by factors and conditions other than agency (in our sense of self-determination) itself.

AGAINST FULL PHYSICAL–BIOLOGICAL DETERMINISM

Human actions are meaningful, and meaning requires a context. *Meaning* refers to the conventional, common, or standard sense of an expression, construction, or sentence in a given language, or of a nonlinguistic signal, symbol, or practice in a particular sociocultural setting (Audi, 1999, p. 545). Therefore, the meaningfulness of human actions requires sociocultural rules and practices, the most important of which are linguistic or language related. Consequently, the only way in which human choice and action could be determined entirely by biological–neurophysiological states and processes is if the sociocultural rules, practices, and conventions are determined by or reducible to such states and processes.

Such a full reduction of societies and cultures to physical biology seems highly implausible, given that we currently do not possess, nor we would argue, ever are likely to possess adequate physical descriptions of sociocultural, linguistic practices. Without such descriptions, attempting to explain agency in solely physical terms is rather like attempting to explain the activity of baseball players without reference to the rules and regulations of the game of baseball. Note that this argument against full biological–physical determinism does not rule out human biology and neurophysiology as requirements for human action. However, requirement alone is not determination.

Furthermore, the meanings found in sociocultural and linguistic practices constitute and are constituted by those very practices. These meanings provide a coherence for the human life-world that does not exist at the level of biology or neurophysiology. So, even if some kind of biological–neurophysiological account of sociocultural and linguistic practices were put forward, such an account itself would only draw its meaning from that very sociocultural–linguistic level that it was attempting to explain.

AGAINST FULL SOCIOCULTURAL DETERMINISM

Socioculturally governed meanings change over historical time. Such change could not occur if past sociocultural rules, conventions, and practices were fully determining of meaning. Therefore, past sociocultural rules, conventions, and practices cannot be fully determinate of meaningful human action; they must be at least partially open-ended.

If sociocultural rules and practices were fully determinate of meaning, there would be no possibility of changes in meaning to accommodate novel facts or features of reality. Yet, such changes are clearly in evidence, especially in the sociocultural world, which is modified and transformed through historical time. Sociocultural rules and practices do not specify how to proceed beyond structured, consensual situations, but go on we do. For example, the current acceptance in many jurisdictions of homosexual families and marriages would have been unthinkable short decades ago, indicating a shift in the social practices and rules that govern meaningful human action.

If sociocultural rules and practices are not fully determinate of meaning, they cannot be fully determinate of meaningful human action and therefore cannot exhaustively or solely determine agency. As Koch (1999) noted,

> [T]hough rules may be guides to action, they cannot be recipes for action. . . . If rules are determinants of actions, the causal distance is very great and the underdetermination immense. Rules, at best are templates through which action is somehow squeezed, and in this process of squeezing, the templates themselves are continuously bent and twisted—sometimes in ways that make apparent the need for new ones. (p. 12)

The open-ended nature of conventional social practices and regulations provides for the development of social meaning in relation to novelty and change and also provides for the dynamic development of personal understanding that creates possibilities for action. But such provision is not determination. Somewhat analogous to the way in which scientific theories are underdetermined by evidence, human understandings and interpretations, and the actions they support are underdetermined by sociocultural practices and regulations. There always exist different understandings and interpretations that are equivalent with respect to their sociocultural constitution because such constitution is only partial. If full sociocultural determinism existed, societies and their individual members would be trapped in static systems of meanings, but they are not.

However, perhaps it is possible still that sociocultural change might arise from factors other than human agency. For example, unorchestrated contact across societies with different rules, conventions, and practices might foster change in the absence of deliberative, individual agency per se. But important as such occurrences might be in human history, much sociocultural change occurs in the absence of contact with other cultural traditions. Moreover, it is extremely difficult to imagine any cultural tradition if one were to subtract the contributions of particular individuals. For example, try to think about contemporary Western culture on the assumption that individuals such as Leonardo da Vinci, Johann Sebastian Bach, René Descartes, and Albert Einstein had never existed. Would some others have undertaken exactly the same kinds of work with the same kinds of sociocultural consequences? Such extreme social determinism seems highly unlikely. Societal change demands the activities of agents whose actions are at least in part deliberative, even if the wider consequences of such actions never can be entirely anticipated and even if relevant sociocultural traditions and practices are required for any such agentic activity to be possible at all.

It should be clear that the foregoing claims and arguments against full biological–neurophysiological and sociocultural determinism also rule out full determination of human agency by any combination of biological and cultural factors and conditions alone. Given that human actions are meaningful and that the meaningfulness of human actions requires sociocultural rules and practices, biology by itself is insufficient. However, because sociocultural rules and practices are open-ended and societies and cultures change, culture by itself also is insufficient. Given this state of affairs, together with the already noted irreducibility of cultural conventions and practices to biology, it seems inconceivable that any combination of insufficient biological and insufficient cultural factors and conditions possibly could fully determine human agency.

Against Randomness and Unconscious Processes Alone

To this point in our argument by elimination, the facts of cultural change and individual action outside of conventional, rule-governed situations have been taken as sufficient grounds for warranting the open-endedness of sociocultural rules and practices required for meaningful human action. But such change and unregulated action may result from nonagentic randomness or unconscious processes, rather than from reflective human agency. To put these possibilities in the most plausible way, sociocultural change may, indeed, reflect the activity of human beings collectively and individually, but this activity may be random and/or nonagentic, reflecting no intentionally engaged understanding, reasoning, and choice of human agents. At this point, it seems necessary to concede the possibilities that some social change may, indeed, come about in such a random manner and that unconscious processes of individuals and collectives may, indeed, influence human activity in the world. In fact, there is good reason to believe that much of everyday, conventional rule-governed human action is engaged by actors without much in the way of explicit, conscious deliberation. However, all that is required for our argument for agency is that social change also may be brought about, at least in part and sometimes by the reflective reasoning and acting of human beings. Therefore, it is easy to understand why so much emphasis in the relevant philosophical canon has been given to phenomenological arguments for reasoned deliberation and the choice of action based on such thoughtful consideration, especially in nonstandard, unconventional situations.

Such arguments rest on the widely shared intuition that we do, in fact, sometimes make decisions to act based on a deliberate consideration and weighing of possible alternatives from our own first-person perspectives concerning our situations and lives. Of course, the reasoning and choosing in which we perceive ourselves to be engaged may be deeply flawed, but if so, this in itself has no bearing on the possibility that our actions are determined in part by our reflective (but errorful) understanding and reasoning. What does bear on this kind of phenomenological argument is the counterargument that intuition of any kind is not a good guide to truth.

On the other hand, it is worth noting that almost all arguments against intuition and therefore against phenomenological evidence for agency have been put forth by those who wish to secure a foothold for nonagentic determinism not for randomness or for unconscious, irrational processes. If randomness, unconscious determination, and agency are the only remaining options (which, having ruled out full sociocultural and/or biological determinism, they now are), phenomenological evidence of reflective deliberation, linked to actions that clearly do seem to make a difference in unfolding sequences of events, becomes much more attractive.

It simply is not sensible to hold that human actions that seem to individuals to follow from their own reflective deliberations should be placed below merely random or unconscious activity alone in the attempt to understand and explain human affairs. Again, this is not to say that what sometimes does, or eventually might, transpire in the sociocultural context is unaffected by random or unconsciously determined activity. After all, the sociocultural context is extremely busy and contested, in which, if anything, many actions may be overdetermined by various competing nonagentic, agentic, and random occurrences and factors. Nonetheless, to deny the possibility of agency in favor of randomness or the unconscious alone, having ruled out other full nonagentic determination, is to us difficult to fathom if the object of the entire exercise is the understanding and possible explanation of human action in the world.

Despite ongoing sociocultural change, a good deal of order is discernible in sociocultural conventions, rules, and practices. Randomness cannot account for such meaningful order. At a purely physical level, random processes might contribute to the establishment of order or patterns in physical systems. However, this kind of order can only be one among many necessary conditions for meaning. Meaning is more than mere organization or patterns—it involves significance as well. Even the recognition of something as a pattern and the evaluation of its significance presupposes meaning. Therefore, the sociocultural meaning that is required for human action cannot be random.

Moreover, humans are, at least partially, aware of many of their choices and actions in ways that converge and coordinate with the observations, accounts, and activities of others. Unconscious processes alone cannot account for such awareness and coordination of human choice and action.

Once again, we accept that change in sociocultural practices, conventions, and rules that guide human choice and action may, and probably often does, reflect human activity that is nondeliberative in the sense of being tacit or inarticulate. However, we submit that our phenomenal experience of ourselves as intentional agents, in combination with our ability to coordinate our actions with those of others to achieve commonly judged, orderly social ends, provides sufficient reason to forego a commitment to fully random or unconscious determination.

AGENCY AS THE SURVIVING, PLAUSIBLE OPTION

Having eliminated full biological and cultural determination of human action and argued against randomness and unconscious processes alone, we are left with the possibility that human choice and action, at least in part and sometimes, result from the irreducible understanding and reasoning of human agents. The underdetermination of human agency by these other conditions and factors does not mean that human agency is undetermined, only that it figures in its own determination. Such self-determination means that human agency is not reducible to physical, biological, sociocultural, and/or random–unconscious processes, even though many of these may be required for agency, and/or help to constitute it.

Of course, it might be argued that some combination of physical–biological, sociocultural, random, and/or unconcious factors and conditions might provide a fully deterministic account that does not require self-determination. Indeed, this may be a logical possibility if one assumes some kind of generative, nonadditive interactivity among these various conditions and factors. However, without an exacting theoretical description and empirical demonstration of precisely such a generative effect (preferably one displayed at the level of everyday events, not one based speculatively on psychologists' and/or philosophers' interpretations of chaos theory or quantum mechanics), such possibilities amount to little more than gestures of faith that assume a determinism that is complete without self-determination. Consequently, they seem to us to beg the question.

At this point, we also should repeat an argument made in the previous chapter to the effect that human agency, understood as self-determination, may not always be exercised. Just as we do not become unable to stand after we have been sitting, we do not become unable to exercise self-determination because there are occasions and circumstances in which our choices and actions reflect no deliberative self-determination. In other words, the fact that we may not always be self-determining does not imply that we can not self-determine at other times and in other circumstances.

We now want to argue more directly for the plausibility of our assertion that human agency is underdetermined by factors and conditions other than self-determination. To recap, our first premise is that human actions are meaningful. Our second and third premises are that the meaningfulness of human actions requires sociocultural rules and practices, but that these are open-ended to account for sociocultural change. As we previously argued, existing sociocultural rules and practices do not allow human actors to go beyond standard, consensual situations, but go on we obviously do. That is, in certain situations, sociocultural rules and practices are insufficient to account for human action.

What we now want to argue is that transformations in social meaning require the positing of human agency as self-determination. It is only through the exercise of self-determination that humans can accommodate to novel situations in ways that become the object of social negotiation and transformation. The open-ended nature of conventional social practices and regulations provides for the extension of social meaning in relation to novelty and change, precisely because it requires interpretation based on the understanding and reasoning of human agents. Consensual elements define the standard situation, but agents must decide for themselves how to act in nonconsensual situations. In these situations, sociocultural rules and meanings can provide only a partially interpreted basis for acting, and agents' understanding and reasoning (i.e., self-determination) must do the rest. Because understanding and reasoning are not entirely situationally bound, different agents in the same situation and with similar histories of past sociocultural participation, may act differently based on their own understanding and reasoning in those situations. It is in this way that human agency is underdetermined by the sociocultural contexts and experiences of biological humans.

In making the foregoing argument for the underdetermination of human agency, we do not wish to be read as implying that agency itself arises mysteriously in the sense of not requiring nonagentic sociocultural and biological factors and conditions. Nor do we wish to deny that some part of our activity in the world may reflect the activity of unconscious or tacit processes over which we exercise little deliberate control. What we believe is that reflective agency arises in an intelligible manner within inescapable physical, biological, and sociocultural contexts. However, once it arises developmentally in these contexts, it cannot be reduced back to these other factors and conditions; instead it always may play a part in its own subsequent development and exercise.

This way of thinking is somewhat foreign to much mainstream psychology and analytic philosophy, both of which often have treated the human agent as somewhat detached from relevant context, as disembodied, and as without a developmental history. (See Kane [1998] and Mele [1995] for some notable exceptions However, even in these instances, possibly relevant developmental theorizing is more suggested than elaborated.) It is entirely possible to discuss "brains in vats," computational "minds," and other such hypotheses and associated arguments about the relation between minds and brains, with little more than a passing nod to human history or culture. The alternative conception of human agency that seems to us to be required, as we hinted in the previous chapter, is that which has been described by contemporary hermeneuts such as Taylor (1985) and Martin and Sugarman (1999), among others (e.g., Richardson et al., 1999). This is a form of agency that draws as much from the hermeneutic tradition within twentieth-century Continental philosophy, as from the kind of analytic tradition with which we are mostly concerned in this chapter. This is an "in-the-world" agency exercised by embodied, developmentally emergent psychological individuals within sociocultural, developmental context. However, before turning to a detailed description of the conditions, development, and exercise of this kind of agency (in chapter 5), we want to spend much of the rest of this chapter in clarifying and refuting several contemporary attempts to frame and argue for the reduction of agentic, psychological to natural, physical and biological kinds.

CONTEMPORARY PROGRAMS OF REDUCTIONISM AND THE IRREDUCIBILITY OF AGENCY

In contemporary philosophy of science, scientific realism has replaced earlier positivistic theories of science. With respect to psychology, positivists understood psychological kinds (what they termed "mental states") as theoretical entities postulated in order to explain empirical regularities in behavior. The resultant psychological behaviorism equated mental states such as desires to displays of particular patterns of behavior. However, as scientific realism replaced positivism, such behaviorism fell out of fashion. When applied to psychology, scientific realism implies that our psychological states should be viewed and understood as natural kinds that feature in causal explanations and generalizations to explain behavior. (With respect to the chronology of events reported in chapter 2, the reductive efforts of behaviorists in the first half of the twentieth century now have been replaced by the reductive efforts of neurophysiological and computational psychologists who subscribe, either explicitly or implicitly, to scientific realism.) The important point here is that by the end of the twentieth century, the Anglo American tradition of philosophy of mind and psychology, influenced by the recently acquired hegemony of scientific realism in the philosophy of science, now understands psychological states as states of a system that are causally responsible for bringing about behavior. It is the characteristics of such states and the system within which they reside that now have become the proper objects for scientific psychology.

For the scientific realist in physical science, physical effects stem from physical causes, and lawful generalizations make reference only to physical kinds, the constitutive features of which provide the required causal mechanisms in causal, scientific theories. Even if such mechanisms cannot be observed directly, they are real by virtue of their causal efficacy and can be taken as legitimate objects for scientific theorizing. When transplanted to psychology, such an approach has insisted that the most pressing task for philosophers of mind and psychology is to provide an account of mental states that establishes the causal role of mental states in a way that is consistent with the causal explanations of physical science (Burwood, Gilbert, & Lennon, 1999).

In what follows, no exhaustive attempt is made to survey all recent and contemporary efforts to relate mental states to physical, brain states in a manner consistent with the demands of scientific realism. Nonetheless, the approaches discussed serve to give a reasonable introduction to such attempts and are sufficient to provide a clear indication of their nature and, in our opinion, limitations with respect to capturing agentic human activity.

CENTRAL STATE MATERIALISM

The most straightforward way of applying the scientific realist program in physical science to psychology is to reduce mental states to physical states. The simplest way of doing this is to assume that what we understand as two different entities (i.e., the physical and the mental) actually are reducible to only one entity (i.e., the physical). Thus, on this view, the psychological descriptions used in everyday, folk psychology actually pick out distinctive physical kinds. Moreover, these kinds are exactly those that can feature in physical causal explanations. In short, what is most important about psychological or mental states is that they really are physical states, in the sense of brain states. What is being claimed in this basic form of central state materialism is that one's love for one's spouse or anxiety about the illness of a family member are identical to some particular brain states. To love or be concerned about a person is the same as being in some particular physical state. This must be so because what causally explains behaviors such as writing letters to one's spouse when away from home or hopping in a car to travel to the hospital are mental–brain states such as "love for spouse" or "concern/anxiety about family member."

A key question for psychological, central state materialists (sometimes called "type/type identity theorists") concerns exactly in what a mental state consists. The reductive model employed to answer this question is one in which lawlike generalizations linking psychological kinds with behavior are derivable from lawlike generalizations employing physical kinds. Bridging laws pair specific psychological kinds with specific physical kinds. This bridging is crucially important because with the proper bridges in place everything that occurs at the level of psychological kinds becomes explicable in terms of the lower-level physical kinds and the systematic body of physical laws that govern them. With respect to the scientific realist project, when all of this is accomplished, we will have uncovered the intrinsic physical properties of psychological kinds. Love and anxiety will be discovered to be actual physical states of the brain in the same way in which water was discovered to be molecules composed of one oxygen and two hydrogen atoms.

From a scientific realist perspective, one problem with type/type identity theory of the central materialist variety is that it seems to rule out the possibility of fashioning truly general laws governing human behavior. This is so because under the terms of type/type identity theorizing a single psychological state (such as love or anxiety) seemingly can have multiple realizations in different people or even in the same person at different times. General laws would seem to require a more obviously consistent patterning than this, unless the requirement of consistent correlation between the physical and the mental might be relaxed.

In an attempt to salvage the materialist aspiration for broad, general physical laws, many materialist theorists faced with the "multiple realization" problem began to propose various kinds of token/token identity theories (cf. Bechtel, 1988). Token/token identity theorists doubt that research ever will support a strong correlation between types of phenomena described mentally and types described or characterized physically. The idea behind all token/token identity theories is that there need not be any systematic link between the different physical states that are identified with a particular mental state on different occasions (and in different people). Such theories maintain that every token of a mental event is a token of a neural event but do not require a strict equation between types of mental and types of neural events. Thus, every time a person is in a particular mental state, this mental state is identical to a brain state, but on other occasions when the same person is in the same mental state, she may be in a different brain state. The problem with such proposals is that ·it is not clear how those different physical states underlying the same mental state might be linked together in a way that bridges to generalizable underlying physical laws, at least without overdetermining human behavior. The prospect of overdetermination arises when two or more independent causes (e.g., two or more brain states) either of which would suffice to bring about a particular effect (e.g., the same mental state) are possibly available.

The seemingly intractable problems of type/type and token/token identity theories, even when viewed from within a scientific realist perspective, have led some theorists to adopt the more radically materialist solution of eliminating psychological kinds entirely in favor of physical kinds. Such theorists (e.g., Churchland, 1981) argue that if those psychological kinds cited in causal explanations of behavior cannot be reduced successfully to underlying physical properties, the reality of psychological kinds is questionable, and they should be eliminated from scientific explanatory theories. Since there seem to be no inner, mental kinds that both fit within our everyday, folk psychology and can function scientifically as required by scientific realists, we should abandon attempts to reduce our folk psychology to scientific psychology by abandoning our folk psychology itself, together with its mentalistic but unrealistic vocabulary. Science can no more retain the language of folk psychology than it can retain the language and conceptions of witchcraft. Some eliminativists (cf. Rorty, 1989) seem willing to retain the terms of everyday folk psychology as convenient placeholders for purposes of everyday discourse, at least for the time being.

However, to many not committed to the scientific realist project for a reductive psychology, attempts to reduce or eliminate our everyday psychological terms and considerations seem scarcely intelligible. As Robert Woolfolk (1998) states,

> [The] theories and constituent concepts [of a physical, biological level of explanation] simply do not connect with most worlds of human practice at the levels those worlds are conceived and carried out. Just as bridge builders never talk much to each other about quarks, it is unlikely that declarations in ordinary language, such as "I love you," will ever be replaced by what would doubtlessly be a very elaborate, lengthy, and unromantic description of limbic system excitations. (p. 14)

The very concerns that fuel psychological inquiry and interest would seem to be lost in such materialist projects. One's love for one's spouse and one's concerns for a family member would seem not so much informed as dissolved in talk about brain states and their physical properties alone. And if our folk understandings of what it means to love and be concerned about others are dissolved into biological states alone, our responsibility for such states also would disappear. If all that binds us to our partners and friends is a neurochemical state called "love," we can hardly be expected to remain loyal when such states change in accordance with biological laws. Such general concerns about central state materialism have encouraged some contemporary philosophers of mind and psychology to recast their reductive attempts in less ontologically demanding terms. In what follows, we have clustered such attempts together under the heading of supervenience and functionalism.

SUPERVENIENCE AND FUNCTIONALISM

Thus far, we have seen that type/type identity theories have difficulty explaining the multiple realization of mental states from different physical states or events without seeming to suggest that mental states or events must, therefore, be overdetermined. On the other hand, while token/token identity theories seem capable of handling multiple realizations, they still assume that individuation into token states or events at the psychological level must coincide with reductive individuation at the physical level. Such an assumption seems to stretch traditional ideas of direct causality by suggesting that there are many versions of a cause and many versions of an effect, to such an extent that it becomes unclear where the lines of demarcation might be drawn with respect to a particular causal event.

In response to such difficulties, some philosophers of mind and psychology (e.g., Kim, 1996) have suggested a different kind of relation, one that sees the required connections between mental (or psychological) and physical states in terms of supervenience or supervenient causation rather than in terms of classical causation. Most basically, supervenience is a relation of dependence between properties or facts of one type (or kind) and properties or facts of another type (or kind). Properties of type "A" supervene on properties of type "B" if and only if two entities cannot differ with respect to their "A" properties without also differing with respect to their "B" properties.

Supervenience models are not reductive in the classical manner. To say that psychological states are supervenient on physical ones is to claim that the mental is fixed by its physical properties (which are the fundamental ones), but that the states concerned are not sufficiently distinct for the relation to be causal in the classical sense. Thus, one's experience of pain may be said to supervene on one's particular neural state at the time, and one's wincing may be said to supervene on one's muscle contraction that is caused (classically) by one's neural state. Here, the relations between mental and physical states are supervenient, while the relation between physical states (i.e., between neural state and muscle contraction) are causal. Moreover, the relation between the mental states or events of pain and wincing is said to be one of supervenience rather than causality. Finally, to allow for the possibility that mental events might on occasion "cause" physical events, some theorists also have suggested that, in relation to this particular example, pain might be viewed as a supervenient cause of muscle contraction.

In supervenience models, mental properties are not considered sufficient for any given set of physical properties because the former may be found with different physical properties on different occasions. Nonetheless, the mental properties, states, or events do not float free; instead, they always are grounded in some set of physical properties, states, or events that are sufficient for them. The important point is that unlike classically reductive models the mental properties remain distinct from each of their many possible physical bases and may even be seen to interact with physical bases in a way that influences the latter (superveniently). The dependency involved is therefore one of supervenience rather than reductive identification. Such a model is not classically materialist or reductive because it allows a dualism of mental and physical properties as long as a sufficient supervenience relation holds between the mental and the physical.

For many philosophers of mind and psychology, acceptance of the supervenience thesis does not give an adequate account of what is involved in having a mental state (cf. Burwood et. al., 1999). It also is difficult to understand how the distinctive character of the mental requires nothing more than the instantiation of physical properties. Finally, if real causation is taking place only at the physical level and if one wishes to grant a real causal role to the mental, then it seems necessary to beat a retreat to the classical reductive picture of central state materialism. It is in response to such concerns that the currently favored perspective in Anglo American philosophy of mind and psychology—reductive functionalism—has been developed (cf. Jackson, 1996).

The functionalist program begins by claiming that classical materialist reductionism erred by describing physical properties in the wrong way. It focused on physical kinds defined in terms of their material constituents (e.g., atomic structures, neural firings). The functionalist proposal is that we should instead understand our physical states in terms of their relational properties and functional roles within the systems of which they are part. If this basic proposal is accepted, it should then be possible to reduce psychological states to physical states thus construed. This is because psychological or mental states are relational and functional. They are inner states whose identity consists of their role in mediating responses to environmental stimuli.

The "function" in functionalist models is causal. Agents are understood as being in particular mental states that play a specific causal role in determining their response to the environment. Causal and supervenient relations of physical and mental states to each other and to environmental conditions and behavioral outputs, all are considered in determining functional roles within a system. Thus, one's belief that it will snow today (mental state, grounded in a particular physical state of expectation) based on one's perception (mental state, grounded in physical, sensing processes) of prevailing weather conditions (relevant environmental factors) causes one to put skis in a car-top ski rack (behavioral output).

Functionalism assumes that mental kinds are identified with functional kinds that supervene on physical kinds. The same functional kind may be instantiated by different physical kinds on different occasions. Thus, the relation between the mental and the physical is mediated by the introduction of an intermediate, functional level. Once psychological kinds are given their appropriate functional characterization, this same functional characterization can be manifested at the physical level. Because psychological states are understood in terms of their functional role, supposedly it is clear how a variety of physical states could play this same functional role in different persons, species, or other systems (most notably, computers) at different times, without risk of overdetermination. Moreover, appropriate classification into functional kinds can yield lawlike generalizations that can be used for prediction and explanation. Even though such generalizations are not derivable from underlying physical states and events, they supervene on such states and their causal interactions.

The issue that divides various functionalist proposals concerns the matter of how we are to arrive at intermediate functional accounts of our psychological kinds. It is in response to this issue that reductive functionalism attempts to characterize the functional roles of psychological states in nonmentalistic ways. For reductive functionalism to work, there must be nonmentalistic functional kinds that are coextensive with our everyday mental kinds. Moreover, these nonmentalistic functional kinds must explain and predict what our everyday psychological kinds explain and predict, as well as capturing what we take to be unique and distinctive about our mental kinds. The functionalist response to this enormous challenge has been to develop computational models of mind.

Computational Models of Mind

Reductive functionalism somehow must demonstrate how psychological characteristics might arise in a material world where privilege is granted to physical kinds and physical science. Two interlocking features of our psychological states are especially challenging to such a project: intentionality and rationality. Intentionality refers to the fact that our mental states are about something, someone, or some actual or imagined state of affairs. Not only can our mental states be directed at objects or states of affairs in the world, but they also can be directed at content that does not correspond to any state of affairs in the world. For example, an author might think about the office in which she writes, or an imaginary world wherein to set her story. Moreover, when we think about objects or states of affairs (actual or imaginary), we think about them in particular ways. The author can think about how her office facilitates or detracts from her writing and how to mold the imaginary setting of her story to the unfolding narrative she wishes to relate. Consequently, human psychological states cannot be fixed by the objects or states of affairs to which they relate. Rather than intentional states being linked causally to their content, they seem to be linked rationally. Such links reflect reasons that relate our intentional states to their contents in logical or conceptual ways. Our author has reasons for arranging her office and for imagining the setting for her story. (Notice in passing that the presence of such reasons does not necessarily make it rational for her to furnish her office in a particular way or to imagine a particular narrative setting.)

Computational theories of mind are used by reductive functionalists in an attempt to make intelligible how a physical system can manifest mentality. The core idea is to compare the mind to a computer. To capture what seems unique about mental states, computational models attempt to formalize intentional states and reason-giving relations. What this means is that such states and relations are spelled out in terms of formal or structural patterns of propositions. This amounts to a claim that the intentional and reason-giving relations that seem to define human mental states are a matter of syntax (structure or form) rather than semantics (meaning). Thus, the first move in comparing minds to computers is to reduce meaning to structural syntax alone.

But this is just a starting point. Two additional moves also are required. A second computational claim is that the structural relations that constitute intentional–reason-giving relations can cause alterations in mental states. In essence, causal transitions at the psychological level (recall the basic model of reductive functionalism) that are anchored in reason-giving relations are reflected in causal transitions at the nonintentional level that are anchored in syntactic linkages. Computers can work only with symbols that are assigned semantic interpretations. Consequently, the causal processes at work in computational models can rely only on formal, syntactic relations and properties. For this reason, purely syntactical manipulations replace reasoning about meanings.

Finally, all of this necessitates a third claim in the computational approach. This third claim is that rationalizing links between intentional states and contents are reducible to patterns of causal transitions between physical and structural states of the computer. The reductive chain now is complete. Meaning has been reduced to syntax alone. Syntactical manipulations have come to substitute for reasoning. And the architecture of the computer stands in place of mind and its mental states and contents.

The foregoing—reductive claims of the computational approach—assume a language-of-thought model in which intentional and reason-giving states and relations are understood as the occurrence of sentence-like structures or maps of propositions inside the head (or inside the computer). Moreover, it is further assumed that if semantic and intentional properties of mental events are to be real, they must be identical with (or supervenient on) physical properties that are themselves neither intentional nor semantic. In particular, if intentional states are to be genuinely causally effective in the way required by the usual notions concerning agency, then they must be firmly and demonstrably anchored in more fundamental causal interactions at the physical level. In the case of computational models of mind, computers provide the required physical, foundational substratum.

What has been said thus far captures the form of reductive functionalism most commonly modeled in computational environments. However, some computationalists (see Horgan & Tienson, 1996) more recently have suggested that it might be possible to accommodate attributions of intentional content and reason giving to psychological states without assuming that the structure of propositions or sentences is mapped at an underlying physical level. Such connectionist proposals are sufficiently complex to defy ready description. For current purposes it is sufficient to note that while other computationalists claim that particular syntactic structures always accompany particular thoughts or mental states, connectionists deny that thoughts or mental events have this kind of syntax. Their counterclaim is that it is the states of a computational network as a whole that can be interpreted as representing our intentional thoughts or propositional attitudes.

Debates between connectionists and other computationalists turn on whether an intermediate level of syntactic description is necessary if intentional and rationalizing relations are to be generated from physical causal or supervenient relations. Nonetheless, all computational models of mind, connectionist or not, require that intentional and reason-giving kinds can be reduced to states and patterns of interaction without an intentional vocabulary and without the kind of normativity and perspective that seem to attend the psychological life of humans in their everyday thoughts and actions. It is to these matters that we now turn.

What Is Missing in Reductive Functionalism and Computationalism?

As already stated, the program of reductive functionalism, whether instantiated in computational environments or not, would have us believe that the intentional and reason-giving relations that typify everyday human experience can be captured adequately in ways that ignore or move abstractly away from the semantic content of our intentional and reason-giving states. Reductive functionalists want to employ only formal and structural features and ultimately reduce through identity or supervenience relations all intentional and reason-giving kinds to an underlying structural level that may be sustained at a purely physical, material level. Can this be done? Donald Davidson (1985), John McDowell (1994), John Searle (1992), and others say that it cannot. Their reasons for rejecting the program of reductive functionalism (and the various other reductive programs summarized previously) revolve around their claim that intentional and reason-giving relations cannot be captured adequately in nonintentional, formal or structural systems. To understand this objection, let us extend a previous example.

Our author wants to arrange the office in which she writes so as to affect her writing in a positive way. She believes, correctly or not, that the physical space in which she works can have what she refers to as a "facilitating effect" of this kind. She also believes that this same space might affect her writing adversely. Moreover, perhaps like the batting rituals of baseball players, what she views as facilitative or adverse changes over time and projects. Sometimes, she reasons that the presence of a previously successful book that she wrote will serve to inspire her. At other times, she finds the presence of this book intimidating and replaces it with a book she wrote that was decidedly unsuccessful, so as to feel that she certainly can do better than this.

The point of this example is to attempt to convey the impossibility of reducing an agent's intentional thoughts (in this case, about writing, books, and reasoning about them) to levels composed solely of nonintentional, reason-absent formalizations that might bear identity relations to purely physical properties. This is not just because, as McDowell (1994) points out, there exists no mechanical test for logical validity in general, because the plausibility of any statement or theory rests on its relation to a complex network of other beliefs, the boundaries of which are not fixed. Indeed, it would be extremely difficult to position the kind of intentions and reasons in this example within any known system of deductive or inductive reasoning. If anything, the reasoning involved is highly informal and predominantly practical. But more important, it is reasoning that reflects an agent's own first-person perspective, a perspective gained by her unique history of experiential participation in the life-world into which she was born and has developed as an agent and a writer. It also reflects the normativity of the sociocultural contexts that she inhabits and has inhabited. All of this acts as an inescapable background to her intentions, reasons, and actions in this example.

Moreover, what allows any of us to understand scenarios such as this is our ability to interpret the intentions, reasons, and actions of human agents—ourselves and others. Such understanding cannot be gained formalistically by reading from a formal syntactical script. It is not a matter of information processing but of reflective, situated interpretation. It simply is not possible to predict today, at least with any consistent accuracy, how our author might reconfigure her writing space tomorrow. For what she does tomorrow, while not undetermined, inevitably will reflect both her history of life-experience within a particular sociocultural background and her own reflective, deliberative self-determination enacted at the moment of her writing in that particular context at that particular time.

Normativity is present in this example in that the author reasons and behaves in part because of societal norms relating to acceptable work, effort, and duty to self, family, and others. But normativity, while itself difficult to capture in reductive, computational systems, is insufficient to capture all that is occurring here. Pointing out that actions conform to norms does not capture our author's recognition and sense that what she is doing at any given moment of rearranging her work space is the thing to do. The kind of reasoning involved here is tied up with the perspectivity of an agent. Her actions are intelligible precisely because she has the perspective of an agent deciding how to act to accomplish a purpose that relates to a life project of being and becoming a successful writer. Anyone who would understand such actions must appreciate them from the position of a situated, deliberative agent.

The normative and perspectival character of human mentality reflects the reality of the human condition. We humans are creatures buffeted like inanimate objects by the world around us and responsive to the demands of our biological bodies, but we also are creatures to whom the world shows itself. Through the course of our experiential development as creatures in the world, we come to take up the facticity of our existence and condition by engaging in the world as it appears to us as situated, reflective agents. Any adequate psychological understanding of human agency will not come about through the pursuit of reductive programs that fail to comprehend human agency as situated in the world and engaged in this way. To understand human agency requires interpretation, not reductive formulation. In our everyday lives, we perceive and understand immediately by virtue of our embedded, situated existence in the sociocultural world we inhabit in ways that are enabled by physical and biological levels of reality, but which are not reducible to these required levels. Only when thwarted do we reflect on our context and condition by engaging a more reflective interpretation that helps us to uncover patterns of intentionality, rationality, normativity, and perspectivity in our agentic makeup and activity. The interpretive explanations that result are not of any classically causal kind, and therefore they escape the reductionists' demand that they ultimately revert to solely physical structures.

SUMMARY AND LINKS

In the previous chapter, after considering the traditional positions for and against freedom of choice and action advanced by libertarians, hard determinists, and compatibilists, we concluded that a viable compatibilist position with respect to self-determination—one that would go beyond dissolutionism or voluntarism to include a modest degree of origination—required two things: First, an argument needed to be made for self-determination that did not beg the question of agency, in the sense of assuming it as a premise in arguments purported to establish it as a conclusion. Second, a viable theory of agency needed to be developed that would explain how human self-determination is possible, without resorting to notions of radical freedom with mysterious origins. We began this chapter by focusing on the first of these projects and proceeded to offer an argument for the underdetermination of agency by biological–physical and/or sociocultural factors and conditions alone. The form of this argument was eliminative. We argued against what we understand to be all of the possible explanations for agency, other than assuming that humans have a unique capacity for self-determination. We concluded that because human actions are meaningful they require sociocultural rules and practices that preclude any reduction of agency to physical–biological factors or conditions alone. However, because sociocultural rules and practices are open-ended, in that human actors embedded within them nonetheless are able to "go beyond" them in nonstandard situations in which their normative routines are stymied, agency also cannot be reduced to sociocultural factors or conditions alone. After dealing with several other, less central possibilities, we went on to claim that transformations in social meaning actually require human agency—understood as the reflective or deliberative activity of a human being in selecting, framing, choosing, and executing his or her own actions in a manner that is not fully determined by factors and conditions other than his or her own authentic understanding and reasoning. Moreover, such agency also is implicated by the phenomenal experience of humans who perceive themselves, at least sometimes, as acting with deliberation from their own first-person perspectives.

In the latter part of this chapter, we turned to contemporary programs in the philosophy of psychology and mind that attempt to reduce human psychological kinds to nonagentic physical kinds. The most popular variant of such proposals—reductive functionalism, a perspective often modeled in computational environments—employs a two-tier form of reduction that involves both claims of identity and supervenience and is compatible with some forms of scientific realism (currently the most accepted position in the philosophy of science). We concluded our review of such programs by emphasizing that for reductive functionalism to work there must be nonagentic functional kinds that are coextensive with our everyday psychological kinds. In addition, these functional kinds must explain what our everyday psychological kinds explain, as well as capture what is unique and distinctive about our psychological kinds. However, after a further consideration of computational models that supposedly indicate the promise of such accomplishments, we concluded that no such reductive program possibly can capture adequately certain central features of our everyday agentic activity in the world. In particular, the intentionality, rationality, normativity, and perspectivity of our everyday thoughts and actions cannot be instantiated in nonintentional systems that are disembodied and disengaged from the kind of historical, sociocultural, and developmental context that provides the necessary background for human mentality and agency.

Having thus argued for an irreducible self-determining agency, we attempt to remove, in the next chapter, what we earlier described as the second major obstacle to an adequate defense of agency in the compatibilist sense of self-determination: the absence of a theory adequate to the task of explaining how such a situated, deliberative agency as we wish to defend can emerge developmentally without resorting to mysterious assumptions concerning the existence of some kind of a priori, radical freedom. As might be expected given the succession of hints dropped in this and the previous chapters, our forthcoming account of situated, emergent, and reflective agency will borrow heavily from some of those theories of agency already outlined: the social constitutionist position of Greenwood (1991), the sociocultural, developmental work of Vygotsky (1986), the social constructionism of Harré (1998; Harré & Gillett, 1994), and especially from the hermeneutic perspectives of Dilthey (1894/1977), Gadamer (1960/1995), Heidegger (1927/1962), Merleau-Ponty (1962), and Taylor (1985, 1995). However, the particular way in which we subsequently develop our theory of situated, emergent, and deliberative agency owes much to related, recent work of our own (Martin & Sugarman, 1999) and others such as Richardson et al. (1999). Having acknowledged these influences, there, nonetheless, are several novel features in the theorizing to follow in chapter 5, which will become clear as our narrative concerning the developmental emergence of human agency unfolds.

CHAPTER FIVE

A THEORY OF SITUATED, EMERGENT, AND DELIBERATIVE AGENCY

THE UNDERDETERMINATION and the irreducibility of human agency mean that any adequate account of psychological kinds must make contact with an adequate theory of human agency. Psychological kinds are agentic kinds. They interact with those classifications, practices, and categories employed to describe and inquire into them (Hacking, 1995, 1999) precisely because they have agentic capability. By psychological kinds, we mean human subjectivity, understanding, actions, and experiences, the agentic reality of which we regard as not reducible to sociocultural, biological, or physical levels of reality. We do regard these other levels of reality as requirements for, and constraints on, psychological kinds. However, it is a mistake to identify psychological, agentic kinds with sociocultural, biological, or physical kinds. The natural scientific methods and explanations entirely appropriate to biological and physical kinds (i.e., natural, indifferent kinds) are incomplete and depending on the precise question or concern sometimes inappropriate when applied to the study of psychological kinds (human, interactive kinds). While psychological kinds require and are constrained by physical and biological levels of reality, they not only require and are constrained by, but actually are constituted at, the sociocultural level of reality. Both the existence of psychological kinds and inquiry into them are dependent on human activity (at collective and individual levels). Only the latter is true of biological and physical phenomena. Moreover, at least some of human activity issues from situated, deliberative human agents capable of exercising some degree of self-determination with respect to their choices and actions.

In this chapter, the various claims that constitute our theory of situated, emergent, and deliberative agency are presented and elaborated. Taken together, these claims explain the emergence, development, interactivity, and status of agency and psychological kinds, as distinct from natural kinds. Our hope and conviction is that with an adequate theory of agency and psychological kinds it will be clear how the subject matter of psychology differs from that of physics, and why the methods and explanations of natural science alone cannot possibly inform psychological studies. Despite disciplinary psychology's long-standing and continuing commitment to psychology as natural science, such a commitment is a basic error that has impeded, and continues to impede, an adequate understanding of psychological kinds.

Our theory of agency is inspired by much of the work we reviewed and summarized previously, especially in chapter 3, but we are not concerned with making our account entirely compatible with any of those other accounts. We want to acknowledge our debt to those symbolic interactionist, social constructionist, sociocultural, developmental, and especially to those hermeneutic lines of work that have influenced our account. Nonetheless, we consider our work in this chapter to have unique features that may or may not be interpreted by readers to fall within the purview of any of these other approaches. Nonetheless, it is clear that much of what we have to say here is at least "hermeneutically inspired."

In the first section of what follows, we explicate a position that we believe helps to establish the reality of sociocultural and psychological phenomena and the relation of these levels of reality to biological and physical levels of reality. With this tiered conception of reality in place, we move on to discuss various existential conditions underlying our theory of agency and briefly elaborate a conception of personhood that includes the kind of agency about which we theorize. We then articulate our developmental theory proper. This leads to a consideration of human care and understanding as these extend possibilities for human being and agency within traditions of living. Finally, we consider the implications of our theory of the developmental emergence of situated, deliberative agency for the understanding of psychological kinds through psychological inquiry.

LEVELS OF REALITY

BEING-IN-THE-WORLD

Heidegger's (1927/1962, 1982) hermeneutic realism avoids the subjective–objective and mind-dependent–mind-independent turmoil that occurs all too easily when traditional doctrines of realism are applied to human activities in the world. It does this by discarding the ontological assumptions that are built into traditional philosophy from Descartes onward. Heidegger undercuts the idea that we are minds or subjects who somehow happen to be in contact with an external world of material objects. For him, being-in-the-world is a unitary phenomenon in which self and world are inter-twined in such a way that there is no possible way of separating them. Heidegger starts afresh with a description of our everyday agency. Our identity as agents is bound up with concrete situations within a world of practices that enable us to find things. Our practices of living largely pre-determine how things show up in our lives. We require the world around us in order to be agents (Guignon, 1991). It is impossible for us to remove ourselves from the world, without ceasing to be human.

For Heidegger, our basic being-in-the-world constitutes the basis for all our theorizing; yet this all-pervasive background of our everyday activity never can be fixed explicitly. There is no external vantage point to be gained from which we can comprehend our worldliness, and human activity keeps the world in constant change. Thus, Heidegger attempts to establish the possibility of an inescapable, dynamic world relation in which humans are lodged at biological birth (a condition he refers to as "thrownness") and in which they develop as agents who are concerned about their own existence and are prone to theorize about it. Heidegger's hermeneutic realism consists of recognizing this state of affairs as given and ceasing attempts to sever the reality of our world relation. On this view, traditional metaphysical and epistemological questions concerning reality, truth, and relativity should be set aside and addressed only after we have worked out a general account of our primordial reality—our situation as being-in-the-world.

Heidegger's project of clarifying our being as agents must proceed at the level of attempting to understand particular problems in context. It should not be engaged at the level of attempting to establish knockdown, once and for all, arguments based on global assumptions that lead to unanswerable questions concerning the existence of the world and how we can know it. For Heidegger, the reality of our world relation is given, and we should get on with understanding our being in this relation, in ways that do not obscure it.

For our purposes, it is useful to focus directly on the implications of Heidegger's hermeneutic realism for human psychology. Taylor (1985, 1995) points out that Heidegger helps us understand that numerous things that are not tangible or that exist only relative to human conception are nevertheless in the world in a straightforward sense. Taylor asks us to step back from our scientific entanglements to see that in everyday life our values and meanings are experienced as "out there" in the world, rather than as "in our minds."

> What normal person could see a child hit by a car and not feel that something bad had happened right there in the street, not just in somebody's mind? It is only a highly specialized and profoundly questionable characterization of "reality" that could lead people to doubt the reality of badness, shamefulness or

goodness in the world. . . . Taylor wants to liberate us from the objectified view of reality and subjectified view of values that we get from modern science. . . . He has tried to show that we would not be able to think and live as we do unless we granted that meanings, imports, significances and values have a real existence "out there." (Richardson et al., 1999, p. 215)

What Taylor (1985, 1995) wants us to realize is that our psychological experiences in the world cannot be regarded as purely subjective in the sense that they exist only or entirely within our minds. Situational imports provide the grounds or bases for our feelings and experiences in a way that is quite independent of whether anyone actually has these feelings or experiences in a particular case. For example, a heroic action is characterized by someone being altruistically brave, whether the person who performed the action has the appropriate feeling–conception. We can say things like "You ought to be extremely proud of yourself" with appropriate feeling, irrespective of the attitude of the person involved. Taylor's point is that the import of the situation is not reducible to the feelings and responses of particular individuals. It is in this sense that human experiences and actions are out there in the situational context itself. Following Heidegger, it may be concluded that psychological actions and experiences are irreducibly in the world.

With respect to the conduct of psychological inquiry, Taylor (1985, 1995) makes a further point that, for our purposes, is useful. He claims that because of the irreducibly interpretive and meaning-laden character of many human phenomena only someone who is embedded within the relevant practices of an experiential world will be able to make sense of what self-interpreting beings in such a life-world feel and do. Thus, in Taylor's view, psychological interpretation is possible because psychologists themselves are self-interpreting beings who are co-participants in a shared linguistic and historical world. In other words, psychologists are "insiders" with a prior grasp of the meanings and evaluations they set out to interpret.

TIERED REALITY

Of the four levels of reality considered in our approach, physical reality may be considered the most basic. Although there is no doubt that the actions of human beings can affect the physical world (e.g., pollution and overpopulation), the physical world came into existence first, presumably, with a "Big Bang" and in general (with the obvious exceptions of dramatic events such as earthquakes, volcanoes, and tidal waves) exhibits the slowest rate of change. At some historical point, biological reality took hold within the physical world. Since this genesis various forms of biological life have evolved in more and more complex and varied ways in interaction with the physical world and eventually with the collective activity and accomplishments of living species themselves. Biological reality is contingent on physical reality, most notably through processes of natural selection, and generally possesses the next slowest rate of evolution. Both physical and biological reality exist outside of human collective or individual perception and constrain (in the sense of limiting possibilities with respect to the development of) sociocultural and psychological realities.

With the historical appearance of human beings and their ancestors, collective practices, creations, and institutions have developed to the point at which they are capable of supporting the developmental emergence of psychological individuals. Sociocultural reality consists of the systems of beliefs and practices shared by members of human collectivities. Sociocultural reality depends on human activity in the world, and consequently varies with such activity, but always within real physical and biological constraints. By way of illustration, the vulnerability of the human biological infant to conditions of the physical world is such that any human society must include some beliefs and practices concerning protective child care. Such a requirement, contingent on physical and biological reality, may manifest in a variety of ways across different societies located in different parts of the physical world, with relatively similar or dissimilar consequences. For example, societies that develop more elaborate, yet feasible, conventions and expectations with respect to cooperative, communal activity in response to the requirement of child care may develop more effective, productive, and differentiated systems of communal responsibility in other areas of sociocultural life as well.

The psychological reality of individual humans (e.g., memories, intentions, imaginings, experiences, and so forth) emerges as a consequence of the immersion and participation of biological human individuals in the societies and cultures into which they are born and within which they grow and develop. In this sense, the psychological reality of individuals is not only constrained but also is actually constituted in large part by socioculturally shared beliefs and practices. For example, when a parent reads to a child a story about friendship, the parent makes available to the child a set of sociocultural practices concerning what it is to be a person with commitments and obligations to others.

Because sociocultural reality is pluralistic, both across and within different societies, individual psychological reality may vary considerably from society to society, from individual to individual, and from time to time. In partial consequence, the rate of change and variation evident in human experiences, intentions, and actions is generally much greater at the psychological level than the other levels of reality in which psychological reality is nested. Unlike physical and biological levels of reality, sociocultural and psychological levels of reality do not exist independently of human perception and activity. However, this does not mean that they are not real in the influences that they can exert on human collectives and individuals. Human understanding, belief, deliberation, purpose, and action have very real consequences. Consider, for example, the lies of a cheating lover or the ardent beliefs and ideological commitments of the political activist.

The most basic historical line of influence in our model is from physical to biological to sociocultural and finally to psychological reality. The physical universe evolves, species emerge and evolve, cultures develop and change, and individuals emerge as psychological persons within historical, sociocultural contexts. Nonetheless, while most basic, this pattern and direction of influence is only one in a much more interactive and reciprocal pattern of dynamic possibilities across these various levels of reality. In particular, the actions of individual psychological humans may have important consequences not only for human sociocultural reality (e.g., inventions and discoveries) but also for the physical and biological levels of reality as well (e.g., the possible acceleration of global warming as a consequence of our prodigious consumption of fossil fuels).

Part of this dynamic interaction is reflected in the social constructionist argument that the psychological reality of individual humans arises from a lifelong appropriation and internalization of the sociocultural, relational practices of the societies into which biological humans are born and within which they develop. In this respect, the conversational practices of a given society are thought to be especially influential (e.g., Shotter, 1993). However, although strong social constructionism emphasizes the way in which the psychological is constituted and constrained by relevant sociocultural reality, it says relatively little concerning the possibility of psychologically inspired, sociocultural change. And yet, as we already have argued in chapter 4, if the psychological agency of individual humans could be reduced entirely to a hard social determinism, there would be little possibility of explaining why societies themselves change and evolve over time, as they very obviously do.

To understand sociocultural evolution, it seems necessary to consider the effects of psychological agents on their societies. And if such effects can push societies beyond prevailing sociocultural practices, means, and shared understandings, it must be the case that psychological reality, reflected in individual psychological agency, is not entirely determined by those same sociocultural conventions. Thus, while the psychological reality of individuals largely derives from sociocultural reality, it is not entirely reducible to these sociocultural origins.

Psychological individuals, through their imaginings, intentions, and actions, are capable of influencing the societies that have spawned them in ways which explain the evolution and change clearly evident in sociocultural history. Societies only exist as aggregates of biological and psychological individuals and evolve only through their feats of imagination and ingenuity. What is social and what is psychological both arise within this dynamic process of ongoing mutable interaction. The psychology of any given individual is emergent within the life span of that individual, while the accumulation of the agentic actions of psychological individuals, and the sociocultural consequences of same, means that societies and cultures are also in constant evolution. And all of this sociocultural–psychological interaction occurs within biological and physical levels of reality that both constrain it and provide the basic physical and biological conditions that make it all possible.

Once again, the basic pattern of nesting of these various levels of reality has the psychological nested within the sociocultural, which in turn is nested within the biological, which in turn is nested within the physical. However, the pattern of real influences that these various levels exert on each other is highly interactive, involving both adjacent and nonadjacent levels in this nested hierarchy. Thus, frequent and powerful interactions are found between the psychological and sociocultural, between the sociocultural and the biological, and between the biological and the physical, respectively. However, there also exists the possibility of dramatic and direct influences between levels that are separated by other levels, as, for example, undoubtedly occurs when human activity at psychological and sociocultural levels affects the physical environment.

It is important to note explicitly the nature of the reality claims that are implicit in the foregoing account of the "levels-of-reality" position. In particular, given current debates in psychology, it is useful to attend to (a) the nonstatic nature of all levels; (b) the nonessential, contingent nature of the sociocultural and psychological levels; and (c) the irreducibility of any level to any other level.

The fact that all four levels of reality are in a constant state of dynamic evolution, owing in large part to their interactions, is a clear indication of the potential inadequacy of any philosophical or psychological system of thought that would assume fixed, foundational, essential, or noncontingent categories of things. This conclusion is especially apparent with respect to sociocultural and psychological levels of reality, which are highly nonessential and contingent in light of the collective and individual actions of human agents. And yet, even at these levels of reality, things are not so ephemeral as to escape entirely human attempts to inquire into them in ways that might yield useful, even if inevitably temporary, and contextualized understandings. After all, the interrelational, communicative practices and conventions of societies and their members make available coordinating systems of meaning and understanding that cannot be changed overnight—or sometimes, as many would-be reformers have discovered, even over years and lifetimes. For example, rules and meanings of communicative exchanges among individuals in a particular society may admit to several viable interpretations, but not to any interpretation whatsoever. Further, systematic inquiry into relevant social practices often can serve to limit further those viable interpretations to ones that are more, rather than less, likely. Although inevitably dynamic, nonessential, and contingent, sociocultural and psychological reality admit to being studied in ways that might yield worthwhile, if not timeless, knowledge of them.

The irreducibility of any level of reality to any of the others also is an important factor in consideration of human inquiry. Even though the patterns of nesting and interaction we have described both enable and constrain the evolution of the various levels of reality, each level invariably contains generative features that perpetuate and extend itself (e.g., tectonic plates, viral mutations, labor surpluses, and purposeful ruminations). Reductions are instructive only if what previously have been thought to be two things operating at different levels can be shown to be the same thing at the more basic level. The generativity evident within each of the levels of reality makes such reductions impossible. The most powerful, comprehensive explanation of phenomena at any level of reality requires consideration of influences across and within the various levels in our model.

AN EXISTENTIAL STARTING POINT AND
A BRIEF CONCEPTION OF PERSONHOOD

Having clarified our tiered ontological realism, we turn now to an articulation of our developmental theory of historically and socioculturally situated, emergent, and deliberative agency. We begin by considering the conditions of human existence that make possible the development of psychological kinds. What we regard as ineluctable is that human biological individuals are born into societies and cultures, the existence of which precedes such individuals. As already discussed, we assume three levels of reality that to us seem incontestably necessary for human psychological being and understanding: the reality of human collective sociocultural institutions and practices existing within a real physical world into which real biological infants are born. Of course, human being within, or understanding of, this layered reality is not pre-given. All human experience, action, and modes of being and understanding emerge contingently within the existential condition of human biological individuals born into and acting within preexisting sociocultural and physical reality. There is no essential, a priori nature of human psychological, agentic kinds.

We want to stress that all psychological kinds emerge and develop contingently within real sociocultural, physical, and biological contexts to make it clear that psychological kinds, while real, differ from natural physical and biological kinds from the very beginning of their unfolding within individual life lines. As we will endeavor to show, because the reality of psychological kinds differs from that of natural kinds, the understanding of psychological kinds requires a different approach than that employed in natural science. Furthermore, psychological kinds also differ from the sociocultural contexts and practices within and through which they are constituted. Although initially constituted by sociocultural practices (especially discursive, relational practices) and continuously formed in interaction with sociocultural practices and contexts, psychological kinds ultimately are not reducible to their sociocultural origins.

It is our position that psychological being, understanding, experience, and action, in the absence of pre-given essences, are free to develop according to particular historically constituted sociocultural practices that are constrained by the physical and biological world. What this means is that many different, socioculturally spawned psychological kinds are possible so long as their interaction with sociocultural practices continues to ensure that human biological infants will receive the care they require for survival. It is the requirement of some form of caregiving that is mandated by the existential condition of the birth of human biological infants into the preexisting physical and sociocultural world. Without the historical sociocultural emergence of some form of communal, cooperative caregiving that protects vulnerable human biological infants from hostile physical elements and ensures their biological nurturance, neither societies nor the psychological agents they foster could persist.

But how is it possible that psychological kinds can come to transcend their sociocultural constitution and physical and biological requirements in the manner we have suggested at various points in our account thus far? To substantiate our position in this regard, we must turn to a more detailed consideration of the developmental context and process within which psychological kinds emerge. But first, it will be helpful to clarify explicitly various aspects of the conception of personhood that has been assumed in what we have said so far.

For us, a person (or psychological person) is an identifiable, embodied individual human with being, self-understanding (self), agentic capability, and personal identity. The adjective *identifiable* references the physical characteristics and social identity of a person. Social identity refers to those socially constructed and socially meaningful categories that are appropriated and internalized by individuals as descriptive of themselves and/or various groups to which they belong (e.g., female, African American, soccer player, attorney, mother, community leader, and so forth). The adjective *embodied* captures the sense of a physical, biological body in constant contact with the physical and sociocultural life-world. *Being* refers to the existence in such a life-world of a single human being (an individual). Importantly, the manner of such being is historically and socioculturally effected within traditions of living. Self, for us, is understanding that discloses and extends a person's being and activity in the world. Thus, our conception of the self is one of relational understanding, not of physical or transcendental substance. Such a conceptual self is dependent on, but very different from the developmentally more primitive, prelinguistic sense of self that equates with one's recognition of one's physical body as distinct from other objects and people. Personal identity, for us, refers to the particular concerns, cares, and commitments to which self-reflective agents direct their actions and efforts.

Finally, as already made clear in the previous chapter, *agency,* in our conception of personhood, refers to the deliberative, reflective activity of a human being in selecting, framing, choosing, and executing his or her actions in a way that is not fully determined by factors and conditions other than his or her own understanding and reasoning. More generally, however, we consider agency to relate intimately to the activity of a person in the world and claim that the philosopher's (and our own) reflective, deliberative agency emerges from prereflective activity as part of the developmental unfolding of an individual life within a collective life-world. It is to the developmental emergence of reflective, deliberative agency and self-understanding that we now turn.

THE DEVELOPMENTAL EMERGENCE OF SITUATED, DELIBERATIVE AGENCY AND PSYCHOLOGICAL KINDS

At the beginning of individual human life, the biological infant is equipped with nothing more than primitive, biologically given capabilities of limited orientation, motion, and sensation and the prereflective ability to remember, in a very limited physical sense, something of what is encountered and sensed. However, over time, given the physical–biological maturation and activity of the human infant within a sociocultural context of relational, linguistic practices, care and understanding gradually emerge as increasingly reflective, psychological characteristics of the developing psychological individual. In this sense, we claim that the ontological status of human individuals shifts gradually within the developmental context from nonpsychological, prereflective to psychological, reflective. Indeed, this ontological shift is precisely what is entailed in becoming a socioculturally constituted psychological person.

In reaction against both the pre-given, isolated individual of modernity and the collectively determined, socially constructed product of some postmodern theorizing, we understand the person as emerging from the practical activity of a biological human infant embedded in the physical, historical, and sociocultural world into which she is born, and within which she develops. Although holding that the person is mostly constituted by sociocultural practices, such practices require the participation of a functioning and maturing biological individual and a physical, as well as sociocultural world. Linguistic and other social practices are indispensable to the formation of persons, but so too is the activity of a biological human organism in both physical and sociocultural context.

Thus, for us the person is an embodied, biological human individual who through interacting in the physical and sociocultural world comes to possess an understanding of her particular being in the world (a conceptual self or self-understanding) that enables her to act as a self-reflective agent with a unique set of commitments and concerns (a personal identity). On this view, the self, agency, and personal identity of a person require the in-the-world activity of a biological human equipped with rudimentary capacities to sense and orient to, and remember (in a primitive, prelinguistic sense) some of what is encountered in the physical, sociocultural world. The sociocultural placement of such a biological infant gives her an initial social identity, and her early, biologically given, orienting movements assist her to acquire a preconceptual sense of self. From these humble beginnings, the conceptual self, reflective agency, and personal identity that define personhood emerge from ongoing participation in the world of human sociocultural practices—practices that are not only linguistic. For example, as Merleau-Ponty (1962) has pointed out, an initial sense of self can emerge from tactile engagement with the world in which prelinguistic, experiential distinctions are sensed between touching inanimate objects, others, and one's own body, and being touched by objects and others. Such preconceptual attainments are the result of practical activity in the world that is not yet linguistically saturated.

Nonetheless, with enhanced mobility and sensibility, the sociocultural world of linguistic and other relational practices comes increasingly to dominate the life-world of the developing infant. Indeed, it quickly becomes that life-world, nested within the ever-present biological and physical world. Caregivers and others interact with the infant, and in the presence of the infant, in ways that furnish the developing infant with the various practices, forms, and means of personhood and identity extant within the particular society and culture in which the infant exists. Psychological development understood as the development of psychological kinds now proceeds as the internalization and appropriation of sociocultural practices as psychological tools—that is, vehicles for language and thought, much in the manner envisioned by Vygotsky (1978, 1986; also see Harré's, [1998] neo-Vygotskian account). In this way, developing psychological individuals come to talk and relate to themselves in much the same way as others have talked and related to them. In so doing, they become engaged in both the ongoing, always present sociocultural practices in which they are embedded and those appropriated, internalized linguistic and relational practices they now employ as means for thinking and understanding (cf. Brandstädter & Lerner [1999], for an extensive review of relevant studies in contemporary developmental psychology).

Important vehicles for the appropriation and internalization of sociocultural practices as psychological understandings and tools are those processes of reinforcement and social, observational learning well-known to most psychologists. However, as Richard Degrandpre (2000) has argued, a full appreciation of the role of such processes in the sociocultural constitution of psychological individuals requires a rather dramatic and nonreductive reconfiguration of this entire area of psychological research. (Much more will be said about the required reconceptualization in chapter 6.) With the appropriation and internalization of sociocultural practices and the thinking and understanding thus enabled, the individual's mode of being is transformed from one of prereflective activity to one in which reflective (or deliberative) intentional agency is possible.

The psychological person is a biological individual who becomes capable of understanding some of what the life-world (in its history, culture, and social relations and practices) and her being in it consists. Such understanding always involves an interpretation of available sociocultural meanings and practices, but as development unfolds, the never-ending process of interpretation and reinterpretation becomes increasingly available to conscious reflection and deliberation, should such reflection and associated deliberation be required. Open to the life-world, the psychological person gradually becomes capable of increasingly sophisticated feats of recollection and imagination. Concomitant with these capabilities of projecting backward and forward in time is the gradual understanding of one's embodied being in the world as a center of experiencing, understanding, intending, and acting. In this way, "self" understanding emerges, and continues to develop, within the historical, sociocultural contexts into which humans are born as biological individuals but come to exist as psychological persons.

Such psychological persons are capable of reflective, intentional thought and action directed outward and inward. The self now has emerged as a particular kind of interpreted, reflexive understanding of an embodied "in-the-world" human being—an understanding that discloses and extends particular, individual existence. When this occurs, thought and action are no longer entirely determined by the sociocultural practices from which they initially were constituted and within which they continue to unfold. Given the inevitably unique history of individual experience within a life-world, and the capacity for self as reflexive, interpretive understanding of experience in that world, psychological persons are underdetermined by their constitutive, sociocultural and biological origins. This does not mean that psychological persons are undetermined, only that together with biological, cultural, and situational determinants, the "self" understanding and deliberations of such persons may, and frequently do, enter into their determination. Even as psychological persons continue to be formed by the relational and discursive practices in which they are embedded, they also come to contribute to those practices in innovative ways that reflect a self-interpreting agency. As Rychlak (1988, 1997) might say, as agents, we are capable of framing "transpredications" (alternative possibilities) that draw on but purposefully transform what we have experienced and learned as participants in sociocultural and linguistic practices and forms of understanding.

For us, agency as self-determination equates with a kind of self-understanding that permits a deliberative, reflective activity in selecting and choosing, framing, and executing actions. Even though there is some limited origination (as opposed to voluntariness alone—see chapters 1 and 3) in this, it is important not to overstate it. Psychological persons never can stand outside of the determining influence of relevant physical, biological, and sociocultural (especially relational and linguistic) factors and conditions. Human possibilities always are limited by the limits of human reflective agency. The explicit understanding enabled by such agency always is partial and incomplete when considered against the always-present background of historical, sociocultural practice from which it is constituted and continues to unfold. Most of what we perceive, think, and do in everyday life escapes our conscious reflection. Our immersion in those linguistic, relational, and discursive practices of which we as psychological beings are part is so complete that we typically take for granted the assumptions and conceptions buried in this background to all of our explicit understanding. Most of what we understand is tacit and unexamined. It is only when our everyday routines are interrupted or disrupted in some way that requires our conscious attention that we may notice certain things about our taken-for-granted world of practices and means, things that previously escaped our reflective consciousness. When this occurs, an opening or possibility is created for extending our explicit, conscious understanding of things already present, but of which we are unaware. In this sense, much of our conscious understanding as psychological beings involves not only attempts to go beyond our sociocultural contexts but also (even mostly) to penetrate the assumptions, conventions, and intelligences implicit and hidden in those contexts and practices of which we are a part. Thus, much of our agency is a matter of selectively picking up sociocultural practices that already are available to us by virtue of our sociocultural embeddedness and adapting and using such possibilities as psychological tools and resources for deliberation, choice, and action. We thus "originate" in the sense of interpretively taking up (and possibly modifying and adapting) practices, ideas, and possibilities for acting that already are available, at least to some extent, in the sociocultural contexts in which we exist.

Once emergent as psychological persons within sociocultural contexts, human individuals no longer can be reduced to their sociocultural constituents, let alone to their physical and biological requirements. There is nothing mysterious about the shifting ontology and underdetermination of psychological agents and kinds. It is just the case that with the developmentally emergent capabilities of reflective thought and intentional action psychological persons can deliberate about, and act purposefully within, their sociocultural contexts and categories in ways that alter and change them. This is simply what is true of human kinds and is not true of natural kinds that are not subject to the developmental trajectory just described.

Of course, emergence, as a processual characteristic of systems is not limited to living, let alone human kinds. In general, something is emergent if it possesses properties possessed by none of its components (Bunge, 1977). For example, refraction is an emergent property of transparent bodies that is not possessed by any of the atomic (or molecular) components of such bodies. Nonetheless, the property of refrangibility may be said to be explained and determined by electrodynamics in terms of the electrical properties of atoms (or molecules) and light. Although human agentic capabilities such as reflective thought and intentional action are not determined in exactly this way, they are, nonetheless, developmentally emergent properties of human persons that are not possessed by any of the physical, biological, and/or sociocultural requirements or constituents of personhood. Nonetheless, such capabilities may be explained and determined by the kind of dynamic, developmental trajectory theorized herein. Moreover, these human agentic capacities, as situated and embodied in the ways we describe, seem undeniably unique to human persons. They are sui generis, irreducible human kinds. (It should be noted that the ascendance of epigenetic theories of human development during the twentieth century was due in no small part to the emergentist features of such theories. In contrast to earlier, performatist views of development in which the embryo was understood as a tiny adult or in which development performed in a genetically programmed sequence, constructive epigenesis posits emergent, qualitative, developmental change—cf. Gottlieb, 1992.)

Although many different conceptions of emergence have been formulated in physical and social sciences and the philosophy of science and mind, the particular conception we have adapted for our purposes has recently been clarified by Jack Martin (2002). We hold that agency and other psychological kinds are ontologically emergent properties of biological humans in dynamic, ongoing interaction with their sociocultural contexts and circumstances. As we consistently have argued, a person's psychological states and properties exhibit features quite unlike those of physical objects. Consequently, the emergence of psychological kinds within physical, biological, and sociocultural requirements and constituents inevitably requires assumptions and speculations that can be expected to differ from those assumptions that have been enshrined in various models and theories of emergence in the physical sciences.

A detailed development of such emergentist theorizing is admittedly unavailable at this writing. Nonetheless, we want to be explicit and clear about the general claim with respect to human agency that any such theorizing must satisfy. This claim is that reflective agency is a constitutive, emergent property of human persons who develop from embodied, biological individuals active within a physical world of constraints and a sociocultural world of practices and conventions. These practices furnish possibilities for psychological kinds such as self-understanding, personal identity, and deliberative agency.

As emergent psychological agents, with the capability of some limited transcendence of our immediate context, our continued development consists mostly of attempting to understand more and more of our context, even as this context itself shifts in interaction with our actions as psychological individuals. In this way, the psychological and the sociocultural exist in a dynamic dance of mutually constitutive interaction. Of course, sociocultural evolution and change typically occur over somewhat longer periods of time and reflect the historical and contemporary activity of many individuals and collectives, while psychological development and change are more time limited within an individual life line. Nonetheless, neither psychological agents nor societies could exist without the other. It is their dynamic interaction that constitutes the human world nested within the natural world of physical and biological reality.

Having briefly described the developmental context within which psychological kinds emerge and exist, it now is possible to clarify further our ontological claims concerning care and understanding. From their primitive biological beginnings as nonpsychological movements and sensations associated with feeding and bodily reactions, care and understanding emerge as psychological kinds exercised in association with the developing reflectivity and intentional agency of psychological beings. Human subjectivity, whatever its contingent historical, sociocultural character, exhibits care in the sense of concern for itself. Psychological persons are ontologically unique in that they care about their own existence. They are self-aware and concerned.

The primary way in which the care of psychological persons manifests is in understanding. Understanding opens possibilities for psychological persons to develop and extend themselves. Because both being and understanding, as psychological kinds, require a background of historical, sociocultural practices, care must be situated within both the individual and collective projects of humans within a tradition or way of life. For psychological persons (agents), understanding always includes a kind of valuing—a finding of significance and personal meaning in the life-world. The interpretation of meaning and significance in lived experience is thus a necessary, ongoing aspect for the understanding and care of psychological persons or agents. It is what takes human psychological development forward at both collective and individuals levels.

UNDERSTANDING AND CARE WITHIN TRADITIONS OF LIVING

To care for itself in a mostly physical and biological world, a nonhuman animal must get by as best it can with a nonreflective, relatively primitive consciousness and agency. However, to care for itself within a historical, sociocultural life-world of discursive and relational practices, the human psychological individual must understand. As already hinted, human understanding is both tacit and explicit. Tacit understanding is the kind of know-how that comes from acting with others in general accord with, but without explicit recognition and articulation of, the conventions, norms, and shared assumptions of the sociocultural context. Explicit understanding is achieved through a more purposefully engaged interpretation of the life-world in relation to particular concerns of a psychological person, concerns that reflect the care of such a being for itself. Tacit understanding may become explicit, particularly when the concerns of a psychological person are thwarted in some way that requires the person to penetrate the tacit, taken-for-granted understanding and the background of historical, sociocultural practices that provide meaning and potential intelligibility to human action and experience. Such penetration requires interpretation and not infrequently is assisted by consideration of the articulated, shared understandings of others within a particular tradition of living.

All understanding opens up possibilities for the enactment of psychological being within a life-world. However, given that tacit understanding typically is sufficient for the execution of everyday routines, it is the opening of possibilities through reflective agency and interpretive activity that enables a psychological person to develop beyond whatever set of tacit understandings currently constitutes that person's way of being in the life-world. Interpretive understanding, as already noted, begins with a concern related to a psychological person's care for herself or himself and involves some kind of inquiry into the world of lived experience. The concern may be relatively minor (e.g., locating an alternative route to work during heavy traffic) or major (e.g., attempting to discover what has gone wrong in an intimate relationship). Concerns may lead to other and further inquiries and to possible reorganizations of relatively small or large areas of understanding, experience, and activity.

As the opening of possibilities for living, understanding always is ongoing, mutable, and incomplete. It ebbs and flows as concerns arise in the course of living and acting. Explicit, interpretive understanding is possible only because of the set of tacit understandings and potential understandings available in the background of practices and assumptions that form a tradition of living. Interpretation involves an attempt at openness to one's own and others' understanding and the historical, sociocultural tradition or traditions within which any understanding takes place. It also involves attempts to apply what is understood within this necessarily dialogical activity to the concerns and questions that motivated the interpretive inquiry. All understanding has this general, highly contextualized form, whether it relates to our everyday attempts to understand ourselves, others, and events or whether it relates to more formalized, collective disciplinary practices such as psychology.

Moreover, all understanding, interpreted or not, is both enabled and constrained by physical, biological, and especially by sociocultural and psychological levels of reality. It is the fact that interpretation is nested in these various levels of reality that makes it possible, and that supplies bases upon which psychological persons can discern and judge the understanding it yields. An example will help to make more concrete the relations among the everyday interpretive inquiries of psychological beings and the various levels of reality in which they exist.

Let us take as illustrative material the hypothetical case of a thirty-five-year-old American woman who is experiencing unexpected ambivalence concerning her desire to continue in a childless marriage of fifteen years' duration. She is aware of several aspects of her married life that seem related to her ambivalence. She wants to have children "before it is too late" but knows that her husband has no such interest. As a dual-career professional couple, she and her husband enjoy a very comfortable lifestyle, and both have found considerable fulfillment in their careers. They feel in control of their lives and good about themselves, at least for the most part. Nonetheless, she has begun to tire of their routine together. Her career seems "stalled" at the moment, and she has begun to question her overall level of happiness. In particular, she does not feel as good about herself as she has been accustomed to feel. She has grown apart from her family and friends and worries that she is being taken for granted in her marriage. For the first time in years, she does not know what she wants to do in the future, and wonders about where her life will go.

We suspect that many North American readers will understand the gist of the concerns confronting the woman in this example, without really stopping to think much about how such understanding is possible. But we want to illustrate the importance of a particular historical, sociocultural background of practices and assumptions in achieving such a seemingly immediate sense of understanding. Some of the historical, cultural ideas and values at play in this example might include the Christian Protestant belief in a personal God who values faithful effort, a standard Western view of an autonomously cogitating self, a sociopolitical sense of individual rights, freedoms, and moral responsibilities, a notion of life as a process of self-actualization and self-achievement, a valuing of hard work and material possessions, and so forth. Moreover, the English language makes frequent, relatively decontextualized use of the personal pronoun "I," and adopts the central idea of a person as an agent. Advertisements on and in American media suggest that we should "be all that we can be," "have it our own way," "find our own place," and "just do it." American family life includes "Hallmark" Christmases and family summer vacations, while the American work place encourages initiative and advancement, and the American educational system wants people to feel good about themselves and their accomplishments. Everywhere in America people seem concerned with whether they are happy, are having fun, and are being successful. The American individual is positive and unique, "in control," stable and consistent, and highly articulated.

As a way of emphasizing the relevance of the American historical, sociocultural, political, and moral life-world to an understanding of concerns such as those experienced by the woman in our example, consider how much more difficult it might be for Japanese readers to achieve an immediate understanding of our example. In Japan, Shinto-Buddhism emphasizes compassion for others, Confucianism focuses on the maintenance of a traditional social order, and Taoism reflects a disciplined Way. The Japanese word for self is *jibun,* meaning to share, and the Japanese language has minimal room for the self as agent. Historically popular proverbs include "the nail that stands out gets hammered down" and "the mature rice bends to the ground." Both legal systems and family structures highlight the importance of duty, remorse, and consideration of others' feelings. Companies employ a family model in which seniority is respected. Teachers encourage persistent endurance and laud the joy of group life and self-effacement. Socially, compliments are refused ("It was nothing"), and others' expectations and preferences are of primary concern. The Japanese individual tries to improve, to fit in, to harmonize, and to be connected.

Obviously, both American and Japanese cultures, like all major cultures, are much more pluralistic than our extended example may suggest, and it is possible that many different kinds of psychological persons might develop within either culture, depending on the specific practices experienced by particular individuals. Moreover, cultures themselves always are "in motion" and probably never more so than in our contemporary world. Nonetheless, there should be no mistaking the rather different historical, sociocultural contexts and traditions of practice extant in our illustration and the ways in which they are likely implicated in the constitution of the understandings and concerns of psychological persons embedded in them. It is only against the horizon of possibilities for living and understanding represented within particular historical, sociocultural traditions that human psychological being and understanding are possible. To understand is in many ways to share, or to come to share, a tradition of living. Human being, understanding, experience, and action (as psychological kinds) always must be interpreted within the traditions of living that form them.

Unlike natural kinds, psychological kinds do not exist outside of such traditions. Although both natural and psychological kinds require human traditions for their understanding, natural kinds do not require such traditions for their very existence. Furthermore, although psychological kinds are in constant, dynamic formation in interaction within traditions of living, natural kinds (rocks, gravity, electromagnetic fields, and so forth) are indifferent to human historical, sociocultural traditions. This is not to say that natural kinds might not be affected by human activity, only that natural kinds do not react and interact with their historical, sociocultural construals, categories, and understandings in the manner of psychological kinds.

For example, the woman in our example, through her attempts to interpret and act on her concerns, may decide that she will not be governed by the middle-class career and relationship ethic extant in her experience of contemporary American culture and will eschew her career and marriage in favor of what she regards as a more family-oriented life in her small hometown. Clearly, her concerns, decisions, and actions continue to be shaped by practices and possibilities extant in her broad sociocultural context, but as a psychological person she is capable of interacting agentically with different combinations and fusions of possibilities available to her. A physical object or force does not interact in this way.

But what happens when human understanding is confronted with the task of judging alternatives and possibilities that arise from different traditions of living or from widely diverse assumptions and practices within a particularly diverse and pluralistic tradition (e.g., modern cosmopolitanism as discussed by authors such as Julia Kristeva [1991]). It is here that it is possible to appreciate more fully the way in which understanding as a reflection of care involves both epistemic and ethical aspects. The interpretation of understandings and practices both within pluralistic traditions (e.g., different life-experiences within a common culture) and across traditions (e.g., cultural divides) requires a respectful openness to the understandings and perspectives of others as sources of possibility. Care and the understanding that sustains it require others as subjects. In this sense, care extends beyond one's subjectivity to that of others, and the traditions of living that support such emergent subjectivity. To appreciate what is being suggested here, it is helpful to elaborate a kind of neo-Gadamerian approach to interpretive understanding (cf. Kögler, 1996).

Both the epistemics and ethics of interpretive understanding require a respectful openness to the general possibility that the perspective of the other person, tradition, or orientation within a tradition might contain some truth that when understood and applied within one's own life-world might enhance the significance that one finds in one's existence. Truth in this sense is not derived from some impossibly neutral, objective vantage point outside of relevant traditions and persons formed within them. Rather, what is true is a result of the application of understanding within a life-world governed by care. Human psychological persons or agents differ from the objects of natural science in that they find significance in their lives. The understanding of things and events matters deeply to psychological persons. It gives meaning to existence and advances the capability of such individuals to care for themselves and their ways of life. The ethics implicit in the kind of dialogical openness to possibility that defines authentic existence and care applies equally to the everyday interpretive understanding of a psychological subject and to the disciplinary inquiry practices of psychologists and other inquirers.

The ethical–epistemological stance of the interpretive, perspectival, and highly contextualized approach to understanding that we are advancing is warranted broadly by three considerations: First, whatever interpretive sense issues from a respectful dialogical engagement with others and other traditions and orientations must cohere sufficiently with participants' existing and evolving sense of things so that the resulting fusion of perspectives can be judged to enlighten the understanding of participants in the dialogue and to enhance their possibilities for acting in the world. Second, when applied within the life-world, such enhanced understanding actually must open up possibilities for living and understanding that advance individuals' abilities to find meaning and significance and to care for themselves, especially with respect to the concerns motivating the inquiry (or attempt at interpretive understanding). In this sense, whatever interpretations and possibilities arise dialogically must "speak to" and "act on" those concerns that fueled the dialogical inquiry in the first place, at least as such concerns themselves persist and are transformed in the course of the inquiry. Third, the possibilities that are opened up must fit within constraints of the real physical, biological, and sociocultural world within which human psychological agents are nested.

In all of this, it is important to remember that the kind of interpretive understanding that is being discussed always occurs within the horizons and fusions dictated by traditions of living within which both interpreters and viable interpretations are constituted and develop. Interpretive understanding is not a matter of detached subjectivity or solipsism. It is human psychological subjects who interpret and understand, but what is interpreted and understood, like human subjects themselves, always is inescapably embedded in traditions of living that are historical, sociocultural, and political and which have an existence outside of any single individual or group of individuals. Human psychology does have a subjective component, but such subjectivity is emergent within and formed by the embeddedness and emergence of human biological persons within historically preexisting societies and cultures nested within a real physical world. Human interpretive understanding is an ongoing dialogical ethical and epistemic excursion into the sociocultural, biological, and physical life-world. It is substantive in a way that goes well beyond, but nonetheless always includes, the subjectivity of dialogical participants.

Imagine that the American woman in our example, motivated by her concerns with respect to her current experience, embarks on an attempt to understand perspectives on marriage and career available in other cultural contexts—in particular, let us say (perhaps because of a close personal friend who comes from Japan), within a Japanese way of life. Given the considerable differences across American and Japanese sociocultural contexts noted previously, such an attempt, if engaged seriously, would require a sustained dialogical exchange and immersion in a Japanese life-world. Further, this attempt would require the maintenance of a continuous openness to the possibilities for life, relationship, and work located in the unfamiliar life-world and a vigilant guarding against the ever-present likelihood of prematurely assimilating what she is attempting to understand within her American tradition and understanding. In fact, in attempting to understand the Japanese life-world, she must penetrate many of the taken-for-granted, unarticulated assumptions and practices of her American life-world. Only in this way, could she possibly come to appreciate the extent and variety of differences she might encounter. (Of course, all of this assumes some sustained effort to learn something of the Japanese language and discursive context as well.) And, ultimately, whatever understanding is genuinely attained always must remain partial and fused with her previous understandings as these continue to evolve.

Although interpretive understanding always is possible to some extent, assuming a respectful openness to the possibility of the other, such understanding may require much effort and struggle over a considerable time. Even within the pluralistic, dynamically evolving sociocultural contexts in which we emerge and develop as psychological persons, interpretive understanding always poses a considerable challenge, requires an ethical–epistemic openness and criticalness, and always must remain partial, nonabsolute, and susceptible to change. Ways of living are in constantly evolving interaction with individual and collective lives. Psychological persons are condemned to care and understand within this dynamic, interactive flux, which in turn is both made possible and constrained by the real biological and physical world. As agents, psychological individuals make choices and act in ways that might extend possibilities for their own understanding and care. In our view, the psychological self is a kind of understanding of what it is to be a particular deliberative human agent situated in a life-world.

Agency is closely linked to the dialogical character of such self-understanding and to the way in which it is sociotemporally situated. For, as we have seen, agency always involves the past and present activity and understanding of persons embedded in the life-world and the imaginative projection of future possibilities for action and understanding in relation to concerns and questions of living. As agents, we draw retrospectively from our lives to date in ways that orient us toward our futures, and we constantly choose among alternatives available within this sociotemporal space of our existence. (For more extended discussions of the temporal dimension of human agency and existence, see Martin Heidegger [1927/1962], Slife [1994], and Mustafe Emirbayer and Ann Mische [1998]. The latter makes extensive use of the unique pragmatism of George Herbert Mead [1934] which contains both important similarities to and differences from the neohermeneutic, sociocultural, developmental position taken herein.)

SUMMARIZING OUR THEORY OF AGENCY AND PSYCHOLOGICAL KINDS

In this chapter, we have theorized about the origins, development, and intelligibility of situated, emergent, and deliberative agency and psychological kinds. In doing so, we have located all psychological kinds, including human experience and action, within contingent, emergent forms and practices of human being and understanding nested in historical, sociocultural traditions of living. The requirements that psychological kinds cohere and have application within traditions of living, together with constraints imposed on the development of psychological kinds by the real biological and physical world, both constrain the psychological kinds that can emerge and make possible their intelligibility.

Our most basic claim is existential and is congruent with the contingent emergence of psychological kinds, not with any pre-given, essentialist characterization of human psychological individuals. Given that human biological individuals are born into real physical and sociocultural contexts that pre-exist them, we maintain that the contingent, historically and socioculturally shaped emergence of some kind of subjectivity, or psychological being, is inevitable. We also make two additional claims with respect to the shifting ontology of human psychological kinds: that whatever its contingent historical, sociocultural character, human subjectivity or being will exhibit care, in the sense of concern for itself and that care manifests in, and requires, understanding, construed as the opening up of possibilities for living.

With respect to the developmental emergence of psychological kinds within traditions of living and understanding, we argue that psychological kinds, while requiring physical and biological realities of world and body, are constituted by the appropriation and internalization of sociocultural means and practices that have evolved within historical traditions of living. However, once emergent within historical, sociocultural traditions, psychological persons and kinds cannot be reduced back to their sociocultural origins. Psychological persons and kinds, by virtue of a reflective consciousness aided by developmentally emergent capabilities of memorial and imaginal construction, are both irreducible to, and underdetermined by, their sociocultural origins and physical–biological requirements. Thus, the ontology of psychological kinds is not fixed but emerges and shifts within the developmental context we have described.

As the opening of possibilities for living, the understanding of human psychological agents always is ongoing, mutable, and incomplete. Moreover, it most often is tacit and taken for granted, becoming explicit only when concerns and questions arise within the course of living and acting. Nonetheless, explicit understanding (the purposefully engaged interpretation of understanding) is possible, even if never exhaustive. Human psychological kinds, including understanding, can be interpreted within the dynamic, historical, sociocultural context within which they emerge and develop. Such interpretation involves sincere attempts to be open to one's own and others' understanding and to the historical, sociocultural traditions within which understanding occurs and unfolds. It also requires the attempt to apply what is understood through this dialogical process to the concerns and questions that motivated the interpretive inquiry in the first place. Understanding and its interpretation, like subjectivity or psychological being, always are both enabled and constrained by relevant sociocultural traditions and physical–biological requirements. As already argued, coherence, application, and constraint act as everyday warrants with respect to the understanding of psychological kinds.

Because the interpretation of psychological being and understanding requires a respectful openness to the understandings and perspectives of others as sources of possibility, the care of psychological beings always exhibits an ethical aspect. Psychological persons (selves and others) are "ends in themselves," the interpretive understanding of which always requires a dialogical, mutual intersubjectivity. Through respectful openness to others and their understandings, combined with critical reconsideration of one's self-understandings, possibilities for living open up in a process of dialogical fusion that draws from different traditions of living and understanding, and from different experiences within those traditions.

In all of this, it should be obvious that the emergence, underdetermination, and irreducibility of psychological kinds (such as the deliberative understandings, imaginings, memories, commitments, projects, desires, and actions of psychological persons) have no direct equivalencies in the natural world of physical, chemical, and strictly biological kinds. Even though Hacking (1995, 1999) did not necessarily intend that his distinction between natural—indifferent and human—interactive kinds should apply to the broader hermeneutic distinction between natural and human science, our development of the closely related distinction between natural and psychological kinds has exactly this intent. When the full weight of the differences between natural and psychological kinds is acknowledged, it becomes stunningly clear why the scientistic, reductionistic inquiry practices and assumptions of much disciplinary psychology over the past 125 years have resulted in so little in the way of a defensible understanding of psychological kinds. Moreover, it also becomes clear the extent to which such practices actually have begun to offer for public consumption an increasingly influential set of constructed categories, findings, and explanations that actually encourage Western individuals to misunderstand their experiences, actions, and ways of being and understanding (cf. Cushman, 1995; Woolfolk, 1998).

Perhaps most important, it becomes more clear the extent to which disciplinary psychology's professional instrumentalism and excessively reductive scientific functionalism have encouraged a retreat from situated, deliberative human agency and what might reasonably be regarded as a proper ethical consideration of human psychological individuals and collectives. These themes will be explored in greater detail in the next chapter of our book. In this final chapter, we reinterpret and extend conventional understandings of psychological inquiry, practice, and the relation of psychology and the broader society in light of the theory of situated, emergent, and deliberative agency with which we have been concerned in this chapter. In particular, we attempt to demonstrate what kinds of psychological understanding might fit with our conception of situated, emergent, and deliberative human agency. As should now be clear, we seek a conception of psychology as the contextualized, interpretive understanding of psychological kinds, a conception positioned outside of what we regard as the unsustainable polarity of a too hard, scientifically reductive determinism versus an obscurantist, radically libertarian humanism.

IMPLICATIONS FOR UNDERSTANDING PSYCHOLOGICAL PHENOMENA

Objectivity is affected by the nature of the phenomena studied and by the methods of study. In physical science, it is primarily the latter that are humanly constructed. However, in psychology, both phenomena of interest and strategies of inquiry are human constructions. Human actions and experiences are unlike inanimate materials, chemicals, and atoms. Understanding psychological phenomena requires interpretation of the meanings of these phenomena within historical, sociocultural, and linguistic context. Psychological reality is constrained by its nesting within physical and biological levels of reality, and it requires interpretation by virtue of its nesting within historical sociocultural reality that includes language. To understand someone's experience of emotional upheaval during and after a domestic dispute, or someone's motives and intentions making a career change, is to penetrate the relevant interpretive contexts within which such emotion and action occur. For example, a professor's decision to move to a different position may be nested within general and particular academic, economic, political, interpersonal, and familial contexts (to name only a few), each of which may contain different, even competing, possibilities for framing and interpreting the career change.

Contexts are far from monolithic in the meanings and interpretations they will support. Consequently, although a viable interpretation of human psychological actions or experiences must fit within relevant physical and biological constraints and within relevant sociocultural contexts of meaning and practice, there can be no ultimate certainty or finality with respect to such interpretation. The nesting of psychological reality within other levels of reality provides both constraints and warrants that militate against an unfettered relativism in the interpretation and understanding of psychological phenomena. However, because such constraints and warrants are themselves located in physical, biological, and especially sociocultural reality that is not static, fixed, nor monolithic, no single, final, complete, or absolute understanding is possible.

Even though physical objects and biological species are natural kinds that exist independently of those studying them, psychological, agentic kinds are defined and constituted, both consciously and unconsciously, by the aims, methods, and activities of human agents. As we have seen, human phenomena may be considered real by virtue of their possible influence, and particularly by virtue of their irreducible occurrence within the sociocultural, biological, and physical world. Because of their embeddedness within sociocultural, biological, and physical reality, there is good reason to believe that psychological actions and experiences are far from chaotic, arbitrary, or fleetingly irrelevant. Such a psychological reality clearly is assumed in the vast majority of psychological inquiry, even if it is treated skeptically by some theoretical psychologists.

Human sociocultural and psychological categories are not arbitrary in that they are definite kinds, even if not natural. As Kurt Danziger (1997) argues, "Human kinds . . . are not natural kinds, but neither are they mere legends. They do refer to features that are real. But it is a reality in which they themselves are heavily implicated, a reality in which they are a part" (pp. 191–192). Because human psychological beings are agents who are aware and reflective (even if never completely so), their courses of action and ways of being are affected not only by the classifications of societies and cultures but also by their own conceptions of, and reactions to, such classifications. Thus, an individual's experience of being mistreated—say for example, as a victim of police brutality—is not simply a social construction but is constituted in part by the individual's own understanding of the significance of being a victim of police brutality. This latter understanding obviously reflects a life of immersion in socioculturally available practices but also is based on a somewhat inevitably unique set of experiences of any psychological individual within those practices (cf. Taylor, 1995). Further, the reflections and actions of classified individuals often result in changes in classification. As mentioned earlier, the sociocultural and the psychological construct each other (Fay, 1996; Martin & Sugarman, 1999). It is this sort of ongoing, mutual interaction between a classification and classified individuals that Hacking (1995, 1999) calls the looping effect of human or interactive kinds, in contrast to natural or indifferent kinds. What Hacking intends to convey by this distinction is that human kinds affect people classified, but that classified people nonetheless are potentially capable of taking matters into their own hands, at least to some extent.

Within all of the dynamic flux that describes the ongoing mutable interaction between societies and psychological individuals, there exists a kind of nonchaotic, nonarbitrary social and psychological reality that is much more than linguistic. It is not simply a matter of how we decide to think or talk, as some postmodernists appear to claim (cf. Kvale, 1992). For thought and language are richly woven systems that will work their performative magic only when the necessary, relevant strands are engaged. When the jury says "not guilty" and the accused is released from the custody of jailers, an entire social system of law, authority, and conceptions and practices of freedom (and the possible lack thereof) is invoked. The jury's deliberations and language perform because they fit into this multilayered sociocultural reality. However, if a jury gets its thinking and expressive language spectacularly wrong in relation to the relevant sociocultural system or if a psychological individual attempts to command a physical force (e.g., commanding the tide to halt), both may end up "all wet." As the levels-of-reality position asserts, the physical, biological, and sociocultural world simultaneously constrains and enables the emergence and interpretation of human psychological kinds.

The reality of psychological phenomena within other levels of reality allows psychologists to warrant claims concerning their interpretive findings by tapping into, and participating within, systems of meaning and practice extant in relevant historical, sociocultural contexts. However, the same reality ensures that our understanding of psychological phenomena never can be absolute, certain, or complete. (The enumeration of specific approaches to psychological inquiry that seem mostly consistent with the general ontological and epistemological situation outlined here, exceeds the aims of the current volume. However, informative discussions of such inquiry strategies may be found in Brian Fay [1996], John Greenwood [1991], Jonathan Smith, Rom Harré, and Luk Van Langenhove [1995], Jack Martin and Jeff Sugarman [1999], and Frank Richardson et al. [1999], among others.)

Postmodern psychologists (e.g., Gergen, 1994) are right to reject the foundationalist idea that psychological and sociocultural reality is characterized by conceptually independent, ahistorical, unchanging forms or laws that can be apprehended objectively. However, on this basis, to conclude that psychological and sociocultural reality is nothing more than a chaotic, random flux, the arbitrary ordering of which reflects only dominant positions and interests, goes too far. On the one hand, this conclusion fails to recognize the extent to which sociocultural and psychological reality is nested within, constrained by, and shaped by biological and physical reality. On the other hand, it ignores the possibility that, although clearly contingent and variable across societies and cultures, such human reality is far from chaotic or ephemeral. Rather, it consists of practices and structures that can be identified and understood in a warranted manner, within an epistemological framework that allows for uncertainty and incompleteness in interpretation, but does not condone an anarchistic relativism.

Such an epistemology is not classically metaphysical. It eschews first principles and certitude. It is primarily concerned with the meaningful explication of human action and experience in context. Such a social psychological contextualism aims interpretively to understand particular actions and experiences associated with particular focal concerns. Its warrants include most importantly a sense of being informed with respect to those concerns that motivate particular inquiries into human affairs. It is a view that has been advanced by such influential and diverse twentieth-century thinkers as Martin Heidegger, John Dewey, and Ludwig Wittgenstein. It also is the general view favored by several contemporary philosophers and historians of psychology who resist a forced choice between modern scientism and postmodern anarchism (e.g., Danziger, 1997; Hacking, 1995; Taylor, 1995). There is room for warranted interpretive navigation between the Scylla of essentialism and the Charybdis of ephemeralism.

A FINAL WORD

One way to understand the implications of our approach to agency as always contextualized, yet emergent, self-determination is to contrast it with a recently influential conceptualization of self-determination that has been advanced by the libertarian Kane (1998).

> To say that persons self determine ... is to say that they perform ... acts and that they have plural voluntary control over their doing so and doing otherwise [right up to the very point of acting]. Agents have plural voluntary control when they are able to do what they will to do, when they will to do it, on purpose rather than by accident or mistake, without being coerced or compelled in doing, or willing to do, it, or otherwise controlled by other agents or mechanisms. (p. 191)

Kane, unlike many other contemporary libertarians, insists that such self-determination need not invoke a mysteriously unique kind of nonoccurrent agent causation. (Nonoccurrent causation is the causation of an action or other occurrence by something other than other occurrences.) His tactic here is to take seriously the possibility that a kind of self-network exists that somehow can be mapped onto neural occurrences, and that all of this (both the conscious experience of agency and the intervening self-network) is somehow related to the quantum character of reality. Here, it is interesting to note just how closely Kane seems to come to the kind of functionalism currently favored by many hard determinists who employ computational, supervenient models in an attempt indirectly to link agentic kinds to an underlying physical level of strict causation (e.g., Kim, 1996).

Although sometimes seen as alternatives to contemporary hard determinist, materialist accounts of agency, functionalist accounts that employ supervenience seem to us mostly to beg the reductive question by purposing an intermediate level of rather mysterious "computational," "connectionist," or "schematic network" kinds that somehow are supposed to mediate between psychological, agentic and physical kinds. As we previously have argued, such efforts experience the same kinds of difficulty as earlier, more directly and obviously reductive, central-state materialist and computational models in accounting for important features of our psychological states such as intentionality, rationality, normativity, and first-person perspective (cf. McDowell, 1994; Searle, 1992). Moreover, they frequently seem to conflate requirement with identity relations in apparently assuming that because human agents require biological bodies they are nothing more than biological bodies, albeit "computerized" and/or "schematized" ones. In all such approaches, sociocultural meanings, rules, conventions, and practices, which for us play critically important background, contextual, and constitutive roles in the development of human self-understanding and agency, receive extremely short shrift.

In contrast to Kane's version of contemporary libertarianism, our own treatment of agentic self-determination is more modest in requiring only that self-determination be an irreducible part of the determination of a particular choice and action. Moreover, for us, such self-determination need not always be active. In addition, we understand self-determination as emerging developmentally, as a kind of reflective self-understanding linked to deliberate action, within the constraints and influences of both biology and culture, but not reducible to either. We thus attempt to avoid both a reduction of agency to neurophysiology and a speculative appeal to microparticulate theorizing that seems ultimately to substitute quantum uncertainty and "indeterminacy" for agentic reason, intention, and perspective. To us, such moves seem to sacrifice precisely what we hope to maintain and try to explain. Interestingly, Kane's (2002) most recent work indicates to us that he recognizes a need to balance the neurophysiological aspect of his theorizing with a kind of emergence, perhaps not totally dissimilar to that discussed herein.

Traditional libertarian and hard-determinist approaches to agency tend to ignore the historical, sociocultural constitution of agency. In the case of libertarianism, this tendency manifests in question-begging assertions of radical freedom emanating from a metaphysically isolated agent somehow disconnected from the physical, biological, and sociocultural world. In the case of hard determinism, this tendency often manifests in implausible attempts to reduce agency to nothing more than physical kinds and causes. By bringing agency "into the world," we hope to have moved some small way toward addressing the problems associated with compatibilist theories that we posed earlier. In the previous chapter, we have attempted a nonquestion-begging argument for agency as self-determination. In this chapter, by elaborating a theory of agentic development, we hope to have shown how this conception of agency may be held coherently as being both determined and determining.

What we claim is that agency arises from the prereflective activity of biological humans embedded inextricably within a real physical and sociocultural world. It is this activity and its consequences that make available sociocultural practices, conventions, and meanings to the increasingly reflective understanding of human persons. That part of such understanding that reveals aspects of the particular being of a human individual is constitutive of the self of that person. With the onset of reflective, "self" understanding capable of memorial recollection, imaginative projection, and reason, a kind of situated, deliberative agency becomes possible. This is an agency that is of nonmysterious origin, being constituted and determined by relevant physical, biological conditions and requirements and sociocultural practices and meanings. Yet because of the reflective "self" understanding and reason upon which it rests, such agency also consists in a kind of self-determination that never acts outside of historical and sociocultural situatedness but which can aspire beyond and cannot be reduced to such situatedness alone nor to its other biological and physical requirements. Moreover, the resultant agency is not only voluntary but also has an aspect of origination, not in any radically free sense, but in the capability of self-interpreting, self-determining agents to selectively take up, modify, and employ available sociocultural practices and conventions as bases for psychologically significant activity. It is in this sense that the situated, deliberative agency we argue for, and theorize about, is both determined and determining.

Our approach is compatibilist in the sense that it relies centrally on an idea of self-determination, but it is not dissolutionist, nor restricted to voluntariness alone. With respect to psychology, we are of the opinion that the kind of compatibilist theorizing we have attempted herein eventually may contribute to an understanding of psychology as a rigorous but nonreductive study of the experiences and actions of human agents in historical, sociocultural, and developmental context. Such a psychology would carry implications for a form of psychological practice that approaches concerns of living within relevant traditions and practices, without forgetting, but also without elevating inappropriately, necessary physical and biological factors and considerations. It is this nesting of the psychological within the historical and sociocultural, which in turn are nested within biological and physical reality, that we regard as a proper "metaphysics" of the human condition. This is not a traditional metaphysics of transcendental or first principles, certainty, and essentials, but a "neo-metaphysics" consisting in historical, situational, and developmental contingencies that are inseparable from the "acting-in-the-world" of embodied, biologically evolved human beings who seem uniquely "culture-capable."

Obviously, there is much of importance to learn about the physical, neurophysiological, and biological requirements, operations, and conditions that permit human agency, just as there is much still unanswered concerning the sociocultural constitution of agency and the developmental contexts within which it emerges. The task of understanding human agency is large and our advances to date small. However, the enormous complexity of the task should not be avoided in favor of overly simplified, reductive models and programs of research that, in our opinion, can be expected to reveal little of what we find significant in our lives.

At the same time, it is important to identify explicitly a likely consequence of our work herein for traditional scientific psychology. We have claimed that the underdetermination of human agency by factors and conditions other than the irreducible understanding and reasoning of human agents does not mean that human agency is undetermined, only that it figures into its own determination. As such, it might be concluded that the possibility of a deterministic science of psychology still exists so long as the self-determination of individual agents can be accessed through methods of scientific inquiry. However, the practical difficulties of achieving veridical access to such self-determination should not be underestimated. It may prove to be the case that our underdetermination thesis with respect to human agency, if true, while not denying the possibility of a deterministic psychological science, may imply the practical impossibility of such a science. For even if human agency is not undetermined, so long as self-determination is admitted, it may prove to be indeterminate in the sense of being outside the reach of the methods of psychological science.

Turning to the practice of psychology, we believe that psychological practitioners are right to insist on the self-determining agentic capability of human persons. However, such insistence should not be instrumentally and/or romantically exaggerated in aid of purely psychological, decontextualized administrations and interventions. Nor should it lay claim to the kind of support common in more appropriately reductive branches of natural, physical science. In psychology, we should not reductively make human beings small as a means of doing large things with them. With this thought in mind, we now turn to a fuller, illustrated consideration of possible implications of our approach to human agency for psychological research, practice, and the contemporary sociopolitical relevance of psychology.

CHAPTER SIX

PUTTING AGENCY
INTO PSYCHOLOGY

A MAJOR THEME in this book has been disciplinary psychology's failure to develop an adequate conception of human agency because of its untenable joint commitments to an overly reductionistic science and a too facile professionalism. To create the perception of success in both these ventures, psychology has committed itself to an impossibly and wrongly detached, unsituated, and reductively automated view of the human agent. This is an agent outside of and separate from history, culture, and society and yet mysteriously able (especially with the help of psychological professionals) to cope, solve, even to dominate her or his situation and circumstances. Jointly committed to incommensurable strands of hard determinism and libertarianism through its scientist–practitioner rhetoric of reductively scientific but somehow life-relevant practice, psychology has become entangled in the determinism–free-will debate in ways that appear sensible only if one views all of this through the rose-tinted lenses of disciplinary psychology.

Our major purpose in this book has been to argue for, and theorize about, a conception of agency as embedded and situated, yet also emergent within historical sociocultural contexts, which in turn are nested in the biological and physical world. This is an in-the-world agency conceptually divorced from the detached, disavowed, and devalued agency pragmatically, but incoherently, endorsed by disciplinary psychology. It is an agency that does not slide chameleon-like between the conflicting poles of hard determinism and radical freedom to suit the purposes of disciplinary psychology. It is an agency that takes its meaning and much of its constitution from its

sociocultural embeddedness, yet always is enabled and constrained by biological and physical factors, conditions, and processes. Nonetheless, while
thus constituted, enabled, and constrained, it is not reducible to any of these
other factors, conditions, and processes. Once emergent within its developmental trajectory, a path that is initiated ontogenetically by the birth of a
human biological infant into the already existing physical and sociocultural
world, it always may figure into its own determination.

This intelligible self-determination is what defines agency as the always-present, even if not always-exercised, capacity for understanding and
deliberative reasoning that we humans use to select, frame, choose, and
execute intentional behavior in the world. It is what makes human agents
both determined and determining, in the sense promised, but mostly unde-
livered, by previous compatibilist theorizing. It is this capacity for agentic
determination that manifests in the uniquely human interpretive, reflective
understanding of our personal existence that constitutes our sense of self as
a core understanding from which we interpret, understand, reason, and act
agentically. The complex of physical, biological, and sociocultural factors,
processes, conditions, and contexts that gives rise to the human agentic
condition is nested and interactive across both phylogenetic evolution and
history, and within ontogenetic development. As such, but especially when
considered together with the emergent human agency it fosters, this complexity is not amenable to the various reductive programs of disciplinary
psychology. This much we hope to have established in the earlier chapters
of this volume.

What remains to be done in this final chapter is to ask what difference
our conception of situated, emergent, and deliberative agency might make
to our understanding of psychological research and practice and to the
broader sociopolitical impact of psychology on contemporary Western society. As indicated at the end of the previous chapter, it is not our intention
to offer any set of recommended methods for the conduct of such research
and practice or for any social, political advocacy that might seem consistent
with our views as expressed herein. As most students of psychology know,
the discipline's literature is awash in such recommendations, many of them
both exacting and detailed. What we want to offer in this chapter is a series
of interpretive demonstrations and suggestions that will make clear what our
conception of human agency has to offer to psychological research and
practice and to an understanding of interactions between psychology and its
broader society. What we plan to do is illustrate the kind of reconfigurations
that result when our conception of situated, emergent, and deliberative
agency is assumed and brought to bear on salient programs of research and
practice within contemporary psychology and society. Once such reinterpretation and reconfiguration have been achieved, methods that psychologists might use to work within these reconfigured programs will be generally
apparent.

In our opinion, the real trick is to cast an appropriate conceptual net over salient, illustrative programs of psychological practice and research. With such conceptual clarification in place, how best to proceed from there is, and should remain, the province of more specialized communities of researchers, practitioners, and social theorists and advocates, familiar with both available methodological tools and the specifics of their particular programs of activity. The conceptual nets that we will cast in this chapter are initiated and animated by the conception of situated, emergent, and deliberative agency that we have argued for, and theorized about, in the preceding chapters.

This final chapter is organized into three sections. We begin by conducting a reinterpretation of reinforcement theory (perhaps the most widely accepted program of scientific psychological research that disciplinary psychology has yet produced) as part of a larger outline for the in situ study of how sociocultural practices come to constitute psychological persons. In the second section, we turn our attention to a reinterpretation and reconfiguration of the increasingly widespread practice of professional psychotherapy. Finally, in the third section, we examine the possible sociopolitical relevance of our conceptions of agency, self, and person against the background of contemporary debates between liberals and communitarians. In doing so, we adopt the general viewpoint of Philip Cushman (1995), Nikolas Rose (1998), and others concerning the influential role played by disciplinary psychology in framing contemporary conceptions of agency and self that animate such debates. To all of these areas of psychological research, practice, and sociopolitical impact, we import our conception of the situated, emergent, and deliberative agent. In so doing, we reinterpret and transform disciplinary psychology's traditional ways of understanding these areas of psychological research, practice, and influence. Of course, what we are after is an overall demonstration of what might be gained when a more realistic, fully developed, in-the-world conception of agency is made available to psychology and psychologists.

RE-ENVISIONING PSYCHOLOGICAL RESEARCH:
REINFORCEMENT THEORY AND BEYOND

REINFORCEMENT THEORY REVISITED

From the 1930s to 1960s in North America, no single program of research in psychology was more prototypic of "psychology as hard science" than the operant psychology developed by B. F. Skinner. Today, principles of operant psychology remain influential in many areas of applied psychology, including clinical, educational, and industrial–organizational psychology. Most commentators seem now to agree that Skinner's radical behaviorism was insufficiently sensitive to genuinely agentic aspects of human experience and action, although they more often speak in terms of an inadequate attention to either cognitive or affective characteristics of human activity. Nonetheless, there have been several attempts to reconceptualize operant psychology to take fuller advantage of its undeniable success at basic empirical and practical levels of inquiry and application. Some of these attempts at reconfiguration can be interpreted as pointing to similarities (or at least to some common ground) between certain aspects of operant psychology and twentieth-century philosophical systems like North American pragmatism and Continental hermeneutics and existentialism (e.g., DeGrandpre, 2000; Fallon, 1992; Lee, 1992). In what follows, we entertain a brief reconceptualization of operant psychology in terms of the theory of human agency with which we have been concerned in this volume.

One of the most central tenets of our theorizing herein is that people act both prereflectively and reflectively, coming to the latter capability on the developmental basis of the former, but without ever foregoing the former. It is in this sense that human agents are both determined and determining. The practical knowledge that human beings acquire is initially a consequence of their prereflective activity in the world, which is largely a matter of trial and error. Learning from the effects of such prereflective activity, human agents extend their practical understanding of the worldly background and context in which they are embedded and compelled to act. Gradually, such understanding manifests in capacities for memory and imagination that enable human agents to engage in deliberative, reflective inquiry. What we want to highlight in our reinterpretation of operant psychology is the powerful role of operant learning as a basic vehicle for the appropriation and internalization of sociocultural meanings and practices. Processes of operant reinforcement, punishment, and so forth not only potentially affect future behavior but more importantly make salient sociocultural meanings and practices that otherwise would remain hidden. And it is these meanings and practices, thus uncovered and revealed, that permit human agents to penetrate their historical, sociocultural backgrounds in ways that extend their horizons of intelligibility.

In effect, what is being suggested is that the operant processes studied by Skinner and others make the world increasingly intelligible to developing agents in ways that expand their possibilities for understanding and finding significance in the physical, biological, and sociocultural world. As primary vehicles for internalization, such processes are not best understood as environmental contingencies that act on people outside of their situated, prereflective and reflective agency. Rather, they should be reinterpreted as dialectical processes that provide agents active in the world with worldly meanings and practices that they can internalize and use to extend their understandings and actions in ways that provide expanded possibilities for inquiry into everyday concerns and for enhanced caring for self and others.

In DeGrandpre's (2000) words,

> However strange it may seem . . . reinforcement as a general
> learning process is not about why or whether reinforcers are
> reinforcers or about how reinforcers affect behavior. Rather, it is
> about how, as one experiences the consequences of one's actions
> in ecological context, the possibility of new meaning emerges.
> This meaning then gives rise to future action, leading to further
> personal experiences that may or may not sustain one's already
> existing sense of one's social and physical surroundings. (p. 725)

> Reinforcement as a basic but fundamental process of meaning
> making remains a powerful conceptual tool for describing the
> ecological origins of psychological experience and action. (p. 736)

Because DeGrandpre (2000) seems to equivocate between the idea of
meaning as embedded in sociocultural practices and what might, in our
view, better be termed "personal, reflective understanding coupled with
significance," he seems to separate reinforcement somewhat from the unity
of the "agent in the world." For us, reinforcement is not so much a process
of meaning making as a process of meaning transmission, appropriation, and
internalization. However, this is a small quibble that should not be allowed
to overshadow DeGrandpre's otherwise powerful attempt at re-envisioning
operant psychology along lines similar to what we have in mind.

More directly in line with our intended re-envisioning of operant
psychology is V. L. Lee's (1992) formulation of the operant as compatible
with a transdermal interpretation that understands actions as units with both
organismic and environmental constituents but which are not reducible as
psychological entities to their organismic and environmental constituents.
Lee understands reinforcement and other operant processes as

> centered in acts or in changes and preventions of change produced
> by the movements of organisms. This transdermal subject matter is
> separable conceptually from the subject matters of biology and the
> social sciences. Such conceptual separability is consistent with apply-
> ing the principle of levels to the distinction between movements
> and acts, and it implies the autonomy of a psychology of acts. The
> traditional distinction between behavior (or organism) and environ-
> ment obscures the transdermal nature of acts. . . . [T]he task . . . is
> not to find the environmental causes of behavior, contrary to what
> acceptance of the dichotomy of organism and environment has
> suggested [, but] to investigate and illuminate both the natural his-
> tory and the internal organization of this transdermal subject matter
> that is centered in acts. (p. 1341)

Not only does Lee insist on the unity of action in the world, but she also hints at a levels-of-reality ontology similar to that which we have proposed in the previous chapter.

What nonetheless still seems missing from Lee's reconceptualization of operant psychology is the explicit insertion of a situated, deliberative agent capable of self-determination in the manner for which we have argued. For us, it is not enough that operant psychology be reinterpreted as a psychology of irreducible acts in the world. We also insist that at least some such acts be understood as self-determined (at least in part) by the situated, deliberative agent. It is the agent acting in the world toward which we want to direct our re-envisioning of operant psychology. Moreover, the nested unity of "agentic worldliness" must not be reduced to other levels of reality by the methodological penchants of psychological researchers.

When Skinner (1959) admonished against "the flight to the inner man" (p. 252), he was asserting very much the sentiment that Merleau-Ponty (1962) asserted when he wrote, "Truth does not 'inhabit' only the 'inner man,' or more accurately, there is no inner man, man is in the world, and only in the world does he know himself" (p. xi). Any reconceptualization of operant psychology in terms of agentic self-determination, thus requires precisely the kind of always-situated agency that we have argued for and theorized about. But it must also include a conception of the deliberating agent that goes beyond Skinner's treatment of beliefs, reasons, and commitments as little more than internalized forms of behavior. For the difficulty here is not so much one of the impossible "inner man," but of the reduction of the historical, sociocultural background to an agent's reasons and beliefs to only the immediate environmental circumstance. Traditions of practice and belief reveal themselves only in the context of an agent's acting in the world. But this world is multilayered in ways seldom articulated explicitly by traditional operant theorists or connoted with their use of the term *environment.* Moreover, the acting involved is not captured well by the use of the term *behavior,* which connotes an insufficient attention to the intentionality of an agent's actions.

When reinforcement is understood as a primary vehicle for the internalization of historically and socioculturally embedded meanings and practices, the vast research in the area of operant psychology can be re-envisioned as describing important aspects of the emergence of situated, deliberative agents in their worldly context. Such re-envisioning is not necessarily consistent with the traditional aims and aspirations of reinforcement theorists. However, it does serve to illustrate the way in which existing bodies of psychological research and theory might be reinterpreted in terms of the theory of agency and agentic development with which we have been concerned in this volume.

What we have attempted to do with this brief example of interpretive re-envisioning is demonstrate that our account of agency does not necessarily require an abandonment of all of the results of existing psychological inquiry. Rather, by proposing an account of the subject matter of psychology that is consistent with the core idea of irreducible, situated, and deliberative agency, we are able to understand important lines of traditional psychological research in new ways. Hopefully, some of these ways might succeed in drawing together findings and results from extant psychological inquiry into a more focused, unified account of human being, action, and experience. Such a project is not narrowly methodological, but interpretive. It is not a matter of devising and experimenting with various combinations of old and/or new methods of inquiry. Rather, it is an exercise in interpretive and reinterpretive framing of existing inquiry and findings through alternative ontological lenses.

BEYOND REINFORCEMENT THEORY

The kind of reinterpretation we have just illustrated can succeed in recasting some of the findings of traditional psychological research to speak directly to the constitution of developing psychological agents. However, reductive psychology ultimately displays limitations in this regard that can be overcome only with a nonreductive recognition of those capabilities that seem to be unique to agentic psychological persons. Consequently, any attempt to research the developmental constitution and emergence of human agentic capability must inevitably be concerned with linguistic, relational practices. Here, of course, the seminal work of Lev Vygotsky (1978, 1986) and neo-Vygotskians like Carl Ratner (1991) and James Wertsch (1985) is of particular relevance (see chapter 3). However, a great wealth of developmental research on social, linguistic contributions to agency and personhood is beginning to emerge from other and related quarters as well.

For example (as also mentioned in chapter 3), Rychlak's research on predication and transpredication (e.g., Rychlak, Williams, & Bugaj, 1986) and the developmental research cited and described by various contributors to Brandstädter and Lerner's (1999) volume *Action and Self-Development* tell us much about how agentic capability, self-understanding, and theories of mind emerge from immersion in the linguistic, sociocultural practices of human societies. Although it is beyond the scope of this volume to provide a thorough commentary on such work, it is perhaps useful to discuss briefly what we regard as one productive and exemplary line of research on the importance of discourse and language in the development of psychological persons. The example we have selected is Jean Quigley's (2000, 2001) recent work on the grammatical construction of the autobiographical self.

Inspired by the developmental theorizing of scholars such as Lev Vygotsky, (1978, 1986) Nathan Budwig (1995), Jerome Bruner (1990), and Rom Harré (1983, 1995), Jean Quigley (2000, 2001) has studied intensively the way in which the psychological person is constructed by her grammatical, language choices and "situated opinions." For Quigley, mind is an intrinsically social phenomenon. This being so, the subject matter of psychology is not what occurs in the minds of isolated individuals but what occurs in the interactions between individuals—what she refers to as the "relationship between words and world." For Quigley, it is language that gives us the world, and this is a world of relationships.

Quigley's empirical work consists of an extremely detailed grammatical analysis of the autobiographical narratives of English-speaking children in which she mines specific linguistic constructions for psychological significance. What she is looking for in particular is the contributions that particular linguistic constructions make to the developing narrative identities of the children in her sample. In this regard, different patterns of verb transitivity are described as prime vehicles for the constitution of identities. Transitivity is concerned with who did what to whom. In Quigley's work, transitivity is understood as a basic building block of the kind of agency we have attempted to describe in this volume. Of particular importance in this regard, is Quigley's insistence that children make transitivity choices by assigning different roles to participants or characters in their narratives, with the consequence that different characters take on distinctive worldviews. Such transitivity markings are a critical part of how the child represents characters as victims of circumstance or as actively in control of events. Clearly, transitivity in discourse is part of the construction of agency.

Because transitive verbs can take direct objects ("she saw the bird") and intransitive verbs do not take an object ("she dances"), the choice of a transitive verb allows an event to be presented from the viewpoint of an agent. On the other hand, the choice of an intransitive verb allows several options. For example, an event may be presented from the viewpoint of an agent who also becomes the object affected ("he cried"), an agent without an affected object ("he was playing"), or from the supposed viewpoint of an object and the action affecting it ("the swing moved back and forth"). Of course, in English, some verbs can be used both transitively and intransitively, and different languages have different modes of transitivity. The overall point is that options for conveying different narrative perspectives depend, in significant part, on choice of verbs within particular modes of transitivity. The grammatical system of transitivity basically sets up two types of situations: it helps identify and constitute agents in narratives (those whose actions make a difference); and it assigns responsibility for actions to those agents. The use of a system of transitivity thus links agency to a moral order.

In general, Quigley's research (2000, 2001) findings indicate an increase in first-person transitive statements with age. Younger children (five-year-olds) refer mostly to the actions of others using transitive verbs and statements from which they are absent altogether or absent as either actor, experiencer, or recipient. In contrast, older children (eight- and twelve-year-olds) employ mostly agentic constructions involving either first-person actions and events, or generic (every-person) scenarios that can reasonably be interpreted subjectively. On the basis of such research and findings, Quigley concludes that the autobiographical (agentic) self develops over the course of childhood as a kind of rhetorical achievement. Self and agency in this research are understood as the vantage points from which an autobiography is told, and the research may be interpreted to indicate some of the many ways in which the linguistic, relational practices of a society and cultural tradition prefigure and constitute agency.

What we want to suggest is that both traditional psychological research in areas such as reinforcement theory, and more recent psychological research on constitutive relations between sociocultural practices and psychological kinds, can tell us a great deal about how agency is achieved developmentally within sociocultural traditions and life-worlds. Although at present such empirical demonstrations are far from complete, there is much in them to support the claims we have made concerning the sociocultural constitution of psychological, agentic persons and kinds. We fully expect that future work of these and related types will succeed in producing ever-more convincing demonstrations of the sociocultural formation of personhood, given the basic existential condition of human biological individuals born into a physical, sociocultural life-world that preexists them.

We now turn our attention from a recasting of psychological research to a reconsideration and reconfiguring of psychological practice in a manner consistent with our theory of situated, emergent, and deliberative agency. Even though contemporary psychological practice has flowed into many areas of society, including schools, hospitals, and the work place, the area of psychological practice most familiar and obvious to many of us is psychotherapy. It probably is here that psychological and everyday conceptions of the isolated, psychically distressed individual attempting to cope single-handedly with life's difficulties are most pronounced. Consequently, if we can shift such a well-entrenched perspective to one more consistent with the kind of theorizing we have attempted, we will achieve a good indication of the difference our theory of agency makes to our understanding of psychological practice.

RE-ENVISIONING PSYCHOLOGICAL PRACTICE

Adoption of the situated, emergent, and deliberative view of human agency for which we have argued in the preceding chapters, based as it is on the argument that there are crucial differences between natural and human kinds, involves significant shifts in how we see the nature of the problems that bring individuals to psychotherapy, the theories we bring to bear on those problems, the treatments arising from those theories, and the education necessary to provide such treatments. These shifts in perspective would parallel, in many ways, those advocated in recent hermeneutic work on psychotherapy (e.g., Cushman, 1995; Martin & Dawda, 1999; Martin & Thompson, in press; Richardson et al., 1999; Woolfolk, 1998). The prevailing view of the problems that clients present in psychotherapy emphasizes their narrowly "psychological" nature, construing them as largely intrapsychic or interpersonal and as amenable to being reduced to and influenced in terms of related but distinct "components" (i.e., biological, cognitive, behavioral, affective, systemic). By contrast, a hermeneutically inspired view consistent with our conception of agency emphasizes the socioculturally embedded, practical, agentic, moral, and at least potentially political nature of such problems. Such a view of so-called psychological problems gives rise to theories that are situated, local, interpretive, and attendant to moral and political matters, and consistent with, rather than scientifically distinct from, everyday understandings. Such theories are in direct contrast to traditional theories that tend to be decontextualized, universal, transhistorical, neutral, predictive, and reductive and which often cast otherwise familiar human conditions in scientistic, technical language.

Unlike the traditional applied science model of psychotherapy, which emphasizes universal, transhistorical theories of human behavior that translate into morally neutral therapeutic techniques, the hermeneutic view emphasizes the socioculturally embedded, morally laden, practical, and interpretive nature of psychotherapy. And consistent with our conception of deliberative agency, much of this work emphasizes the crucial importance of various forms of situated self-understanding (e.g., Cushman, 1995; Martin & Thompson, in press; Woolfolk, 1998). Acceptance of the emergent and socioculturally embedded and constituted nature of both human agency and psychotherapy involves a crucial shift in perspective on psychological practice: a shift from viewing psychotherapy and counseling as decontextualized applied sciences to viewing them as social institutions that reflect and perpetuate features of their sociocultural and historical context. Once this shift in perspective is made, the inherently moral, practical, and interpretive nature of psychological practice comes into view. Emphasis is now placed on a deepening of clients' understandings of not only the self (as emphasized in traditional forms of psychotherapy) but also of the sociocultural as a source of possibilities for enhanced understanding and for the exercise of human agency. When humans exercise the kind of agency for which we have argued, they take practical decisions and actions that have moral and political (rather than purely personal or interpersonal) implications, the possibilities for which are constrained and constituted by, but cannot be reduced to, their biological, physical, and sociocultural heritage. Thus, the available possibilities can be seen only to the extent that the context, or background, is understood, and selves can only be understood through a knowledge of their context.

In light of our view of agency, we believe that psychotherapy is best understood as a relational and discursive practice devoted to assisting individuals to enhance their understanding of the constraints (perceived and real) and possibilities of their agency, including their moral responsibility for the impact of their choices and actions on their own lives and on the lives of others. We see psychotherapy as a morally laden social institution that has political as well as personal consequences and involves dialogue aimed at penetrating and interpreting practical, everyday agentic, moral concerns embedded within particular sociocultural contexts and within idiosyncratic personal histories. Thus, psychotherapy is an exercise in moving, insofar as possible, from tacit understanding of oneself and one's background to explicit interpretive understanding of significances and personal meanings in the life-world. The desire for such understanding is most likely to arise when everyday routines are disrupted such that we attend consciously to the previously taken for granted. The kind of "self" understanding that we believe is sought, and sometimes achieved, in psychotherapy permits enhanced self-determination through deliberative reflection, choice, and action—that is, it allows for the thoughtful exercise of human agency.

THE NATURE OF PSYCHOTHERAPY

Sociocultural embeddedness and a rejection of reductive scientism are central and pivotal themes both in hermeneutic work on psychotherapy and in our vision of human agency. If human agency is emergent in and constituted by, but not reducible to, its sociocultural context (nor to its biological–physical origins) and if human kinds differ substantively from natural kinds, then discursive human social activities such as psychotherapy are better construed as social institutions than as applied sciences. Woolfolk (1998) argues that all forms of therapy have in common the social functions of alleviating distress, regulating social behavior, constructing worldviews, and explaining the self. As such, psychotherapy is not only a "psychotechnology" or an applied science, but it is also a social institution that both reflects and shapes modern society. Psychotherapy, according to Woolfolk, is the modern world's solution for establishing what is good and bad, right and wrong, worthy and unworthy in human conduct. To achieve legitimacy in a modern age in which science had been granted almost exclusive epistemic authority, psychotherapy has had to be secular and at least to appear to be scientifically based. Thus, psychotherapy, which serves many of the functions of traditional institutions such as religion, has become a Weberian secular theodicy in that it provides "scientific" definitions of reality that make the human condition more bearable. Although striving for "scientificity and value neutrality," psychotherapy is, in fact, a morally laden enterprise that often conflates fact and value, equating sin with sickness and virtue with health.

> [E]very form of therapy comprises prescriptive as well as descriptive elements. Every system of therapy has an underlying

ideology. A therapy may disclose its aesthetic, cognitive, and moral values through the explicit location of thought and conduct on the continuum of health and sickness. Or values may operate tacitly in influencing patterns of therapeutic exploration, in establishing grounds for therapeutic intervention, or in promoting implicit guidelines for the attitudes and conduct of clients. Each system of therapy has its apotheoses. Psychoanalysis offers the ideal of the genital character, humanistic psychology the self-actualized individual, and cognitive-behavior therapy the rational, assertive individual. (Woolfolk, 1998, pp. 18–19)

Similarly, in his expansive historical study of psychotherapy theories and practices, Cushman (1995) argues that the usual decontextualized presentation of such theories and practices has ensured that they "inevitably reproduce the very cause of the ills they treat by implicitly valorizing and reproducing the isolated, empty individual" (p. 7). Based on his survey of the self and psychotherapy in America and on his analysis of the latter half of the twentieth century in particular, Cushman concludes:

Without psychotherapists realizing it, our theories have often reflected the post–World War II consumer landscape, normalized its necessary ingredients such as the empty self, and explained away its unavoidable consequences, such as emotional isolation, selfishness, drug addiction, and the nihilistic use of others. Psychotherapy theories consider these consequences to be anomalies, deviations from the healthy norm, and therefore we set out to heal them. If we were to historically situate our practices we might consider that these consequences are in fact not anomalies but the norm, and that when we medicalize and pathologize the norm, we ignore the dangers of the status quo and unknowingly perpetuate it. (p. 278)

Cushman (1995) argues that psychotherapists are involved in "unintentionally . . . using the approved practices of their era to carry on a disguised moral discourse to justify a particular view about what is the proper way of being" (p. 333). Psychology and psychotherapy have mistaken value judgments for objective scientific truths and have thereby unwittingly reproduced the status quo in a number of ways. For example, many theorists and practitioners of psychotherapy have emphasized the value of the true, expressive, creative, honest self; have configured the self as masterful, bounded, and empty; and have employed theories based on the metaphors of consumerism. Each of these moves involves moral judgments with political implications rather than bald scientific facts. Labeling some behaviors and characteristics of the self as "true," according to Cushman, is a political move made from a privileged "scientific" epistemological position that obscures the underlying ideology. Similarly, he argues that when psychotherapists assert that the bounded modern self is a natural occurrence rather than a social construction, they ignore the political functions served by such a self and thereby engage in the dangerous practice of exercising power while disguising it: "If psychology is one of the guilds most responsible for determining the proper way of being human, then psychology wields a significant amount of power, especially in our current era, in which the moral authority of religious and philosophical institutions has been called into question" (p. 336).

The failure of psychotherapy to adopt a fully interactive perspective has, according to Cushman, led to further denial of its sociopolitical role. This denial involves medicalizing and psychologizing human suffering while failing to see political causes of such suffering and defining freedom as "the *absence* of social influence and political allegiances" (p. 340). The consequence of this approach is that "we condemn ourselves to denying the effects of the macrostructures of our society. Therefore we will leave those structures intact while we blame the only positions in our cultural clearing that show up as responsible, culpable entities: the individual and the dyad" (p. 337). Cushman suggests a "politically subversive" hermeneutic antidote to these problems: a "3-person psychology," (p. 348) in which the third person is "the ever present, interpenetrating social realm" (p. 350) whose presence ensures the sociohistorical situation of psychological practices and theories.

The consequence of situating psychotherapy theories and practices, then, is the recognition that rather than being neutral and scientific they, in fact, reflect and perpetuate their context, which makes them inherently moral and political. Indeed Cushman (1995) indicates that historically situating psychotherapy theories and practices yields a vision of psychotherapy as an "unavoidably—although unintentionally...moral discourse with political consequences" (p. 281). Richardson et al. (1999) also emphasize the inherently moral nature of psychotherapy in their hermeneutic reconceptualization, suggesting that psychotherapy is a form of hermeneutic dialogue focused on "how to best live our lives in concrete situations where we already are defined by some serious commitments and identifications but have a measure of freedom to work out how they might best be reinterpreted" (p. 263).

Our view of human agency further reinforces hermeneutic arguments for acknowledging the moral and political nature of psychotherapy. In fact, one might argue that a view of human agency such as that which we have described is necessary to the hermeneutic argument that psychotherapy is a moral enterprise, for only if we abandon reductive, deterministic notions of human behavior can we claim that anything an individual chooses or does has moral implications. Psychotherapy involves assisting individuals as they struggle to solve problems by enhancing their understanding, making choices, and taking action based on such choices. That is, such problems are usually "solved" through the exercise of agency understood as the kind of self-determination for which we have argued. In this way, individuals decide to confront family members about past wrongs, choose to leave or stay in relationships, learn to say no to what they decide are unreasonable requests, and so forth. When individuals exercise their agency, in part as a result of understandings gained through therapeutic conversations, they are exercising a freedom (constrained though it may be) to make and act on choices that make a difference in their own and others' lives. This nonradical, intelligible freedom of self-determination clearly carries with it personal and moral responsibility for the impact of one's choices. The same can be said about the agency that therapists exercise throughout psychotherapy, as they make choices about theoretical orientation, interventions, and the like. The very nature of psychotherapeutic change both assumes and requires the morally saturated exercise of human agency on the part of both clients and therapists.

The nested, dynamic view of reality underlying our conception of agency lends itself well to describing how psychotherapy, which is a sociocultural phenomenon, can effect psychological change (see Martin, 1994). It also has implications for how we think about the potential outcomes of psychotherapy. Given the possibility of frequent and powerful interactions between the psychological and the sociocultural, for example, psychotherapists cannot and should not assume that they are effecting only psychological change. As feminist therapists have also argued repeatedly, from this perspective, the personal may well be the political, with changes in psychological reality influencing sociocultural change. The political may also become the personal (as for example, Cushman argues is the case when consumerism is unwittingly incorporated into psychotherapy theories, thus influencing our ways of seeing ourselves and others).

Our view of psychotherapy as a morally laden social institution is directly contrary to the American Psychological Association's current marketing strategy for psychological practice, which involves the promotion of "empirically validated treatments" (Task Force on Promotion and Dissemination of Psychological Procedures, 1995). The empirically validated treatments movement sells the applied science model of psychotherapy by giving official stamps of approval to manualized treatments that have been subjected to "scientific" testing. Although the movement has some merits in terms of, for example, encouraging critical evaluation of the efficacy of varying forms of treatment, it overlooks some equally important issues that simply are not visible as long as one uncritically accepts the applied science model. For example, it could be argued, following our view of agency and hermeneutic critiques of psychotherapy, that there is very little truth in advertising involved; that what are being promoted are not scientifically proven, neutral treatments but particular moral worldviews that may be of assistance to some individuals with some problems. As Robert Fancher (1995) has argued, "We need to think about mental health care differently than we now do . . . *its recommendations are essentially moral and social programs . . . understanding the culture of a school of care, and thinking about it as social, cultural critics, is our best bet*" (pp. 3–4). The problem, according to Fancher, is not that the schools of psychotherapy are cultures of healing, but that we have come to mistake cultural artifacts for natural facts, and, in doing so have limited our choices. "If schools of care are indeed best understood as cultures, a substantial portion of their beliefs and practices are optional" (p. 37).

The technical, prescriptive approach of the empirically validated treatments movement also overlooks one of the key problems (see chapter 2) inherent in the attempt to treat human kinds as if they were natural kinds— potentially mistaking generalizations not only from what was to what is and will be but also from what was or is to what ought to be. Once again, moral precepts simply cannot be drawn from empirical results alone.

Finally, it could be argued that the entire movement is an example (on many levels) of what happens when psychology fails to situate itself historically. Because of this failure, it unwittingly reflects and perpetuates its sociocultural, historical context—in this case, by reflecting the scientistic, procedural, "accountable" flavor of modern society in order to ensure political and economic ends (i.e., a "fair" share of increasingly scarce health care funding and of the status accorded to the health professions). Thus, professional psychology, though often critical of the practical relevance of psychological science, also uses science to legitimize its practices and to maintain its political power and economic status in the face of societal commitments to scientism, proceduralism, and efficiency—all of which commitments are more suitable to technical production than to human affairs.

The centrality of the kind of agency we have described to any conception of the psychological, making room as it does for understanding the real but constrained freedom to act with deliberation, further highlights another theme evident in hermeneutic reconceptualizations of psychotherapy: its practical nature. Woolfolk (1998) argues that practical self-understanding "is central to what is sought and found in psychotherapy" (p. 108). Practical self-understanding is action oriented in that we use it to decide what to do in everyday life and, as such, it has significant implications for our happiness and well-being. Woolfolk emphasizes that psychotherapy is aimed at solving real-world problems as played out in the unique, complex, and variable life contexts of self-interpreting human beings. Because of the practical and complex nature of the enterprise, he argues, psychotherapy can never derive from the behavioral sciences to the extent that, for example, mechanical engineering derives from physics. Rather, "Psychotherapy will always involve wisdom as well as expertise, pedagogy as well as technology" (p. 109).

Woolfolk argues that science is predicated on what Heidegger termed "everydayness," on our pre-understandings of what Edmund Husserl termed "the life-world." Although Woolfolk concedes that there are some similarities between scientific and everyday thinking, he argues that the disinterested, incredulous, and intellectually meticulous stance of scientists is neither possible nor appropriate in everyday life. Nor, therefore, should we expect psychotherapy, which is a practical enterprise, to be based on scientific thinking alone. For Woolfolk, science cannot supersede the life-world because there are at least two aspects of the life-world it cannot assimilate: "(1) the background of tacit assumptions and practices on which science, and all abstract knowledge, is based and (2) the sociohistorical context of human interests that both shape science and ultimately determine its application" (p. 111). He argues that all everyday and theoretical activities are underlain by a background of pervasive tacit assumptions, taken-for-granted knowledge, and norms that cannot be made entirely explicit.

THE PRACTICE OF PSYCHOTHERAPY

Our emphasis on a situated, emergent, and deliberative agency suggests that the aim of psychotherapy is the ongoing achievement of a practical, interpretive understanding that applies to our being-in-the-world and that helps us to become effective moral agents. This kind of understanding is achieved when our mostly tacit understandings of being-in-the-world are penetrated, such that we work out possibilities for understanding and action within particular contexts—possibilities that are not determined by pre-given, universal principles (Martin & Thompson, in press). One of the challenges faced by practicing psychotherapists as they assist others to penetrate their tacit understandings is the need to tack between the general and the particular; between, for example, cultural mores and beliefs or psychological theories on the one hand and, on the other hand, the idiosyncratic meanings, significances, and interpretations of these by particular individuals. In light of the idiographic nature of self-understanding and its importance to psychotherapy, Woolfolk (1998) describes the epistemological situation of "scientific" psychotherapy as precarious due to the difficulty of applying what is known generally to particular cases. Given the variable, underdetermined nature of human kinds, this challenge is unlikely to be met through the application of prescriptive treatments based on reductively deterministic, universal theories. What, then, does our view of agency mean for the practice of psychotherapy?

Our emphasis on the socioculturally embedded, situated nature of agency suggests that the typically inward gaze of psychotherapists and their clients (indeed, given psychology's impact on the culture at large, the inward gaze of a psychologized society) needs to be balanced by an outward gaze. This outward gaze appreciates the importance of understanding the context or background, indeed, the necessity of some understanding of the context to any interpretive attempts, including attempts, as in psychotherapy, to understand others. Sass (1988) has argued that from a hermeneutic perspec-

tive, interpersonal understanding does not depend on humanistically capturing the inner experiences of others, "it requires only the careful elucidation
and interpretation of shared and objectified forms" (p. 250). The notion of
dispensing with one's prejudices in an attempt to understand another is seen
by hermeneuts as "not only futile but even self-deluding" (p. 251) because
the foreknowledge that constitutes horizons is always present and is necessary to the act of interpretation. This productive view of understanding
means that the interpreter's prejudices, his or her sociocultural and historical
baggage, play a positive role in the fusion of horizons that is characteristic
of understanding.

Similarly, Sass (1988) has suggested that an appreciation of the "horizonal
non-transparency of human experience" (p. 262) also has implications for
how we understand one of the common outcomes of psychotherapy, conscious insight.

> The hermeneutic view of insight would see it as an exploratory,
> dialogic interpretive process in which therapist and patient play
> closely analogous roles—each in a nondogmatic way bringing to
> bear habitual preconceptions in order to illuminate meanings
> that lie, in a sense, not in the patient's mind but in the text-
> analogue they have before them, i.e., the patient's actions and
> reported experiences. A hermeneutic appreciation of the role of
> horizons also suggests that conscious insight is both more com-
> plex and potentially dangerous than it might otherwise seem.
> For, if insight thematizes what was previously horizonal, then it
> involves not just a discovery but also a radical transformation
> (and, possibly, an alienation) of what had previously been a taken-
> for-granted foundation for existence. (p. 262)

A hermeneutic approach to interpersonal understanding and insight in
psychotherapy thus emphasizes the importance of both therapists and clients
cultivating an openness to the life-world and one's being in it, a focus that
is more outward, in terms of its attention to context and to the shared
construction of meaning, than has been traditional in many forms of psychotherapy. It is through such openness that greater understanding of practical possibilities for exercising agency in relation to concerns is achieved.

Cushman (1995) has described the cultivation of this openness to the
life-world using a hermeneutically derived "horizon metaphor" (p. 302).
With this metaphor, Cushman wishes to emphasize that we each exist
within, and, indeed, conspire in creating, a particular clearing with a particular horizon that allows for particular things to be seen, that is, allows for
particular ways of being. Psychotherapy is about becoming aware of this
clearing and shifting its horizon such that different ways of feeling, behaving,
and thinking become possible. The core idea is that the psychotherapist can

assist clients to shift their horizons, thus creating clearings that allow for new perspectives, feelings, and actions. One might think of psychotherapists bringing to therapeutic conversations perspectives that are not yet available to their clients and inviting a collaborative interpretive dialogue that shifts both their own and their clients' horizons of intelligibility (cf. Martin & Dawda, 1999). From our perspective, part of what Cushman describes but does not name is the mostly invisible player in psychotherapy and psychology: human agency. Psychotherapy, to reinterpret Cushman's perspective, is about discovering and taking responsibility for how we have employed the limits and possibilities of our agency and about making informed decisions concerning how and when we can exercise it in the future, and with what results for ourselves and others. When we see our agency, we find ourselves in the clearing from which Cushman speaks: a clearing in which we recognize that, if we have agency, then we are capable of choosing and acting, and that our choices and actions carry with them personal moral responsibility for their impact.

Thus, our hermeneutic focus on sociocultural embeddedness and on moral questions and practicalities leads to a different, somewhat expanded notion of what is to be explored, understood, and interpreted through psychotherapeutic conversation. As Sass (1988) has suggested, a hermeneutic approach would lead to less exploration and interpretation of clients' unique and private subjectivities in order to make more room for exploration of moral and practical concerns such as "one's relationship to shared ethical norms, of the truth or adequacy of one's understanding of external social reality, and of the meaning, interpersonal impact and appropriateness of one's concrete actions in the world" (p. 262). Openness to exploring clients' problems in terms of their moral import would also lead to less focus on unquestioningly promoting the elimination of symptoms of distress and suffering by the most efficient means possible and to more consideration of understanding and interpreting the meaning and significance of distress and suffering. Consistent with our view of human agency, emphasis on volitional choice or human freedom would be balanced with a recognition that biological, cultural, and historical contexts are a part of the fabric of being rather than obstacles to self-fulfillment. Recognition of the nested reality in which human agency is situated would assist psychotherapists in identifying problems that might be better tackled through intervention, advocacy, or activism focused at the societal, cultural, economic, or political level.

Finally, our rejection of the tendency to treat human kinds as natural kinds, which involves assuming that they are amenable to being understood and manipulated through the application of reductive, scientistic theories, draws attention to two further aspects of psychotherapy's efforts to influence human agency. First, we hope that it draws attention to the tremendous complexity and difficulty of the task faced by psychotherapists—agency, in our view, is not malleable and manipulable through the application of facile, recipe-book interventions based on universal assumptions about human kinds. Second, we believe it draws attention to the potential value of "everyday" understandings of human experience—including those provided by individuals described as having common sense, wisdom, or maturity (not always experts, with the authority of scientific expertise) and those evident in great works of literature (rather than scientific, academic texts)—and to the means by which individuals arrive at such understandings.

THE EDUCATION OF PSYCHOTHERAPISTS

We began this reconceptualization of psychological practice by claiming that our conception of agency necessitates seeing clients' problems, theories about and treatments for those problems, and the training of psychological practitioners differently. What appears in the clearing created by our conception of agency is a picture of psychotherapy as a largely Western set of institutionalized helping practices intended to assist individuals with everyday practical, agentic, moral problems. Moreover, such helping practices make use of theories that, because they are situated, are necessarily local, moral, and interpretive. These are theories that have personal and interpersonal, as well as political, implications and consequences. So, how might we educate psychotherapists if we accept this characterization of psychotherapy? At the very least such education should include (a) a sustained critical analysis of psychotherapy (Woolfolk, 1998), (b) more educational breadth, and (c) more focus on the nature and development of practical wisdom.

Cushman (1995) has argued that the failure to historically situate psychological practices is due at least in part to psychotherapists' lack of training in philosophical and political analysis of the sort that would illuminate the many complex and subtle ways in which "social practices *inevitably* reproduce the status quo" (p. 248). Indeed, because we have accepted the view of psychotherapy as an applied science or a behavioral technology, the need for such education has simply not shown up in our clearing. Similarly, Fancher (1995) argues that current training models are overly focused on narrowly defined fields of knowledge and that "we expect far too little broader humane knowledge of health professionals" (p. 316). Therapists, he suggests, need significant knowledge of anthropology, evolutionary disciplines, social psychology, sociology, history, other cultures, philosophy, ethics, and religion. With "the lives of patients, which are themselves contextualized within a background of tacit knowledge" (Woolfolk, 1998, p. 115) as their subject matter, Woolfolk argues that psychotherapists must have tacit knowledge of the profession (including, e.g., knowledge about the craft of therapy) as well as tacit knowledge about tacit knowledge (e.g., knowledge about the cultural background and how it might affect an individual and knowledge about the ways of the world). The narrowly scientific research training of psychotherapists would also need to be reexamined, perhaps with the aim of developing interpretive skill (Packer & Addison, 1989), familiarity with and more use of methods and perspectives from the humanities (Sass, 1988), and with greater appreciation for the value of everyday understandings.

We are also sympathetic to the views of Woolfolk (1998) when he claims that psychotherapists are involved in the development and exercise of the Aristotelian virtue of phronesis. Phronesis is practical wisdom, which "involves grasping the particularities of a concrete, real world situation and ascertaining the means *and ends* appropriate to that situation" (p. 120). It is distinct from two other intellectual virtues: techne (technical skill), which involves competent use of a means to achieve preestablished ends, and episteme (scientific knowledge), which involves knowledge of universal laws. Techne and phronesis involve practical know-how or the application of general knowledge to particular situations. However, phronesis involves choosing both what means and what ends should be pursued, whereas techne involves the choice and application of means in situations in which the end is preassumed.

Woolfolk's (1998) analysis highlights the shortcomings of the scientist–practitioner model, which is based on the notion of psychotherapy as an applied science and which emphasizes techne (e.g., mastery of research and clinical skills) and episteme (e.g., mastery of theories) at the expense of phronesis. The scientist–practitioner model misses an important component if one accepts the argument that psychotherapy is an inherently moral enterprise. In the scientist–practitioner model, the ends are pre-assumed— existing as facts in psychological theories. However, from a hermeneutic perspective, such ends miss the mark because the theories from which they are derived do not recognize the moral nature of their assertions.

Fancher (1995) parallels Woolfolk's discussion of Aristotelian virtues through his assertion that clinicians can claim expertise over "knowing how" to be present to those in distress and how to apply relevant theory to particular cases. Clinicians do not, however, have a privileged knowledge base in "knowing what" is right or wrong or ill or healthy. Rather, schools of psychotherapy and their practitioners have "mistaken their cultural creations for natural facts" (p. 322). Although the adoption of a hermeneutic approach may lead psychotherapy to "lose . . . [its] grip on the powerful social status that is granted to scientific practices and theories" (Cushman, 1995, p. 249), there is also much to be gained by ceasing to insist that psychotherapy is an applied science in the manner of physical science.

Richardson et al. (1999) point out that a hermeneutic view of psychotherapy might better prepare therapists to deal with the inherently moral questions (e.g., deciding who and why to marry, whether to end a relationship, how to make sense of uncertainties and tragedies, and so forth) of their clients by making clear the inescapable nature of our social ties and obligations and by casting such obligations in a more positive light (as contrasted with seeing them mostly as impediments to individuation and autonomy).

A hermeneutic view of psychotherapy, with its emphasis on the interpretive nature of the enterprise, might also bridge the gap between practitioners and researchers (Packer & Addison, 1989). For example, the acknowledgment of the importance of phronesis would lend credibility to serious exploration of qualities such as clinical judgment, common sense, maturity, and character. Such "virtues" have long been of interest to psychotherapy educators when selecting and supervising students. However, their importance has been eclipsed and forced underground by what has been seen as a more appropriately "scientific" focus on "measurable" behaviors such as mastery of discrete counseling skills and strategies (techne), knowledge of a narrow, empirically derived literature (episteme), and so forth. Even though there certainly is nothing wrong with such foci, they are by themselves inadequate for the interpretation of agentic lives emergent within the historical, sociocultural life-world.

Thus concludes our example of how psychological practice might be reinterpreted to fit within the kind of socioculturally spawned, developmental theorizing that has typified our approach to human agency, and to psychological kinds in general. The third, and last section of this final chapter explores the possible relevance of our conception of agency to contemporary sociopolitical life in Western democracies. Such a concern may seem far removed from psychological research and practice and the struggles of disciplinary psychology to achieve a coherent conception of agency appropriate to its aspirations. Nonetheless, as theorists such as Cushman (1995) and Rose (1998) have argued, psychology has been instrumental in framing the ways in which contemporary Westerners think about themselves as individual persons. As such, it has been an influential source of those conceptions of personhood that animate much contemporary political theory and practice. According to Rose (1998) psychology has given us a psychologized conception of ourselves such that our "psychological being is now placed at the origin of all the activities of loving, desiring, speaking, laboring, sickening, and dying" (p. 197). Psychology has given an interiority to our conceptions of ourselves as psychological beings that flows from

> all those [psychological] projects which seek to know [persons] and act upon them in order to tell them their truth and make possible their improvement and their happiness. It is this being, whose invention is so recent yet so fundamental to our contemporary experience that we today seek to govern under the regulative ideal of freedom—an ideal that imposes as many burdens, anxieties, and divisions as it inspires projects of emancipation, and in the name of which we have come to authorize so many authorities to assist us in the project of being free from any authority but our own. (p. 197)

What Rose implies is that the impact of disciplinary psychology has been such that contemporary Westerners now demand a kind of governance at a societal level that seems consistent with a psychological view of themselves as radically free individuals capable of harnessing all of the powers of contemporary science and social science to enhance their freedom further. In short, disciplinary psychology has contributed instrumentally to the creation of an everyday psychological profile consistent with its own labored tacking between the poles of reductive scientism and mysteriously detached freedom.

What we want to do in what follows is illustrate the ways in which our conception of situated, emergent, and deliberative agency might animate a critical reformulation of two prominent contemporary political theories that have been animated by rather different conceptions of personhood. These are conceptions that, particularly in the case of contemporary neoliberalism, we understand to have been informed significantly by disciplinary and professional psychology in the general manner indicated by Rose (1998). Consequently, our discussion of contemporary liberalism and communitarianism in terms of the kinds of agents they assume is intended to be broadly illustrative of the sociocultural influence of disciplinary psychology and how such influence might be transformed under our conception of the situated, emergent, and deliberative agent.

THE SOCIOPOLITICAL CONSEQUENCES OF SITUATED, EMERGENT, AND DELIBERATIVE AGENCY

Since the seventeenth century, political theorists have been divided by two competing ontological commitments. On one side, political legitimacy is understood to issue from the separateness and independent agency of individuals. Under this construal, individuals constitute the most fundamental level of social and political analysis. Persons are conceived as rational beings capable of fashioning themselves and shaping their existence through autonomous acts of reflection. Societies and cultures are aggregates of individuals competitively or cooperatively pursuing their self-determined ends. The politics of individuality, as it has found expression in varieties of liberalism and libertarianism, is concerned largely with assuring the freedom in which individuals can exercise choice over their beliefs, values, and actions, and do so unencumbered by obligations not of their own choosing. To this end, adherents typically advocate for individual rights, limits on the authority of government, and the equality of all persons before the law. (As Rose [1998] convincingly argues, it is this kind of liberal individualism that currently benefits so much from the increasingly prevalent social impact of disciplinary psychology with respect to the kinds of persons we are and should strive to be.)

On the other side of the political divide, the social and cultural is regarded as ontologically prior to the individual. Individuality is conceived fundamentally as a social and historical inheritance rather than as an object of autonomous self-determination. Societies and cultures are not simply the contingent arrangements of independent presocial atoms but, rather, the enactment of relational practices that exert a constitutive force in the formation of persons and selves. In turn, the kinds of persons and selves that societies and cultures create act in ways that sustain the particular sociocultural practices and institutions by which they are created. In political philosophies such as communitarianism, socialism, Marxism, nationalism, and feminism, individuals are understood to be bound ineluctably to one another by language, belief, values, and obligations inherited from sociocultural traditions. Individuals are conceived as expressions of collective identity, shared moral goods, and public practices. In the politics of collectivity, bonds of association and responsibility take precedence over individual pursuits. Obviously, the impact of traditional disciplinary psychology is much less apparent with respect to the fostering of this kind of collective, socially constrained personhood. Nonetheless, as we described in chapter 2, current work in some postmodern and social constructionist psychologies certainly is consistent with a strongly socially determined agent.

As the history of ideas attests, from the self-certain ratiocinator of Descartes to the fragmented, unessentialized postmodern self, ontological presuppositions concerning agency and the constitution of persons and selves undergird the sociopolitical conditions advocated by different political philosophies. Although there is an important distinction to be made between ontology and advocacy, there appears to be no way of remaining ontologically agnostic about human agency or its disposition in the realm of political theory. The way in which agency, personhood, and selfhood are construed licenses certain sociopolitical possibilities over others. As Taylor (1995) explains, "Taking an ontological position does not amount to advocating something, but at the same time the ontological does help to define the options which it is meaningful to support by advocacy" (p. 183).

In what follows, we examine briefly liberal and communitarian sociopolitical views and discuss the possible relevance of our account of a developmentally emergent, situated agent capable of "self" understanding and self-determination to debates between liberals and communitarians. We wish to note that our purpose is not to explore these views in detail but to outline them sufficiently so that we might meaningfully discuss the position we advance within the context they provide.

LIBERALISM AND COMMUNITARIANISM

From its inception, liberal thought has been directed at two fundamental problems. One regards abuses of state power and encroachment of the state on individual liberty and self-determination. In ancient and medieval doctrines, persons were conceived of as essentially social beings who inherited obligations and roles from tradition, frequently including a duty of strict obedience to the authority of an absolute monarch and the church. Individuals' rights and obligations were enjoined by their particular position in a social hierarchy in relation to powers deemed absolute in authority. Early liberal thinkers disdained the servility, intolerance, civil and religious strife, corruption, and oppression that appeared to follow from the wide discretionary powers assumed and all too readily exercised by church and state. Contemporary liberals retain concerns about the reach of political power in individual life.

The second problem with which liberals are occupied stems from increasing recognition, developed over at least the last four centuries, of differences among persons with respect to their conceptions of the good life. It now is acknowledged that there exists a plurality of goods and ways of life that individuals may esteem and pursue and that they reasonably may disagree over the relative merits of such goods and lifestyles. In this context the problem becomes how to specify the terms and conditions of political association that permit peaceful coexistence.

The remedy liberals prescribe for the first problem is to wrest authority for individual self-determination from the state and delegate it to individuals themselves. To limit potential for political coercion, liberals argue that the state must remain neutral with respect to notions of the good life. A liberal polity does not presuppose or promote any particular ends or goods but grants as much latitude as possible to individuals to formulate and pursue their own conceptions. Connectedly, the remedy to the second problem is to provide terms of association that as many people as possible can abide, despite inevitable differences concerning the worth of goods and ways of life. To this end, liberals have attempted to articulate neutral, impersonal principles that are intended to avoid countenancing any particular goods or ways of life over others. Tolerance, fairness, and pluralism are advanced as neutral principles from which procedures can be derived for minimizing conflict and maximizing individual freedom.

The framework of justice advanced by contemporary liberals asserts priority of the right over the good. In principle, no one individual's rights may be subordinated to a state-imposed common good. There are notable and nuanced contrasts among contemporary liberal theorists, in the emphasis accorded particular principles. For example, some theorists, such as Ronald Dworkin (1977), emphasize rights as "trumps" that individuals hold against state power, while others, such as Robert Nozick (1974), assert that market mechanisms and property rights can be used to prevent intrusion by the state. Nonetheless, liberal theorists are united in championing state neutrality and a procedural republic committed to rights while, at the same time, remaining purposefully uncommitted to any specific goods. Moreover, liberals are joined by another common thread; namely, their convictions about human agency and the constitution of self.

Liberal politics follow from an ontological view of humans as radically autonomous individual selves. Behind a liberal polity is a human agency that can take charge of its own life by virtue of its ability to deliberate, make choices, and execute actions according to its own self-chosen reasons and values. The liberal self is an independent agent capable of self-legislation. State neutrality and a procedural republic are intended to accommodate such selves. These kinds of conditions correspond with a conception of selves as essentially autonomous agents, unencumbered by traditions and capable of independently seeking their own goods and authoring their lives as they see fit.

Central to liberal doctrine is the ontological claim that the self is not constituted by any of the particular identifications, ends, or attachments it chooses but by its fundamental capacity to make choices. This is the import of John Rawls's (1971) oft-cited formulation that "the self is prior to the ends which are affirmed by it" (p. 560). Our various identifications, ends, values, and attachments issue from an agency that comes already equipped to choose. For liberals, the just political order is one that secures conditions for the possibility of individuality in a manner that accords with this ontology of individual being. The liberal political order supports the notion of a self that manifests its essential nature through choice. But there is something else at stake here. Liberalism presents a possibility for being—a certain conception of ourselves as human agents—such that we endorse liberal political arrangements and voluntary associations as consistent with a liberal understanding of self. This is why one of the foremost communitarian critics of liberalism, Michael Sandel (1984), states that liberalism "has a deep and powerful appeal" in our contemporary, psychologically minded society, and that "it is our vision, the theory most thoroughly embodied in the practices and institutions most central to our public life" (p. 82).

The communitarian movement in political theory has arisen as an effort to redress what many regard as deficiencies of modern liberalism. (See Stephen Mulhall and Adam Swift [1996] and Shlomo Avineri and Avner De-Shalit [1992] for overviews of the debates between communitarians and liberals and summaries of works of the major contributors.) The main thrust of the communitarian critique is that the individualism on which liberal theory is founded provides an illusory and untenable conception of the self. Liberal preoccupation with exalting individual liberty comes at the sacrifice of values and bonds that are intrinsic to, and constitutive of, both individual and collective life. Communitarians object to the liberal notion of agents as socially independent atoms who enter into relationships and entertain obligations only if and when it suits them.

According to communitarians, the liberal interpretation not only obfuscates deep and important communal ties and relations but works invidiously to undermine and dissolve them. The ideal liberal self is completely unencumbered by any reliance on, or attachment to, others. It is a radically autonomous, rational chooser. Such a vision demands an idea of human agency that is abstracted from the vicissitudes of history, culture, language, and experience. It is to suggest that human beings can be understood without knowing anything whatsoever about their goods, aims, values, terms of expression, and those of their forebears. Communitarians ask, in the absence of these features, what is left to understand? They charge that it is fantasy to suggest that the multifarious values, ends, goods, and attachments with which individuals identify, and which can be attributed to the character of their sociocultural and communal involvements, are entirely contingent and can be shed through rational reflection. Consequently, Sandel (1982) characterizes the liberal attempt to bracket substantive moral concerns and sociocultural commitments and involvements as a "thin" rendering of persons and selves.

In the communitarian view, our individuality cannot be understood as prior to, or apart from, the social, cultural, historical, and communal bonds that preexist us and into which we are born. Communitarians argue that the values, ends, and goods sustained by communal practices and adopted by individuals are constitutive. They constitute the individual's understanding of himself or herself. The moral goods and ends by which we live define us as the persons and selves we are. We depend on our communal attachments for the very ways in which we think, including the ways in which we think of ourselves as individuals. In contrast to the liberal self, the communitarian self is thickly constituted and considers not only what it wants but who it is. Communitarians claim that our choices always are contextualized by a sense of identity, and our identities, in turn, are interwoven with obligations and allegiances that are part of a sociocultural inheritance. In this light, an understanding of oneself can be achieved only by reference to a community of others.

Communitarians, of course, do more than subscribe to an account of persons and selves that stands in contradistinction to liberal individualism. Their idea of community also departs from the liberal view. From the communitarian perspective, community is not an aggregate of instrumental associations among autonomous individuals. Rather, it is a unity to which individuals belong. Drawing on Jean-Jacques Rousseau and Georg Hegel, communitarians frequently make use of the organic metaphor in understanding community. For many communitarians, community is a collective body that manifests a unified will and coheres in a shared moral orientation and set of intrinsic values. Communitarians grant that individuals are likely to differ with respect to particular judgments. Nonetheless, even in disagreement, members of a community retain a basic commitment to terms of reference, norms, values, and the moral framework that undergirds and organizes communal life. The fact that disagreements can be articulated, understood, and occasionally resolved by disputing parties depends on shared traditions of language and argumentation.

Some communitarians, notably Michael Walzer (1983), contend that the specific features of cultural traditions are vital to any claims concerning the way in which a community should order itself. Communitarians insist that because individuals are constituted by their sociality and facticity any proposals about justice or political right can make sense only in the context of shared understandings and practices that comprise a particular way of life. Communitarians assert that the major implication of a socioculturally and historically informed ontology is a politics that affirms the values of community over the values of individuality. They argue that if community has ontological priority, then it also must have moral priority. Even though communitarianism comprises a broad spectrum of thought, communitarians tend to advocate a politics in which the common good supersedes individual rights—a politics that advocates commitment to, and participation in, community life.

Liberals respond to communitarian critics on a number of fronts (Etzioni, 1996). They allege that communitarianism opens the door to a majoritarian politics, and that majoritarianism is simply an expression of mass opinion concerning values. Liberals admonish communitarians for underestimating the extent of disagreements and conflicts of interest and belief and warn that communitarian appeals to consensus and tradition could be used for purposes of coercion and the subjugation of individuals to state interests (Fairfield, 2000). Further, although communitarians have provided much criticism regarding liberals' adherence to ontological individualism, they have not been forthcoming with a clear account of what is meant by "community," nor have they articulated specifically what the common good or goods of the contemporary sociopolitical context ought to be. Wilfred McClay (1998) alleges that in the absence of any compelling proposal, talk of "community" has become "a form of mood music" (p. 101), lulling us with vague sentimentality into overlooking the more detestable aspects of our communal practices, organizations, and institutions.

The Political Disposition of a Situated, Emergent, and Deliberative Agency

We now turn to some features of our account of a developmentally emergent, situated agent capable of "self" understanding that might be used to cast light on the disposition of such an agency with respect to a collective politics. It is not our intention to venture deeply into the domain of political advocacy but to mention some potential contributions our arguments for the irreducibility of agency and conception of self as a kind of understanding might make to liberal and communitarian conversations.

To begin, the notion of a developmentally emergent, situated agent capable of "self" understanding and self-determination can be used as a corrective to the abstracted, unencumbered, radically independent self on which liberalism has been fashioned. In this sense, our prescription for liberalism closely parallels our prescription for psychotherapy. The interests of individuals are never simply individual interests; they always are embedded and emerge from within an inescapable background of normative, sociocultural, and historical perspectives. Nor are our interests, and ability to choose from among them, simply given. They develop and change as our capacity to reflect and understand develops and changes. So long as the developmental context is ignored and the individual is conceived as an ontologically prior, rational chooser with fixed boundaries and an autonomous essence, liberalism will be susceptible to communitarian challenges that it falters on ontological grounds.

We believe our account of self as a kind of developmentally emergent understanding that discloses and extends particular being provides a plausible alternative to the ahistorical, asocial, essentialist, and individualist ontological interpretation of self. Our notion of self as a kind of understanding is predicated on assumptions that are existential, not essential. The actual forms and content of self are historically contingent and socioculturally constituted. As a result, selves are not pre-given and static but emergent and continuously dynamic in their realization within communal traditions of living.

At the same time, assuming that humans only acquire their goods, ends, and identities from appropriating traditions can entail a kind of sociocultural reductionism that narrows the self and human agency in ways that also are mistaken (see chapter 2). As a corrective, our account achieves a viable conception of an irreducible human agency. As we have elaborated, with the development of reflexivity, the nature of human experience and activity shifts from unmediated and prereflective to mediated and reflective. Human agents are underdetermined in that they can reflect on their lives and circumstances in ways that enable them, at least potentially, to move mildly beyond extant traditions. Once again, our thesis of underdetermination holds that while psychologically capable agents have their origins in their sociocultural embeddedness, once emergent in the manner we have described, they no longer can be reduced to their biological and sociocultural origins, even though they continue to be affected by their biological bodies and the sociocultural contexts in which they live and act.

Claims similar to our thesis of underdetermination recently have been made by Paul Fairfield (2000) in his attempt to resuscitate liberal theory. According to Fairfield, the task facing contemporary liberals is to recognize the historical and sociocultural constitution of self while preserving the liberal tradition's commitment to instituting conditions that facilitate and protect individual liberty and self-determination. Fairfield accepts much of the communitarian critique but argues that liberals can shed the "metaphysical embarrassment" of ontological individualism without jettisoning the principles of liberal politics. Crucial to Fairfield's argument is his "revisability thesis," which also underscores the underdetermination of self:

[M]oral agents, while situated beings with situated capacities, are nonetheless capable of revising their moral ends, questioning convention, reasoning about norms, reflecting on practices, refashioning their identity, reconstituting traditions, and unseating consensus. . . . [E]ach of these capacities, like all human capacities, is finite yet sufficiently robust as to make it possible for individuals to revise the ends that they inherit from tradition. . . . Persons are social yet separate beings. They are factical selves, yet their facticity underdetermines their being. (p. 129)

Fairfield (2000) argues that what is needed to rehabilitate liberalism is a conception of rational deliberation that situates the human ability for critical reflection within both an underdetermined agency and the modes and traditions of understanding with which critical reflection is accomplished. Our account of a situated, emergent, and deliberative agency asserts that the sort of reasoning of which human agents are capable is not a purely procedural and rule-governed instrumental activity that somehow is given antecedently to sociocultural and historical contexts. In light of the developmental framework we have described, our reasons for judging and acting come largely from our having been initiated into a life-world comprised not only of means and practices for reflection but also of goods and ends that contribute substance and direction to our deliberations. This sociocultural and historical life-world, replete with meanings and significances, is an ever-present tacit background to all our attempts to deliberate and understand.

At the center of human deliberations is care, or concern for self. Without constitutive concerns, it is difficult to comprehend the position from which any deliberation could take place, let alone any purpose for the developmental emergence of human capacities for mediated, reflective deliberation. In contrast to a view of deliberation that hinges on instrumental rationality, we pose our conception of understanding. Individuals deliberate and exercise choice not simply for the instrumental gratification of desires but to create possibilities for an existence that is both meaningfully connected to the life-world and something of their own agentic making. The development of a capacity for reflective, explicit understanding makes it possible for us to achieve some measure of critical distance from tradition and, in so doing, critique and revise our practices, ends, and, inevitably, ourselves. The fact that in daily life we continually are faced with normative considerations implies not only the possibility of second-order alteration of immediate inclinations but also that some measure of self-transformation is possible. From this perspective, it indeed may not be necessary for liberals to abandon completely their political agenda if at the root of liberal politics is not the ideal of a transcendent, rational chooser but self as a possibility rendered by the developmental emergence of a psychologically capable human agency.

What we humans share in common is not a definable essence or discoverable "nature" but the existential condition of thrownness (Heidegger, 1927/1962). This is the starting point for construing our political and ethical involvements. The emergence of self as a kind of understanding that discloses and extends particular individual being depends on language and relational practices, institutions, and other contingencies that situate us within culture and history. These traditions of living are suffused with at least some minimal agreement about what kinds of life are worth living and how we ought to go about dealing with others. The implication of thrownness is that we already are constituted by politics and ethics long before we become capable of reflecting on them. At least since Plato, it has been recognized that political institutions are culpable for prescriptive, formative practices of "soulcraft." Yet theorists often have overlooked the prereflective engagement that precedes the developmental emergence of abstract reflection. In light of our thrownness, the issue is not whether we are ethically or politically situated but what our ethical and political commitments should be.

However, traditions of living are best seen as a seeding of possibilities. The situated development of "self" understanding also is largely a matter of agency. "Self" understanding is being asserting itself as a subject of action. It is not simply an autobiographical collection of interpretations that have accumulated over time. It reflects the self-identified, self-chosen, and self-executed actions of a human agency. Our account of the irreducibility of agency gives some currency to the notion of persons as morally accountable. This moral accountability is not founded in the fiction of an a priori sovereign autonomy but the developmental emergence of a situated, deliberative agency capable of understanding. As we have argued, psychological agents are dynamically emergent and underdetermined by any fixed physical, biological, sociocultural, or psychological essence. Seeing ourselves as situated agents, but, importantly, in nonessentialist terms, is to reject all ontological reductions of agency. It is to spurn the sort of misbegotten apologia increasingly being heard and given credence in our public institutions that attribute the sole cause of an individual's actions—from marriage to murder—to inescapable genetic, sociocultural, environmental, or evolutionary scripts.

Our antireductionistic arguments go further in their ethical force. They speak against those reductions of agentic action and capability to race, ethnicity, gender, class, or other categorizations of persons that have been implicated in so many inequities and atrocities. Although classifications of these kinds figure dominantly in our identities and "self" understandings, even indispensably so, they are not grounds for substantive reductions that would dismiss or unnecessarily restrict agentic possibilities for understanding and action. (Interested readers may want to note for themselves similarities and differences between what we say here and attempts by some postmodern thinkers, such as Ernesto Laclau and Chantal Mouffe [1985] to fashion a radically democratic strategy for conceptualizing social action in a world without clear foundations.) The notion of a developmentally emergent, situated agent capable of "self" understanding suggests that ethical and political beliefs and ideals need not sacrifice individual differences in the name of communal solidarity nor be limited to them under the banner of individual autonomy. At the same time, it insinuates ethical warrants for strongly rejecting some kinds of discourse.

Communitarians rightly criticize liberals for an account of deliberation that, ideally conceived, is sanitized of all personal and collective goods. However, this criticism rebounds as a problem for communitarians in the absence of explicit formulations of common goods for contemporary sociopolitical arrangements that could supplant those based on individualism. Our conception of self as a kind of developmentally emergent understanding may help to illuminate the kinds of goods that meaningfully connect individuals to their communities and provide impetus for the sorts of communal involvements and commitments to social and cultural institutions that communitarians seek to encourage. Perhaps understanding, conceived as an opening of possibilities, not only constitutes the disposition of self but functions as a constitutive common good that implicitly binds individuals to their communities.

As an example, nowhere may this way of thinking have more applicability than with respect to education. If it is to operate optimally as a situated, agentic understanding that opens possibilities for particular being, self (as formulated herein) must not be unduly restricted by cultural narrowness or enforced ignorance that may stem from highly dysfunctional or impoverished interpersonal and/or economic niches within a given society. If unduly shackled in such ways, self-understanding cannot achieve those feats of socially spawned, yet potentially transforming, imagination and projection so essential for a satisfying personal life and a progressive, collective polity. Given the central importance of relational practices, especially dialogue, to such a self, conversational virtues and principles such as freedom of expression, tolerance, civility, open-minded critique, and plurality must be allowed purchase as political, educational conditions for peaceful communal accommodation and personal agency. Only in this way can a desired balance be achieved between self-development and self-restraint in relation to a common welfare.

Clearly, the sort of communal participation and commitment that communitarians have in mind is not undertaken purely in the interests of private gain. Placing the good of the community before that of the individual entails a certain measure of good will in decisions and actions that affect not only one's own life but the lives and futures of others, as well as that of the community as a whole. This particularly is the case if one is concerned with creating conditions directed at enhancing developmental and educational opportunities for increasingly sophisticated capacities for language and thought and expanding possibilities for understanding.

In such a context, deliberation takes place not instrumentally from static principles and procedures but within a mutable, dynamic sphere of perspectives that encompasses each issue, within which participants, through dialogue, may genuinely attempt to understand each others' perspectives. This kind of communal participation and commitment provides possibilities for interpreting and considering other perspectives and ways of life that may be unfamiliar and for incorporating them into one's own worldview. The good becomes the engagement of others as a way of opening and expanding one's own understanding, thereby transforming oneself and potentially transforming the community. In turn, the development of a more differentiated and sophisticated outlook joined with the broader concerns not only of one's own community but of other cultures and the past engenders more and varied opportunities for continued and sustained development. We are convinced that the disposition and goods to which we are alluding are hermeneutic as described in the work of some contemporary hermeneuts such as those we have mentioned (Cushman, 1995; Kögler, 1996; Richardson et al., 1999; Woolfolk, 1998—also see Martin & Sugarman, 2001).

Any notion of political order inevitably embodies certain ontological assumptions about human possibility. We submit that possibilities for individual and collective being are rooted in agentic understanding. It is in understanding and its instantiation in individual and collective projects that the interests of self and community may converge. Admittedly, this faint gesture toward agentic understanding as a constitutive good leaves much unexplored. Nonetheless, it does hint at a possible bridging of liberal and communitarian politics in which the cultivation of certain conditions and requirements basic to the common good, also may further a certain kind of self-determination and self-development.

In this final chapter, we have attempted to indicate the kinds of difference that adoption of our theory of situated, emergent, and deliberative agency might make to psychological research and practice and to the general influence that psychology does and might exert on contemporary sociopolitical life in the Western world. Such possibilities are admittedly speculative, but our intention in offering them is to indicate why conceptions of agency matter—that is, why they should be of concern to psychologists. Our own conclusion is that if psychology is to achieve an overall coherence in its scholarly, research, and professional pronouncements and impact, one of the undertakings it must successfully achieve is a defensible articulation of human agency. After all, psychology is concerned with human actions and experiences, which are agentic kinds. And as we consistently have argued, agentic, psychological kinds require modes of inquiry that must go beyond those available in the physical and biological sciences alone. Psychological kinds are meaningful and significant because they are embedded in historical and sociocultural traditions of living. It is within such a life-world that human biological individuals emerge as psychological agents. And both the sociocultural practices constitutive of agents and the psychological kinds that make up the in-the-world activity of agents require forms of interpretive consideration and study that go well beyond the methods of physical science.

To ignore these realities and to persist in treating psychological kinds solely with the methods of reductive, physical science is to engage in a kind of scientism. This is a scientism that treats physical scientific understanding as the most important and fundamental kind of human understanding and insists on the application of the methods of physical science beyond those matters and questions for which they are appropriate. On the other hand, to fail to recognize that human psychological reality is determined in large part by sociocultural practices and both enabled and constrained by physical and biological levels of reality is to embrace a kind of obscurantism. This is an obscurantism that frequently manifests in mysteriously detached forms of radical human freedom that somehow place human beings as psychological agents beyond the reach of any kind of systematic human inquiry. What we have attempted to offer is a path between the excesses of scientism on the one hand and obscurantism on the other hand.

A CONCLUDING COMMENT

In his famous Rede lecture, delivered in the Senate House in Cambridge, England on May 7, 1959, C. P. Snow (1959/1998) diagnosed much of the modern cultural malaise of Western civilization as emanating from the loss of a common scientific, intellectual culture. According to Snow, the problem is that educated persons have divided themselves into two opposing camps of scientists and what he called "literary intellectuals." That these camps actually constitute two distinctive cultures is attested to by the fact that they appear to share very few assumptions concerning what is most important and potentially informative with respect to conceptions of what it is to be human and of how to inquire into human life and circumstances. The resulting polarization of worldviews means that persons educated with great intensity cannot communicate across their background beliefs and commitments, which leads to a serious reduction in our collective creative capacity to confront contemporary concerns, to learn from the past, and to anticipate the future.

More recently, Simon Critchley (2001) has revisited Snow's dilemma in a manner closely connected to the general and specific concerns with which we have been engaged in this volume. Although Critchley applies the distinctions he draws to disagreements between Anglo American analytic and Continental philosophy, much of what he says applies equally well to disputations between scientifically minded psychologists and more romantically minded psychological practitioners.

> On the one hand, there is a risk of obscurantism . . . where social [and psychological] phenomena are explicated with reference to

forces, entities, and categories so vast and vague as to explain everything and nothing at all. . . . Any aspect of personal and public life might be seen as evidence of the disciplinary matrices of power, the disintegration of the "Big Other" and the trauma of the real, the multiple becomings of the body without organs, or whatever. . . . But, on the other side of my mini-pathology, there is the risk of a chronic scientism. . . . The assumption of such scientistic approaches is that there is a gap that can be closed through a better empirical explanation. (pp. 119–120)

Critchley goes on to say that in his own view the real gap is between knowledge and wisdom and that such a gap cannot be closed through empirical inquiry because the meaning of life is not reducible to empirical inquiry. For Critchley, the felt gap between knowledge and wisdom is "the very space of critical reflection" (p. 120), and that in cultural life we need to "clip the wings of both scientism and obscurantism" (p. 120).

With respect to human agency, we believe that Critchley's (2001) injunction may best be served by a refusal to reduce our everyday experiences to physical kinds alone, for seemingly no better reason than that it is at the physical level of reality that modern science has proven to be so very successful. There simply is no point in such a reduction if what is reduced is lost in the reductive process. In psychology, we must deal with agentic kinds. Such kinds differ from physical kinds in important ways. There is simply no adequate physical description of agency (including intentionality, first-person perspectivity, normativity, and rationality) because agency is emergent and socioculturally constituted, even though it obviously requires relevant biological and physical levels of reality. One may as well seek the physical–chemical formulae for conversation and history as an adequate physical reduction of human agency. For all of its very obvious strengths and accomplishments, physical science has clear limitations in the arena of human sociocultural and psychological activity. To understand such activity, especially the subset of agentic activity within it, one must adopt developmental conceptualizations and inquiry strategies. Such strategies are as concerned with the evolution of sociocultural, linguistic practices (including agentic contributions to such evolution) as with the evolution of biological features and kinds within the ever-present demands and constraints of the physical world.

In her most recent novel, Jill Paton Walsh (2000) describes a scene in which a formerly aristocratic mother is reunited with her Communist daughter immediately following the collapse of Soviet Communism in Eastern Europe. The two women are surveying and discussing the physical and psychological damage inflicted on their homeland during the past several decades. In response to the mother's entreaty to "Just look at it, just look what you have done," the daughter replies, "But is this what we have done, or is it what happened to us?" (p. 326). Physical kinds are not similarly concerned.

REFERENCES

Allport, G. W. (1935). Attitudes. In C. Murchison (Ed.), *A handbook of social psychology* (pp. 798–844). New York: Russell & Russell.

Angell, J. R. (1913). Behavior as a category in psychology. *Psychological Review, 20,* 255–270.

Aristotle. (1953). *The ethics of Aristotle: The Nicomachean ethics* (J. A. K. Thomson, Trans.). Harmondsworth, England: Penguin. (Original work published *ca.* 350 B.C.E.)

Audi, R. (Ed.). (1999). *The Cambridge dictionary of philosophy* (2nd ed.). Cambridge, England: Cambridge University Press.

Austin, J. L. (1966). Ifs and cans. In B. Berofsky (Ed.), *Liberation from self* (pp. 295–321). Cambridge, England: Cambridge University Press.

Avineri, S., & De-Shalit, A. (1992). *Communitarianism and individualism.* Oxford, England: Oxford University Press.

Bakan, D. (1966). *The duality of human existence: Isolation and communion in Western man.* Boston: Beacon.

Bandura, A. (1986). *Social foundations of thought and action: A social cognitive theory.* Englewood Cliffs, NJ: Prentice-Hall.

Bandura, A. (1995). Exercise of personal and collective efficacy in changing societies. In A. Bandura (Ed.), *Self-efficacy in changing societies* (pp. 1–45). Cambridge, England: Cambridge University Press.

Bandura, A. (1997). *Self-efficacy: The exercise of control.* New York: Freeman.

Bandura, A. (2001). Social-cognitive theory: An agentic perspective. *Annual Review of Psychology, 52,* 1–26.

Barone, D. F., Maddux, J. E., & Snyder, C. R. (1997). *Social cognitive psychology: History and current domains.* New York: Plenum.

Bechtel, W. (1988). *Philosophy of mind: An overview for cognitive science.* Hillsdale, NJ: Erlbaum.

Berlin, I. (1970). *Four essays on liberty.* New York: Oxford University Press.

Bidell, T. R., & Fischer, K. W. (1997). Between nature and nurture: The role of human agency in the epigenesis of intelligence (pp. 193–242). In R. J. Sternberg & E. L. Grigorenko (Eds.), *Intelligence, heredity, and environment.* New York: Cambridge University Press.

Bowman, M. (1997). *Individual differences in posttraumatic response: Problems with the adversity-distress connection.* Mahwah, NJ: Erlbaum.

Bradley, F. H. (1927). *Ethical studies*. Oxford, England: Oxford University Press.

Brandtstädter, J., & Lerner, R. M. (1999). Introduction: Development, action, and intentionality. In J. Brandtstädter & R. M. Lerner (Eds.), *Action and self-development: Theory and research through the life span* (pp. ix–xx). Thousand Oaks, CA: Sage.

Bridgman, P.W. (1952). *The nature of some of our physical concepts*. New York: Philosophical Library.

Bruner, J. S. (1986). *Actual minds, possible worlds*. Cambridge, MA: Harvard University Press.

Bruner, J. S. (1990). *Acts of meaning*. Cambridge, MA: Harvard University Press.

Budwig, N. (1995). *A developmental–functionalist approach to child language*. Hillsdale, NJ: Erlbaum.

Bunge, M. (1977). Emergence and the mind. *Neuroscience, 2,* 501–509.

Burwood, S., Gilbert, P., & Lennon, K. (1999). *Philosophy of mind*. Montreal, Quebec: McGill–Queens University Press.

Butler, J. (1997). *The psychic life of power*. Stanford, CA: Stanford University Press.

Carver, C. S., & Scheier, M. F. (1998). *On the self-regulation of behavior*. New York: Cambridge University Press.

Churchland, P. M. (1981). Eliminative materialism and the propositional attitudes. *Journal of Philosophy, 78,* 67–90.

Cohen, J. (1994). The earth is round ($p < .05$). *American Psychologist, 49,* 997–1003.

Critchley, S. (2001). *Continental philosophy: A very short introduction*. Oxford, England: Oxford University Press.

Cushman, P. (1995). *Constructing the self, constructing America: A cultural history of psychotherapy*. Reading, MA: Addison-Wesley.

Danziger, K. (1990). *Constructing the subject: Historical origins of psychological research*. Cambridge, England: University of Cambridge Press.

Danziger, K. (1997). *Naming the mind: How psychology found its language*.Thousand Oaks, CA: Sage.

Danziger, K. (1998). The historical formation of selves. In R. D. Ashmore & L. Jussim (Eds.), *Self and identity: Fundamental issues*. New York: Oxford University Press.

Davidson, D. (1985). Replies. In B.Vermazen & M. Hintikka (Eds.), *Essays on Davidson: Actions and events*. Oxford, England: Oxford University Press.

Dawda, D., & Martin, J. (2001). Psychologists on psychology: Inquiry beliefs of psychologists by subdiscipline, gender, and age. *Review of General Psychology, 5,* 163–179.

Degrandpre, R. J. (2000). A science of meaning: Can behaviorism bring meaning to psychological science.? *American Psychologist, 55,* 721–739.

Dennett, D. (1995). On giving libertarians what they say they want. In T. O'Connor (Ed.), *Agents, causes, and events: Essays on indeterminism and free will* (pp. 43–56). New York: Oxford University Press.

Dilthey, W. (1977). *Descriptive psychology and historical understanding* (R. M. Zaner & K. L. Heiges, Trans.). The Hague, Netherlands: Martinus Nijhoff. (Original works published 1894 and 1927)

Dworkin, R. (1977). *Taking rights seriously*. Cambridge, MA: Harvard University Press.

Edelman, G. M. (1987). *Neural Darwinism*. New York: Basic Books.

Emirbayer, M., & Mische, A. (1998).What is agency? *American Journal of Sociology, 103,* 962–1023.

Epictetus. (1983). *Handbook of Epictetus* (N. White, Intro. & Trans.). Indianapolis, IN: Hackett.

Etzioni, A. (1996). A moderate communitarian proposal. *Political Theory, 24,* 155–171.

Fairfield, P. (2000). *Moral selfhood in the liberal tradition.* Toronto, Ontario: University of Toronto Press.

Fallon, D. (1992). An existential look at B. F. Skinner. *American Psychologist, 47,* 1433–1440.

Fancher, R. (1995). *Cultures of healing: Correcting the image of American mental health care.* New York: Freeman.

Fay, B. (1996). *Contemporary philosophy of social science: A multicultural approach.* Cambridge, MA: Basil Blackwell.

Fischer, J. M. (1994). *The metaphysics of free will: A study of control.* Oxford, England: Basil Blackwell.

Fonagy, P., Steele, H., & Steele, M. (1991). Maternal representations of attachment during pregnancy predict the organization of infant–mother attachment at one year of age. *Child Development, 62,* 891–905.

Fowers, B. J. (2000, August). *Human agency, character, and the good life.* Paper presented at the annual meeting of the American Psychological Association, Washington, DC.

Frankfurt, H. G. (1971). Freedom of the will and the concept of a person. *Journal of Philosophy, 68,* 5–20.

Gadamer, H.-G. (1995). *Truth and method* (J. Weinsheimer & D. G. Marshall, Trans.) (2nd rev. ed.). New York: Continuum. (Original work published 1960)

Galton, F. (1908). *Memories of my life.* London: Methuen.

Gergen, K. J. (1991). *The saturated self.* New York: Basic Books.

Gergen, K. J. (1994). *Realities and relationships.* Cambridge, MA: Harvard University Press.

Gergen, K. J. (1997). The place of the psyche in a constructed world. *Theory and Psychology, 7,* 723–746.

Giorgi, A. (Ed.). (1985). *Phenomenology and psychological research.* Pittsburgh, PA: Duquesne University Press.

Glover, J. A., & Ronning, R. R. (Eds.). (1987). *Historical foundations of educational psychology.* New York: Plenum.

Gottlieb, G. (1992). *Individual development and evolution: The genesis of novel behavior.* New York: Oxford University Press.

Greenwood, J. D. (1991). *Relations and representations: An introduction to the philosophy of social psychological science.* New York: Routledge.

Guignon, C. B. (1983). *Heidegger and the problem of knowledge.* Indianapolis, IN: Hackett.

Guignon, C. B. (1991). Pragmatism or hermeneutics? Epistemology after foundationalism. In D. R. Hiley, J. F. Bohman, & R. Shusterman (Eds.), *The interpretive turn: Philosophy, science, culture* (pp. 81–101). Ithaca, NY: Cornell University Press.

Hacking, I. (1995). The looping effect of human kinds. In D. Sperber, D. Premack, & A. J. Premack (Eds.), *Causal cognition: A multi-disciplinary approach* (pp. 351–383). Oxford, England: Clarendon.

Hacking, I. (1999). *The social construction of what?* Cambridge, MA: Harvard University Press.

Hanson, N. R. (1958). *Patterns of discovery.* Cambridge, England: Cambridge University Press.

Hare-Mustin, R. T., & Marecek, J. (1990). *Making a difference: Psychology and the construction of gender.* New Haven, CT: Yale University Press.

Harré, R. (1983). *Personal being: A theory for individual psychology.* Oxford, England: Basil Blackwell.

Harré, R. (1995). The necessity of personhood as embodied being. *Theory and Psychology, 5,* 369–373.

Harré, R. (1998). *The singular self: An introduction to the psychology of personhood.* Thousand Oaks, CA: Sage.

Harré, R., & Gillet, G. (1994). *The discursive mind.* Thousand Oaks, CA: Sage.

Harré R., & Krausz, M. (1996). *Varieties of relativism.* Oxford, England: Basil Blackwell.

Haug, W. (1986). *Critique of commodity aesthetics.* Cambridge, England: Polity.

Hegelson, V. S. (1994). Relation of agency and communion to well-being: Evidence and potential explanations. *Psychological Bulletin, 116,* 412–428.

Heidegger, M. (1962). *Being and time* (J. Macquarrie & E. Robinson, Trans.). New York: Harper & Row. (Original work published in 1927)

Heidegger, M. (1982). *The basic problems of phenomenology* (A. Hofstadter, Trans.). Bloomington: Indiana University Press.

Higgins, E. T. (1988). Development of self-regulatory and self-evaluative processes: Costs, benefits, and trade-offs. In M. R. Gunnar & L. A. Sroufe (Eds.), *Minnesota Symposium on Child Psychology: Vol. 23. Self processes in development* (pp. 125–165). Minneapolis: University of Minnesota Press.

Hobbes, T. (1962). *The English works of Thomas Hobbes* Vol. 1 (W. Molesworth, Ed.). London: Scientia Aalen.

Holiday, A. (1988). *Moral powers.* Brighton, England: Harvester.

Honderich, T. (1988). *The consequences of determinism.* Oxford, England: Oxford University Press.

Horgan, T., & Tienson, J. (1996). *Connectionism and the philosophy of psychology.* Cambridge, MA: MIT Press.

Howard, G. (1993). Steps toward a science of free will. *Counseling and Values, 37,* 116–128.

Howard, G. (Ed.). (1994). Freewill and psychology [Special issue]. *Journal of Theoretical and Philosophical Psychology, 14,* 1–101.

Hudson, L. (1975). *Human beings: The psychology of human experience.* Garden City, NY: Anchor.

Jackson, F. (1996). *Philosophy of mind and cognition.* Oxford, England: Basil Blackwell.

James, W. (1909). The dilemma of determinism. In W. James, *The will to believe and other essays.* New York: Longman.

Jenkins, A. H. (1997). Free will and psychotherapy: The enhancement of agency. *Journal of Theoretical and Philosophical Psychology, 17,* 1–12.

Jennings, H. S. (1962). *Behavior of the lower organisms.* Bloomington: Indiana University Press. (Original work published 1906)

Jensen, J. P., Bergin, A. E., & Greaves, D. W. (1990). The meaning of eclecticism: New survey and analysis of components. *Professional Psychology: Research and Practice, 21,* 124–130.

Kagan, J. (1984). *The nature of the child.* New York: Basic Books.

Kane, R. (1998). *The significance of free will.* New York: Oxford University Press.

Kane, R. (2002). Free will, determinism, and indeterminism. In H. Atmanspacher and R. Bishop (Eds.), *Between chance and choice: Interdisciplinary perspectives on determinism* (pp. 371–406). Thorverton, UK: Imprint Academic.

Kant, I. (1949). *Critique of practical reason* (L. W. Beck, Trans.). Chicago: University of Chicago Press. (Original work published 1781)

Kegan, R. (1983). A neo-Piagetian approach to object relations. In B. Lec & G. G. Noam (Eds.), *Developmental approaches to the self* (pp. 267–307). New York: Plenum.

Kempen, H. J. G. (1996). Mind as body moving in space: Bringing the body back into self-psychology. *Theory and Psychology, 6,* 715–731.

Kim, J. (1996). *Philosophy of mind.* Boulder, CO: Westview Press.

Koch, S. (1981). The nature and limits of psychological knowledge: Lessons of a century qua "science." *American Psychologist, 36,* 257–269.

Koch, S. (1992). Psychology's Bridgman vs. Bridgman's Bridgman. *Theory and Psychology, 2,* 261–290.

Koch, S. (1993). "Psychology" or the "psychological studies?" *American Psychologist, 48,* 902–904.

Koch, S. (1999). *Psychology in human context: Essays in dissidence and reconstruction* (D. Finkelman & F. Kessel, Eds.). Chicago: University of Chicago Press.

Kögler, H. H. (1996). *The power of dialogue: Critical hermeneutics after Gadamer and Foucault* (P. Hendrickson, Trans.). Cambridge, MA: MIT Press.

Köhler, W. (1947). *Gestalt psychology.* New York: Liveright.

Kristeva, J. (1991). *Strangers to ourselves.* London: Harvester Wheatsheaf.

Kvale, S. (Ed.). (1992). *Psychology and postmodernism.* Thousand Oaks, CA: Sage.

Laclau, E., & Mouffe, C. (1985). *Hegemony and socialist strategy: Towards a radical democratic politics* (W. Moore and P. Cammack, Trans.). London: Verso.

Lee, V. L. (1992). Transdermal interpretation of the subject matter of behavior analysis. *American Psychologist, 47,* 1337–1343.

Marsella, A., DeVos, G., & Hsu, F. L. K. (Eds.). (1985). *Culture and self: Asian and Western perspectives.* New York: Tavistock.

Martin, J. (1994). *The construction and understanding of psychotherapeutic change: Conversations, memories, and theories.* New York: Teachers College Press.

Martin, J. (2002, October). *Emergent persons.* Paper presented to the Institut für Grenzgebeite der Psychologie und Psychologiene, Freiburg, Germany.

Martin, J., & Dawda, D. (1999). Beyond empathy: A hermeneutically inspired inquiry into interpersonal understanding in psychotherapy. *Theory and Psychology, 9,* 459–481.

Martin, J., & Sugarman, J. (1999). *The psychology of human possibility and constraint.* Albany, NY: State University of New York Press.

Martin, J., & Sugarman, J. (2001). Interpreting human kinds: Beginnings of a hermeneutic psychology. *Theory and Psychology, 11,* 193–207.

Martin, J. & Thompson, J. (in press). Psychotherapy as the interpretation of being: Hermeneutic perspectives on psychotherapy. *Journal of Constructivist Psychology.*

McAdams, D. P., Hoffman, B. J., Mansfield, E. D., & Day, R. (1996). Themes of agency and communion in significant autobiographical scenes. *Journal of Personality, 64,* 339–377.

McClay, W. M. (1998). Communitarianism and the federal idea. In P. A. Lawler & D. McConkey (Eds.), *Community and political thought today* (pp. 101–107). Westport, CT: Praeger.

McDowell, J. (1994). *Mind and world.* Cambridge, MA: Harvard University Press.

Mead, G. H. (1934). *Mind, self, and society from the standpoint of a social behaviorist.* Chicago: University of Chicago Press.

Meehl, P. E. (1967). Theory testing in psychology and physics: A methodological paradox. *Philosophy of Science, 34,* 103–115.

Mele, A. (1995). *Autonomous agents: From self-control to autonomy.* New York: Oxford University Press.

Merleau-Ponty, M. (1962). *Phenomenology of perception* (C. Smith, Trans.). London: Routledge & Kegan Paul.

Morrow-Bradley, C., & Elliot, R. (1986). Utilization of psychotherapy research by practicing psychotherapists. *American Psychologist, 41,* 188–197.

Mulhall, S., & Swift, A. (1996). *Liberals and communitarians* (2nd ed.). Oxford, England: Basil Blackwell.

Nozick, R. (1974). *Anarchy, state, and utopia.* New York: Basic Books.

Packer, M., & Addison, R. (Eds.). (1989). *Entering the circle: Hermeneutic investigation in psychology.* New York: State University of New York Press.

Paton Walsh, J. (2000). *A desert in Bohemia.* London: Doubleday.

Polkinghorne, D. E. (1988). *Narrative psychology.* Albany: State University of New York Press.

Prilleltensky, I. (Ed.). (1994). *The morals and politics of psychology: Psychological discourse and the status quo.* Albany: State University of New York Press.

Quigley, J. (2000). *The grammar of autobiography: A developmental account.* Hillsdale, NJ: Erlbaum.

Quigley, J. (2001). Psychology and grammar: The construction of the autobiographical self. *Theory and Psychology, 11,* 147–170.

Ratner, C. (1991). *Vygotsky's sociohistorical psychology and its contemporary applications.* New York: Plenum.

Rawls, J. (1971). *A theory of justice.* Cambridge, MA: Harvard University Press.

Richardson, F. C. (1998). Beyond scientism and postmodernism? *Journal of Theoretical and Philosophical Psychology, 18,* 33–45.

Richardson, F. C., Fowers, B. J., & Guignon, C. (1999). *Re-envisioning psychology: Moral dimensions of theory and practice.* San Francisco: Jossey-Bass.

Risser, J. (1997). *Hermeneutics and the voice of the other: Re-reading Gadamer's philosophical hermeneutics.* Albany: State University of New York Press.

Robinson, D. N. (1985). *Philosophy of psychology.* New York: Columbia University Press.

Rogers, C. R. (1961). *On being a person: A therapist's view of psychotherapy.* Boston: Houghton Mifflin.

Rorty, R. (1989). *Contingency, irony, and solidarity.* Cambridge, England: Cambridge University Press.

Rose, N. (1998). *Inventing ourselves: Psychology, power, and personhood.* Cambridge, England: Cambridge University Press.

Rottschaefer, W. A. (1991). Some philosophical implications of Bandura's social cognitive theory of human agency. *American Psychologist, 46,* 153–155.

Rychlak, J. F. (1988). *The psychology of rigorous humanism* (2nd ed.). New York: New York University Press.

Rychlak, J. F. (1997). *In defense of human consciousness.* Washington, DC: American Psychological Association.

Rychlak, J. F. (1999). Social constructionism, postmodernism, and the computer model: Searching for human agency in the right places. *Journal of Mind and Behavior, 20,* 379–390.

Rychlak, J. F., Williams, R. N., & Bugaj, A. M. (1986). The heuristic properties of dialectical oppositionality in predication. *Journal of General Psychology, 113,* 359–368.

Safranski, R. (1998). *Martin Heidegger: Between good and evil* (E. Osers, Trans.). Cambridge, MA: Harvard University Press.

Sandel, M. (1982). *Liberalism and the limits of justice.* Cambridge, MA: Cambridge University Press.

Sandel, M. (1984). The procedural republic and the unencumbered self. *Political Theory, 12,* 81–96.

Sappington, A. A. (1990). Recent psychological approaches to the free will versus determinism issue. *Psychological Bulletin, 108,* 19–29.

Sass, L. A. (1988). Humanism, hermeneutics, and the concept of the human subject. In S. B. Messer & L. A. Sass (Eds.), *Hermeneutics and psychological theory: Interpretive perspectives on personality, psychotherapy, and psychopathology* (pp. 222–271). New Brunswick, NJ: Rutgers University Press.

Sass, L. A. (1992). The epic of disbelief: The postmodernist turn in contemporary psychoanalysis. In S. Kvale (Ed.), *Psychology and postmodernism* (pp. 166–182). Thousand Oaks, CA: Sage.

Searle, J. R. (1992). *The rediscovery of the mind.* Cambridge, MA: MIT Press.

Shotter, J. (1993). *Conversational realities: Constructing life through language.* Thousand Oaks, CA: Sage.

Skinner, B. F. (1959). *Cumulative record.* New York: Appleton-Century.

Skinner, E. A., Chapman, M., & Baltes, P. B. (1988). Control, means–ends, and agency beliefs: A new conceptualization and its measurement during childhood. *Journal of Personality and Social Psychology, 54,* 117–133.

Slife, B. D. (1994). Free will and time: That "stuck" feeling. *Journal of Theoretical and Philosophical Psychology, 14,* 1–12.

Smedslund, J. (1988). *Psycho-logic.* New York: Springer-Verlag.

Smith, J. A., Harré, R., & Van Langenhove, L. (Eds.). (1995). *Rethinking methods in psychology.* Thousand Oaks, CA: Sage.

Smith, M. B. (1994). Selfhood at risk: Postmodern perils and the perils of postmodernism. *American Psychologist, 49,* 405–411.

Snow, C. P. (1998). *The two cultures.* Cambridge, England: Cambridge University Press. (Original works published 1959 and 1963)

Sohn, D. (1999). Experimental effects: Are they constant or variable across individuals? *Theory and Psychology, 9,* 625–638.

Sperry, R. W. (1993). The impact and promise of the cognitive revolution. *American Psychologist, 48,* 878–885.

Spivak, G. C. (1996). *The Spivak reader: Selected works of Gayatri Chakravorty Spivak.* New York: Routledge.

Strawson, P. (1959). *Individuals.* Routledge: New York.

Strawson, P. (1962). Freedom and resentment. *Proceedings of the British Academy, 48,* 1–25.

Task Force on Promotion and Dissemination of Psychological Procedures. (1995). Training in and dissemination of empirically-validated psychological treatment: Report and recommendations. *The Clinical Psychologist, 48,* 2–23.

Taylor, C. (1964). *The explanation of behavior.* London: Routledge.

Taylor, C. (1985). Self-interpreting animals. In *Philosophical papers: Vol. 1. Human agency and language* (pp. 45–76). Cambridge, England: Cambridge University Press.

Taylor, C. (1988). Wittgenstein, empiricism, and the question of the "inner": Commentary on Kenneth Gergen. In S. B. Messer, L. A. Sass, & R. L. Woolfolk (Eds.), *Hermeneutics and psychological theory: Interpretive perspectives on personality, psychotherapy, and psychopathology* (pp. 52–58). New Brunswick, NJ: Rutgers University Press.

Taylor, C. (1995). *Philosophical arguments.* Cambridge, MA: Harvard University Press.

Tiryakian, E. A. (1962). *Sociologism and existentialism: Two perspectives on the individual and society.* Englewood Cliffs, NJ: Prentice-Hall.

PSYCHOLOGY AND THE QUESTION OF AGENCY

Tolman, C. (1994). *Psychology, society, and subjectivity.* London: Routledge.

Valsiner, J. (1998). *The guided mind: A sociogenetic approach to personality.* Cambridge, MA: Harvard University Press.

Vygotsky, L. S. (1978). *Mind in society: The development of higher psychological processes* (M. Cole, V. John-Steiner, S. Scribner, & E. Souberman, Eds.). Cambridge, MA: Harvard University Press.

Vygotsky, L. S. (1986). *Thought and language* (A. Kozulin, Trans.). Cambridge, MA: MIT Press. (Original work published 1934)

Wallach, M. A., & Wallach, L. (1998). When experiments serve little purpose: Misguided research in mainstream psychology. *Theory and Psychology, 8,* 183–194.

Walzer, M. (1983). *Spheres of justice.* New York: Basic Books.

Wertsch, J. V. (1985). *Vygotsky and the social formation of mind.* Cambridge, MA: Harvard University Press.

Wertsch, J. V. (1998). *Mind in action.* New York: Oxford University Press.

Wertz, F. J. (1995, August). *The scientific status of psychology.* Paper presented at the meeting of the American Psychological Association, New York.

Westcott, M. R. (1988). *The psychology of human freedom: A human science perspective and critique.* New York: Springer-Verlag.

Williams, R. N. (1992). The human context of agency. *American Psychologist, 47,* 752–760.

Williams, R. N. (1994). The modern, the post-modern, and the question of truth: Perspectives on the problem of agency. *Journal of Theoretical and Philosophical Psychology, 14,* 25–49.

Winch, R. H. (1908). The transfer of improvement of memory in schoolchildren. *British Journal of Psychology, 2,* 284–293.

Woolfolk, R. L. (1998). *The cure of souls: Science, values, and psychotherapy.* San Francisco: Jossey-Bass.

INDEX

Made in the USA
Lexington, KY
04 October 2012